# Mario Vargas Llosa

## Twayne's World Authors Series
### Latin American Literature

David Foster, Editor
*Arizona State University*

TWAS 762

MARIO VARGAS LLOSA
(1936–     )
*Photograph courtesy of Foto Agusti Carbonell*

# Mario Vargas Llosa

## By Dick Gerdes

*University of New Mexico*

*Twayne Publishers • Boston*

*Mario Vargas Llosa*

Dick Gerdes

Copyright © 1985 by G. K. Hall & Company
All Rights Reserved
Published by Twayne Publishers
A Division of G. K. Hall & Company
70 Lincoln Street
Boston, Massachusetts 02111

Book Production by Elizabeth Todesco
Book Design by Barbara Anderson

Printed on permanent/durable acid-free
paper and bound in the United States of
America.

**Library of Congress Cataloging in Publication Data**

Gerdes, Dick.
  Mario Vargas Llosa.

  (Twayne's world authors series; TWAS 762. Latin American literature)
  Bibliography: p. 199
  Includes index.
  1. Vargas Llosa, Mario, 1963–      —Criticism and interpretation.
I. Title.  II. Series: Twayne's world author series; TWAS 762.
III. Series: Twayne's world author series. Latin American literature.
PQ8498.32.A65Z668   1985       863       85–5447
ISBN 0–8057–6612–X

for Aída, Nicole, and Jeff

# Contents

# About the Author

Dick Gerdes is associate professor of Spanish at the University of New Mexico (Albuquerque). He received the B.A. from Colorado State University in 1964, the M.A. from Texas A&I University in 1971, and the Ph.D. from the University of Kansas in 1975.

He is the author of several articles dealing with diverse topics—the Argentine theater, the Peruvian short story, the Mexican novel, Colombian poetry, and Chicano literature—which have appeared in such scholarly journals as *Hispania, Journal of Spanish Studies: Twentieth Century, Kentucky Romance Quarterly, American Hispanist, Bilingual Review/Revista bilingüe,* and *Plural.*

Professor Gerdes has been the recipient of a Fulbright-Hays Overseas Scholar Research Grant to Peru (1979–80), served as associate director for academic affairs of the Latin American Institute at the University of New Mexico (1980–81), coordinated the University of New Mexico Summer School Program in Spain (1984), and participated in a faculty exchange program at the University of Münster in Germany (1984–85).

# Preface

This book is an introduction to the work of Mario Vargas Llosa. It presents a comprehensive view of the more significant thematic and technical elements that rank Vargas Llosa's fiction among the great literary achievements of this century. Each chapter contains, first, a thorough plot synopsis of each work and, second, an analysis of the principal characteristics of the structure inherent to each one. Structure refers here to the organizational principles in fiction writing that are determined in large part by concepts of space and time. Equally important to this analysis of Vargas Llosa's works is the concept of narrative point of view. The author's special treatment of these narrative components is aimed toward the creation of a sense of multiple time frames and spatial diversity, concurrent action, and myriad points of view, which, taken together, evoke the sensation of many lives experienced simultaneously.

Since the dynamic nature of each work is based on these different factors, the reader is challenged to comprehend the shifting perspectives of seemingly illusive texts. Paradoxically, however, each work is highly structured and carefully organized, and once engaging patterns created through repetition, dualities, contrasts, and parallels are established, the works grow clearer. It is here that Vargas Llosa makes a statement about the nature of modern life and the role played by literature in making human existence more comprehensible. My aim, then, is to identify the dynamic qualities of his texts that shed light on certain ideological underpinnings, therefore making Mario Vargas Llosa a consummate twentieth-century professional writer.

Many of the literary concerns treated in this book are the topics of analyses in several critical studies of Vargas Llosa's works. Diverse approaches and equally engaging comments are found in such works as Rosa Boldori's *Vargas Llosa: Un narrador y sus demonios*; Luís A. Díez's *Mario Vargas Llosa's Pursuit of the Total Novel*; Casto M. Fernández's *Aproximación formal a la novelística de Vargas Llosa*; José L. Martin's *La narrativa de Vargas Llosa: Acercamiento estilístico*; José Miguel Oviedo's *Mario Vargas Llosa: La invención de una realidad* (which also contains the most complete bibliography of primary and secondary sources), and Armando Pereira's *La concepción literaria de Mario Vargas Llosa.* I am also indebted to several other literary critics—including Sara Castro-Klarén, Ronald Christ, Alexander Coleman, Frank Dauster, Joel Hancock, Wolfgang A. Luchting, George McMurray, Michael Moody, Raymond Williams—for their excellent interpretive commentary in numerous articles.

The advice, suggestions, and support I received from colleagues and friends are deeply appreciated. I extend a special note of gratitude to Floyce Alexander, Tamara Holzapfel, Alfred Rodríguez, and John Brushwood. I also wish to express my appreciation to the University of New Mexico for the sabbatical leave and research funds that enabled me to write this book.

Dick Gerdes

*University of New Mexico*

# Chronology

1936    28 March: Mario Vargas Llosa born in Arequipa, Peru; only son of Ernesto Vargas and Dora Llosa, who were separated before he was born. Lives with his mother in the home of her parents.

1937    Moves with his mother to Cochabamba, Bolivia, where his grandfather is consul.

1945    They take up residence in Piura (northern Peru).

1946    Early attempts at literary writing disconcert his father. Parental differences are resolved and the family moves to Lima.

1951    Obtains summer employment as a newspaper writer at *La Crónica* (Lima).

1952    Abandons military school, returns to Piura to finish high school (where he organizes a student strike), and initiates a literary career. Works as a columnist for local newspapers, directs his play, *La huída del Inca* (The escape of the Inca), written a year earlier in Lima, and publishes poetry.

1953–1957    Initiates studies in literature and law at San Marcos University in Lima. Holds several part-time jobs, including positions as newscaster, librarian, and collaborator in magazines and literary journals. Two short stories, "Los jefes" ("The leaders") and "El abuelo" ("The grandfather") appear in *Mercurio peruano* and *El Comercio*. Edits literary journal, *Cuadernos de conversación*, with Luis Loayza and Abelardo Oquendo. Completes bachelor's degree, and at age nineteen his marriage to Julia Urquidi, a distant relative by marriage, creates family unrest.

1958    Assists in editing another journal, *Literatura*. Wins *Revue française* short-story competition for "El desafío" ("The Challenge") and briefly visits Paris. Receives scholarship to University of Madrid, works on doctoral thesis; creates a folklore group, Inca Dancers, wins a competition, and tours Spain. Writes a travelogue, "Crónica de una viaje a la selva" (Chronicle of a trip to the jungle), for *Cultura peruana*.

1959   *Los jefes* ("The Leaders"), short-story collection, wins
       Leopoldo Alas literary prize. Moves to Paris and in-
       itiates several years of self-imposed exile in Europe.

1960   Unstable economically, lives precarious existence in
       Paris; teaches Spanish at Berlitz Schools, then works
       at Agence Frances-Presse, and later at the French
       Radio-Television Network. Meets important Latin
       American writers.

1962   Finishes first novel, covers Cuban missile crisis, visits
       Peru briefly, and returns to Paris. Meets Carlos Barral
       and submits work to the Seix-Barral Biblioteca Breve
       competition for novel.

1963   *La ciudad y los perros (The Time of the Hero)*, novel,
       wins Biblioteca Breve prize, Premio de la Crítica Es-
       pañola, and is awarded second place in Prix Formen-
       tor. An edition of *Los jefes* is published in Lima.

1964   Travels to Peru, revisits jungle region, and prepares
       material for second novel. Divorces Julia Urquidi.

1965   Judges literary competition for *Casa de las Américas*
       awards in Cuba and serves on the journal's editorial
       board. Marries a cousin, Patricia Llosa.

1966   *La casa verde (The Green House)*, novel. Invited to
       International PEN Club meeting in New York. Writes
       for *Caretas* magazine in Lima. A son, Alvaro, is born.
       Judges literary competition in Buenos Aires. Changes
       residence to London and teaches at Queen Mary
       College.

1967   *Los cachorros (The Cubs)*, short novel. *The Green House*
       wins three prizes: the Peruvian Premio Nacional de
       la Novela, Premio de la Crítica Española, and the
       $22,000 Venezuelan Rómulo Gallegos award, for
       which he writes his famous speech "La literatura es
       fuego" ("Literature Is Fire"). Writes prologue to Se-
       bastián Salazar Bondy's *Obras completas,* in which he
       discusses the writer's vocation. A second son, Gon-
       zalo, is born.

1969   *Conversación en La Catedral (Conversation in The Ca-
       thedral)*, novel. Writes prologue to Joannot Marto-

rell's novel of chivalry, *Tirant lo Blanc*. Teaches at the University of Puerto Rico (Río Piedras).

1970     *Literatura en la revolución y revolución en la literatura,* literary essays (with Julio Cortázar and Oscar Collazos). Moves to Barcelona. Resumes work on doctoral thesis (the fiction of Gabriel García Márquez). Publishes an important article, "Latin American Literature Today," in *Books Abroad.*

1971     *García Márquez: historia de un deicidio* (García Márquez: history of a deicide), literary essay. *Historia secreta de una novela* (Secret history of a novel), essay (explaining how *The Green House* was written). Severs ideological ties with Cuban revolution; supports Paris-based literary journal *Libre.*

1973     *Pantaleón y las visitadoras (Captain Pantoja and the Special Service),* novel. Coauthors literary essays with Angel Rama, *García Márquez y la problemática de la novela* (García Márquez and the problematic nature of narrative).

1974     Establishes permanent residence in Peru, ending self-imposed exile. A daughter, Morgana, is born.

1975     *La orgía perpétua: Flaubert y "Madame Bovary"* (The perpetual orgy: Flaubert and "Madame Bovary"), literary essay. Special focus on *Conversation in The Cathedral* in *Review 75.*

1976     President of International PEN Club; travels extensively. Lectures at University of Jerusalem. Codirects and has walk-on part in film version of *Captain Pantoja and the Special Service.*

1977     *La tía Julia y el escribidor (Aunt Julia and the Scriptwriter),* novel. Travels to Europe, Russia, and the United States as PEN Club president. He is the focus of the Sixth Oklahoma Conference on Writers of the Hispanic World. Lectures at the University of Oklahoma and teaches at Cambridge University. *Texas Studies in Literature and Language* devotes an issue to his work.

1978     *World Literature Today* devotes an issue to his work.

1979    Writer-in-Residence, Smithsonian Institution (Washington, D.C.). Wins Godó Llallana prize (awarded by Barcelona newspaper *La Vanguardia*) for his commitment to intellectual and artistic freedom.

1980    Lectures and travels in Japan.

1981    *La señorita de Tacna* (The señorita from Tacna), play; opens in Buenos Aires and Lima, winning Premio Anual de la Crítica in Argentina. *La guerra del fin del mundo (The War of the End of the World)*, novel. *Entre Sartre y Camus* (Between Sartre and Camus), collected essays. Directs and hosts twenty-six episodes of the Lima current-events television program "La torre de Babel."

1982    Receives Premio Iila of the Instituto Italo Latinoamericano (Italy).

1983    *Kathie y el hipopótamo* (Katy and the hippopotamus), play. "Inquest in the Andes," *New York Times Magazine* (July), narrative chronicle. Symposium dedicated to Vargas Llosa, Barnard College, New York.

1984    *Contra viento y marea* (Against all odds), collected essays.

# Chapter One
# Biographical Introduction

Mario Vargas Llosa was born into a middle-class family in Arequipa, Peru, in 1936. The following year his mother and father were separated and she took young Mario to live in Cochabamba, Bolivia, where his grandfather was consul. Vargas Llosa recalls those first eight years in Bolivia as happy and uncomplicated; he had many friends, played games, and dreamed of becoming a trapeze artist or a bullfighter. He states, however, that "happiness, you know, is unproductive in a literary sense, and none of the things I thought about in those years has been a literary inspiration to me" (Harss and Dohmann 1967, 352). Yet Vargas Llosa remembers reading books at the time about "Sandokan, the musketeers, Tom Sawyer and Sinbad, books by Nostradamus and Cagliostro, stories about pirates, explorers, bandits and romantic love, and the poems my mother hid in the night table. (I read them not because I understood them but because they had the allure of what has been forbidden.) Since it was unthinkable that the books I loved should ever come to an end, I sometimes made up new chapters or invented new endings for them" ("A Passion for Peru," 79).

In 1945 the family returned to Peru and moved to Piura, a desert city of the north, where Vargas Llosa's grandfather became prefect. There his idyllic childhood came to an abrupt end; young Vargas Llosa found it difficult to make adjustments to a new school, where he was much younger than his classmates. After living in Piura for a year, his parents reconciled their differences and the family moved to Lima, where he attended a parochial secondary school. This experience provided the background for his short novel *Los cachorros* (*The Cubs,* 1967), which deals with his adolescent years in middle-class Lima. From 1950 to 1952 Vargas Llosa attended the Peruvian government's Leoncio Prado military school in Lima. Vargas Llosa explains that his father, an enigmatic figure whom he never trusted, "thought the Leoncio Prado would make a man of me. For me it was like discovering Hell—an unknown reality, the opposite side of life. It marked me to the core" (Harss and Dohmann 1967, 352).

1

At issue was Vargas Llosa's incipient literary creativity; his father "had found out that I was writing poems, feared for my future (a poet is doomed to die of hunger) and for my 'manhood' (the belief that poets are homosexual is still very widespread), and to protect me from these dangers he decided that the perfect antidote was Leoncio Prado Military School" ("A Passion for Peru," 99–100). Vargas Llosa sums up his two years of experience as a cadet and its relationship to literature:

Ever since I was in the Leoncio Prado I wanted to write about it. Although the idea of writing was something I had before. It was one of the reasons why there were always disagreements between my father and myself. I used to write in Piura, I remember, and my grandparents, my uncles, applauded me for it. They thought it was cute. When my father discovered that inclination in me he was frightened. He thought something was seriously wrong. The Lima bourgeoisie thinks that being a writer or an artist is only a pretext for being either a pansy or a good-for-nothing. The saddest part about it is that in many cases they're right. So my vocation grew and solidified a bit secretly. It was an outlet for my revolt against the Leoncio Prado. At that time literature became something very important for me. Also something hidden. Because in school one didn't dare show any sign of that. (Harss and Dohmann 1967, 354)

This direct confrontation with Peruvian reality was much more violent and revealing to him than the insights he gained from life in Piura. He later transformed this experience into fiction. *La ciudad y los perros* (The city and the dogs, 1963; published in English as *The Time of the Hero*) is the story of a young cadet's transition into manhood. The military academy of the real world is transformed into a fictional microcosm of Peruvian society.

For Vargas Llosa Peruvian society tends to exalt masculinity and male chauvinism. The overpowering presence and destructive force of the male element as a cultural determinant in society becomes a dominant theme in his later novels. Very early in his career, Vargas Llosa's secret revolt crystallized into a passionate literary rebellion against society's ills, particularly the Peruvian middle class, which, he says, "is the worst thing under the sun: an absolutely noxious class, infected with prejudices, ignorant, and hypocritical" (Harss and Dohmann 1967, 354). This hostile stance toward mediocrity is one among several constants in his work, and it appears regularly in other novels as well as in *Kathie y el hipopótamo* (Katy and the hippopotamus), a two-act play published in 1983 that contains characters from earlier works, one of whom discovers that he has always detested the bourgeoisie, "those whom we hated for ideological and moral reasons" (62).

After spending two years at Leoncio Prado, Vargas Llosa returned to Piura in 1952 to finish high school. There he was one of the instigators of a student strike, an incident that later became the fictionalized plot of his short story "Los jefes" ("The Leaders"). In addition, he began to write articles for a local newspaper, while concurrently writing and producing his first play, *La huida del Inca* (The escape of the Inca). The social and cultural milieu of Piura and the local stories and legends that Vargas Llosa avidly absorbed with great curiosity created unique experiences for the Peruvian writer that were later incorporated into his second novel, *La casa verde* (*The Green House*, 1963).

Mario Vargas Llosa's journalistic apprenticeship continued in Lima. He worked one summer during high school as a local news editor of *La Crónica*, which put him in direct contact with Lima's dark side; a corrupt underworld of crime and prostitution. This experience, in addition to others, forms the basis of his third major novel, *Conversación en La Catedral* (*Conversation in The Cathedral*, 1969). Just as his stay at Leoncio Prado had yielded new insights into Peruvian reality, such experiences served to enlighten Vargas Llosa's perception of Peru's social environment.

By the summer of 1952 Vargas Llosa was immersing himself in the French novel, from Victor Hugo to Jean-Paul Sartre. From Sartre in particular he learned that modern fiction was very different from the regional folklore narratives that still prevailed in Spanish America. He learned about interior monologue, variable narrative point of view, and multiple levels of time and space. In 1953 Vargas Llosa enrolled in law and literature courses at San Marcos University in Lima. In doing so he rebelled against his family's wishes: they "wanted me to go to Catholic University, the school attended by scions of what were then known as 'good families.' But I lost my faith between the ages of 14 and 15, and I didn't want to be a 'good boy.' In the romantic way that children discover prejudice and social inequality, I had discovered, in my last year of high school, that the country had severe social problems. I wanted to be identified with the poor and to be part of a revolution that would bring justice to Peru. San Marcos, a national, secular university, had a tradition

of nonconformity that attracted me as much as its academic reputation" ("A Passion for Peru," 107).

While studying at the university, Vargas Llosa became involved
in socialist causes; yet he began to lose enthusiasm for orthodox
communist ideology when others began to support the official literary aesthetic, socialist realism. At the same time, Vargas Llosa
had to resort to several part-time jobs in order to relieve financial
pressures brought on by his marriage in 1955 to Julia Orquidi, a
distant relative; in one job, he prepared news bulletins for a Lima
radio station. This period in Vargas Llosa's life is humorously re-
created in his fictional autobiography *La tía Julia y el escribidor* (*Aunt
Julia and the Scriptwriter,* 1977).

Vargas Llosa had also been increasing his literary horizons by
reading Henry Miller, James Joyce, Ernest Hemingway, Marcel
Proust, André Malraux, Jorge Luis Borges, and William Faulkner,
among others. Faulkner's works have always been significant to him:
"Perhaps the most lasting part of my years at the university is not
what I learned in the classroom but what I discovered in the novels
and stories that recount the saga of Yoknapatawpha County." In
those novels he learned "about the infinitely complex shades of
meaning, the illusiveness, and the textual and conceptual richness
that a narrative could have, to realize how much a prestidigitator's
technique was required to tell a good story" ("A Passion for Peru,"
108).

In 1957 Vargas Llosa's short stories began appearing in journals
and newspapers. He also edited the literary journals *Cuadernos de
composición* and *Literatura* with his friends Luis Loayza and Abelardo
Oquendo. The following year his story "El desafío" ("The Challenge") took first place in a literary competition sponsored by *Revue
française,* a prize that provided him a brief trip to France. About
the same time, Vargas Llosa traveled through the Peruvian jungle,
further exposing himself to the diversity of Peru and its social
problems. On his voyage, he journeyed along the upper Marañón
River and visited various Indian tribes. The trip opened his eyes to
an extremely primitive, harsh, and violent region to the east of the
Andes mountains. He wrote a chronicle of the trip for *Cultura
peruana,* and those experiences were also transformed into fiction in
his second novel, *The Green House.*

Vargas Llosa won a scholarship to the University of Madrid, where
he worked on a doctoral thesis that later became an exhaustive

thematic and stylistic study of Gabriel García Márquez's narrative fiction. This early period in his already intense literary career reached its culmination in 1959 when his first book of fiction, *Los jefes* (The leaders, translated in *The Cubs and Other Stories*)—the short stories that he wrote between the ages of sixteen and eighteen—won the Spanish Leopoldo Alas award and was published in Barcelona.

But Vargas Llosa's dedication to writing, his desire to become a good novelist, and his ability to survive economically were severely tested at the time. He managed to find part-time jobs, but his life was very unstable. After finishing his studies in Madrid and moving to Paris, he requested another scholarship from Peru that would have allowed him to remain in France. He did not receive the scholarship, and the two-month wait with his wife in Paris left him penniless. Although that period did not provide for favorable writing conditions, he began to revise the rough draft of his first novel. Through his work at the French radio-television network, Vargas Llosa met prominent Latin American writers such as Julio Cortázar, Jorge Luis Borges, Alejo Carpentier, Miguel Angel Asturias, and Carlos Fuentes. This period in his life also marked the beginning of a fifteen-year self-imposed exile, which ended in 1974.

*The Time of the Hero,* his first novel, was published in 1962. It gained international recognition (it has been translated into almost two dozen languages) and established the author as one of the most promising writers of his generation. The novel won several literary prizes and was lauded for its technical mastery, stylistic innovations, and thematic relevance. In Peru the novel precipitated a curious reaction: a thousand copies were publicly burned on the grounds of Leoncio Prado Academy to protest the author's criticism of the military. If Vargas Llosa's personal experiences at Leoncio Prado had changed him forever, his fictionalized version of those experiences in *The Time of the Hero* propelled him directly from a position of relative anonymity to one in which he could never again avoid public scrutiny.

By this time in his career, Vargas Llosa had become deeply concerned about the writer's role in society. On the one hand he was captivated by Sartre's concept of dialectics, while on the other he was seduced by Albert Camus's anarchistic reformism. During the next twenty years Vargas Llosa wrote several essays that have been collected into one volume, *Sartre y Camus* (Between Sartre and Camus, 1981). Together, as the author explains, the essays present a contradictory but entirely acceptable attitude toward the two French thinkers that demonstrates how his preferences in the 1960s veer from Sartre's cynical realism and demand for revolution to Camus's political idealism and moral stance toward human injustice in the 1980s.

While revising *The Green House*, Vargas Llosa returned briefly to Peru in 1963 and once again traversed the jungle area in search of additional information similar to the material he had gathered and written about five years earlier. As is his custom when writing, he was already voraciously reading all types of books concerned with the setting of his latest novel.

Vargas Llosa's presence in the literary world began to expand rapidly. He was invited to Cuba in 1965 to judge the literary competition for *Casa de las Américas,* and became a member of the journal's editorial board. His eight-year marriage ended in divorce, and a year later he married his cousin Patricia Llosa in Peru. They returned to Paris, and Vargas Llosa finished writing *The Green House,* which came out early in 1966.

With *The Green House* Vargas Llosa invites and even requires further reader participation in the creation of the novel's plot, themes, and aesthetic interpretations. Structurally, Vargas Llosa's novels work from concepts of discontinuity and simultaneity. They demonstrate a technical mastery of multiple perspectives that is the key to what Vargas Llosa strives to achieve in his narratives: the "total" novel. In 1966 in Montevideo, Vargas Llosa presented a lecture (later published), containing personal insights about the nature of fiction, the concept of "literary vocation," the influence of French writers on his thinking, and discoveries about the medieval novels of chivalry. The medieval romancers were masters in presenting reality from multiple levels—namely, objective, subjective, mythic, and instinctual—which enabled them to embrace and re-create all of reality. In his article "Vargas Llosa and the End of Chivalry" Frank Dauster (1970b) states that "this attempt to capture complexity accounts for the very real difficulties of reading Vargas Llosa" (43).

Upon the birth of his first son, Alvaro, in Lima in 1966, Vargas Llosa moved with his family from Paris to London, where he taught Latin American literature at Queen Mary College. He began to write articles for Peru's popular *Caretas* magazine, simultaneously putting the finishing touches on his novella *Los cachorros (The Cubs).* In the meantime, positive reader reaction to *The Green House* gained for it the prestigious Venezuelan Rómulo Gallegos award. At the award ceremony in 1967 the Peruvian writer delivered his celebrated "Caracas Speech," which was spontaneously accepted as a valid perspective on the nature of literature and on the writer's responsibility to society and to himself. The speech "La literatura es fuego" ("Literature Is Fire") focuses on the difficulties that Latin American writers face in societies where literature seemingly has no purpose, no publishers, and not even a reading public. Vargas Llosa views literature as a process of continuous, never-ending insurrection against ignorance and exploitation in society. The title of the speech underscores the writer's sense of rebellion, for Vargas Llosa views the source of the writer's vocation as stemming from his discontent with society.

While Vargas Llosa was in Caracas in 1967 he met García Márquez, whose novel *One Hundred Years of Solitude* had just appeared. In Bogotá and Lima, they collaborated in public discussions on fiction writing that resulted in *La novela en América Latina: Diálogo* (1968). By 1967 the Latin American "boom" novel had reached maturity with García Márquez's seminal novel. In referring to the explosion of the Spanish American novel, Chilean writer José Donoso states that "there exists the fortuitous circumstance that on the same continent, in twenty-one republics where more or less recognizable varieties of Spanish are written, and during a period of a very few years, there appeared both the brilliant first novels by authors who matured very or relatively early—Vargas Llosa and Carlos Fuentes, for example—and the major novels by older, prestigious authors—Ernesto Sábato, Onetti, Cortázar, which thus produced a spectacular conjunction. In a period of scarcely six years, between 1962 and 1968, I read *The Death of Artemio Cruz, The Time of the Hero, The Green House, The Shipyard, Paradiso, Hopscotch, About Heroes and Tombs, One Hundred Years of Solitude,* and other novels all recently published at that time. Suddenly, there burst into view about a dozen novels, noteworthy at the very least and populating a previously uninhabited space" (Donoso 1977, 3).

Vargas Llosa's newly acquired prestige—through his worldwide travel, numerous lectures, conferences, and interviews, plus participation in the international PEN Club—did not detract from his writing: his short novel *The Cubs* came out in 1967, with a prologue by Seix Barral editor Carlos Barral and photographs by Xavier Miserachs. Like his short stories and first novel, this novella deals with the theme of adolescent initiation into society. Here Vargas Llosa strives once again to create the "total" novel by inserting objective and subjective levels of reality into the story through the simultaneous—even collective—points of view of several young people who are never permitted to grow up. The juxtaposed planes of exterior and interior reality create a special rhythm and establish a unique relationship between text and reader, the latter transformed into an eavesdropper as the story unfolds. Vargas Llosa's use of a multidimensional point of view in *The Cubs* demonstrates an acute awareness of the sensitive relationship that exists between the theme of the work and its form and style.

Gonzalo, Vargas Llosa's second son, was born in 1967. The author spent much of the following year lecturing in Western Europe, Russia, and the United States. He was writer-in-residence at Washington State University, where he continued to revise a gargantuan narrative, originally published as a 675-page, two-volume work, *Conversation in The Cathedral,* which probes Peruvian society from a political perspective. Once again Vargas Llosa depends on a plurality of narrative points of view, the structural dispersion of the narrative, and the interpenetration of different levels of reality. Narratives, he feels, are essential to our understanding of reality. The fragmented and complex world of Vargas Llosa's fiction becomes meaningful through the intelligent application of such ordering devices. These do not present a positivistic or mimetic view of reality, but a new reality, the hidden inner connections between the self and the world, uncovered in the reading process.

After teaching at the University of Puerto Rico at Río Piedras in 1969, Vargas Llosa took up residence in Barcelona in 1970; there he resumed work on his doctoral thesis: a penetrating critical study of the rational and irrational, conscious and unconscious elements that molded García Márquez's life experiences into fiction. Vargas Llosa focuses on the Colombian's convictions and obsessions as initiators of the creative act. Vargas Llosa's ideas about the development of the novel in general and the Latin American novel in particular appeared in an interpretive article, "The Latin American Novel Today," published in an issue of *Books Abroad* dedicated to Latin America. Vargas Llosa attributes its renewed literary success to three elements: a thematic shift from nature to man; an expanded concept of reality; and the utilization of the urban experience. Vargas Llosa believes that art creates an autonomous reality; the new "creative" novel, as opposed to the earlier "primitive" novel (which, he says, is impressionistic, mimetic, rhetorical, and naturalistic), depends more on its intrinsically persuasive story for success, and rather than depending on a direct "correlation between the story and its real life model," the new novel relies on "its ability to improve itself upon the reader as a living and coherent reality in and of itself" (8). Accordingly, the "authenticity of a story is not dependent upon its plot but rather upon the means by which the plot is embodied in a particular written form and in a particular structure" (8).

The 1970s was indeed a remarkable decade for Vargas Llosa, not only in terms of his novelistic production—two novels—but also for his work in the area of literary theory and textual analysis. Between 1971 and 1972 Vargas Llosa published his literary analysis *García Márquez: Historia de un deicido* (García Márquez: History of a deicide); and *Historia secreta de una novela* (Secret history of a novel), a study of how *The Green House* came into being. Vargas Llosa's analytic focus and literary judgments in these works are, collectively, a refinement and expansion of the vocational and technical concerns that he presented in *La novela* in 1966. Basically Vargas Llosa sees the novel as an attempt to recover something lost or hidden from humanity; to write a novel is to commit oneself to a grave undertaking in which the writer, in conflict with reality, attempts to rescue from oblivion certain key personal experiences that have remained in one's memory and have become anguishing obsessions or "demons" from which one hopes to free oneself.

The role of art in society has been a burning issue for contemporary writers in Latin America. Some writers and critics contend that literature must serve mainly political ends, while others believe that literature must serve primarily literary ends. The ideas about the ways in which literature is produced and functions precipitated a polemic between Vargas Llosa and other writers who do not see literature as an expression of an autonomous, self-existing reality. For Vargas Llosa, a person writes because he or she has a creative literary concern and not because he or she wants to communicate a particular ideological stance. This position led to a series of polemical essays by Oscar Collazos, Julio Cortázar, and Vargas Llosa that appeared in *Literatura en la revolución y revolución en la literatura* (1975). Controversy surrounding the nature of Vargas Llosa's theoretical stance toward literature served to create a healthy dialogue among Latin American writers and literary critics, allowing the

Peruvian author the opportunity to clarify, expound upon, and defend his ideas.

Mario Vargas Llosa's growing disillusionment with the Cuban revolution reached a breaking point in 1971 after the Cuban government apparently coerced writer Heberto Padilla into confessing to "false" accusations with regard to Cuba. Vargas Llosa protested by resigning his post on the editorial board of *Casa de las Américas*. He impugned Cuban cultural authorities for negating what in the beginning had stimulated him to embrace the ideals of the Cuban revolution and fixed his decision to fight for human justice without sacrificing the rights of the individual.

The 100,000 first-edition copies of Vargas Llosa's fourth novel, *Pantaleón y las visitadoras (Captain Pantoja and the Special Service)*, published in 1973, is a good indication of the commercial success of this substantially different but still typical Vargas Llosa novel. Adapted to the cinema, the novel is both a critical portrayal of distorted social values and an unabashedly funny satire of institutional and individual fanaticism. Vargas Llosa ridicules the military and, in a parallel theme, he derides religious zealots caught up in a primitive cult revival. The novel raises a gale of laughter as the author makes a travesty of the story about the blindly dedicated military "organization man," Capitan Pantaleón Pantoja, who is charged with the establishment of a group of prostitutes in the Peruvian jungle in an effort to pacify soldiers whose ardent sexual desires have driven them to assault women in isolated villages.

With *Captain Pantoja and the Special Service*, Vargas Llosa not only caused a national scandal (again), but also demonstrated even greater narrative dexterity by taking technique a step beyond his previous novels. He molds a heterogeneous set of social speech types and individual voices into an artistically unified and structurally coherent work of literature. He juxtaposes a combination of styles—oral and written, everyday and literary, slang and official language—and demonstrates how effectively to re-create this stratified and fragmented language system novelistically. Vargas Llosa also probes the nature of the creative act in *Captain Pantoja and the Special Service*, a thematic interest further developed in his sixth novel, *Aunt Julia and the Scriptwriter* (1977). Vargas Llosa had long been fascinated with the process surrounding the origin of narratives, which is also a central concern of his 1981 play, *La señorita de Tacna* (The señorita from Tacna). His writing arises as much from the enjoyment of telling a story as from the story itself.

During the 1970s Vargas Llosa became much more aware of his narrative, theoretical, vocational, and political concerns, and of his influence as a public figure. After his third child, Morgana, was born in 1974, he ended a long period of self-exile and moved back to Peru. Living overseas for fifteen years, however, had never presented a major problem for him. Rather than cutting off cultural contact with Peru, his European exile in Paris, London, and Barcelona enriched his perspective on life and made him much less nationalistic in outlook. But his interest in Peru and in Peruvian literature and culture never abated; for example, he wrote several prologues to reprints of novels by Peruvian writers. Before he returned to Peru, the Military Revolutionary Government that came into power through a coup d'état in 1968 initiated sweeping socialist reforms. His critical position vis-à-vis Peruvian politics, which had been exacerbated early on owing in part to the censorship in Peru of the movie version of *Captain Pantoja and the Special Service,* continued throughout the 1970s. Three articles in the *New York Times* during that period confirm the critical stance that Vargas Llosa had taken concerning the Peruvian military: "Famed Novelist Clashes with Peru's Military Rulers" (21 February 1975); "Peruvian Novelist Turns Film Maker and Tangles with the Army" (22 March 1977); and "Peru Novelist Warns Against Military Nationalism" (15 February 1979). In particular, Vargas Llosa became concerned about the nationalization of the press, radio, and television. He quickly realized that the process had not liberated the media but continued to subject it to the same abuses of power and partisan censorship that it had faced under a free-enterprise system.

Another major work of literary analysis *La orgía perpetua: Flaubert y "Madame Bovary"* (The unending orgy: Flaubert and *Madame Bovary,* 1975), reveals as much or more about Vargas Llosa's own literary concerns and obsessions as it does about Flaubert's novel. Vargas Llosa considers Flaubert the first modern writer: The Frenchman possesses not only an acute technical awareness of novel writing but also adheres strictly to a philosophy of literary vocation that thrives on life's "negative experience." This position separates the writer from reality, requiring that he create another (fictional) reality. Vargas Llosa describes his unique personal relationship to Flaubert's novel, analyzes the text, and places it within the perspective of

literary history. The concept of the "total" novel is carried over
from his study of García Márquez's works and applied to his study
of *Madame Bovary*. Of particular interest is Vargas Llosa's minute
analysis of the concept of narrative point of view. He studies the
function of Flaubert's "free indirect style" (a subtle combination of
narration and dialogue) that he himself utilizes, alters, complicates,
and molds to fit the narrative situations in each of his own novels.

Vargas Llosa's ideas and concerns with regard to a program of
personal ethics, the writer's vocation and his social responsibilities—
as well as his fear of the terrorizing nature of ideological fanaticism
and the abuses of political power in modern societies—grew during
the 1970s. Vargas Llosa reread Camus's *The Rebel* and found it
completely relevant. In a lecture, "Albert Camus y la moral de los
límites" (Albert Camus and the morality of limits), delivered to the
Club Israelita de Lima in 1975, he analyzes Camus's position on
literature and life. He discovers a direct parallel between Camus's
stance as a writer during the ideological struggle of the Cold War
in the early 1950s and his own vocational role as a writer in Latin
American society during the 1970s.

Both Camus and Vargas Llosa see the need to cultivate a sense
of artistic beauty and to demonstrate a rigorous respect for individual
freedom through civility, restraint, reason, and moderation. In order
to accomplish these utopian but nevertheless "desirable" goals, one
must reject fanaticism outright; moreover, one must recognize one's
own ignorance and understand humanity's limits in the world. Vargas Llosa states that Camus's "horror of dogma" is like a burning
fire in his heart. Camus was convinced that all dogma—he cited
Christianity and Marxism—which is proposed in absolute terms,
would sooner or later end up justifying crimes and lies. This position
led Camus to his concept of the "morality of limits," that is, the
necessity to accept the possibility that one's adversary may be right
and, hence, to push for a plurality of perspectives. According to
Vargas Llosa, within this scope the writer-intellectual plays a key
role: he is not a revolutionary who kills in order to impose dogma
but a rebel who is a moralist—a voice of reason and moderation.
Unable to disassociate his fight against social injustice and human
exploitation from his struggle for individual freedom, Vargas Llosa
uses the biblical analogy of David and Goliath—the writer and
society's problems—to represent the writer's obligation to rebel
against world injustice. The unfortunate irony of this admirable

position—which Vargas Llosa steadfastly maintains despite the continual attacks on his ideas that have led to an intellectual "cold war" between Vargas Llosa and Latin American Marxist intellectuals— is that while he was delivering his speech in Lima the Israeli-Palestinian war was being waged with heavy casualties occuring for the sake of ideology.

In his weekly column "Piedra de toque" (Touchstone), which appeared from 1966 to 1968 and from 1974 to the present in the popular Peruvian magazine *Caretas,* Vargas Llosa had assumed the role of David, and the stones began to fly. As a severe critic of diverse problems confronting Peru and the world, his opinions cover a wide range of topics—from reportedly supporting right-wing political parties before Peru's national elections in 1980, making literary judgments that were easily misinterpreted with regard to José María Arguedas's "naive" and "simple" literary perspective, and demanding that Peruvian higher education depoliticize itself, to arbitrarily labeling the thinking of intellectual leftists as shallow (O'Hara 1980, 40).

Seemingly Vargas Llosa's political ideas had by 1975 led to contradictions. In an interview he declared that "since I'm not registered with any political party and my discrepancies with the Left are greater, there are times when I ask myself if I continue to be a leftist or not" (O'Hara 1980, 40). It is important, however, to understand that contradiction, self-acknowledgment, and an individual's consequent changeableness are vital to Vargas Llosa's philosophy. This process allows the writer the freedom necessary to rebel against injustice, which is his moral obligation as the watchdog over the abuses of State terrorism in modern dictatorships. As president of the International PEN Club in 1976, Vargas Llosa published in *Index to Censorship* an open letter to the President of Argentina protesting the ill treatment received by artists, intellectuals, and journalists in that country: "I urge you to end this persecution of ideas and books, to respect the right of dissent, to safeguard the lives of citizens and to allow Argentine writers freely to fulfill the role which they have in society and thus contribute to its progress" (5).

In the latter part of the 1970s, special journal issues dedicated to Vargas Llosa and his work, interviews, and public lectures brought him increased international recognition and stature. He traveled extensively for the International PEN Club, lectured at the Uni-

versity of Jerusalem, and visited Europe and Russia. In the United
States his work served as the focus of the Sixth Oklahoma Conference
on Writers of the Hispanic World. The journal *Texas Studies in
Literature and Language* devoted a special issue to him, and the New
York Center for Inter-American Relations journal *Review* focused on
*Conversation in The Cathedral.*

Vargas Llosa's sixth novel, *Aunt Julia and the Scriptwriter,* was
published in 1977. A further deviation from his original social
neorealist stance of the 1960s, this novel is, on the surface, an
autobiographical spoof of the writer's first marriage (from 1957 to
1964) to his older Aunt Julia, loosely retold along with the life of
an egocentric Bolivian writer of radio soap opera scripts whose fanatic
dedication to his "art" drives him insane. The melodramatic, maud-
lin, and comic tone of the work captivated a large audience, especially when the translated version was hailed in the United States
as one of the top five novels of 1982. A serious side to the novel
presents the reader with more than an entertaining piece of casual
reading. Here, Vargas Llosa intensifies his theoretical and practical
concerns about the art of fiction writing. *Aunt Julia and the Scriptwriter* opens the door for Vargas Llosa's world of "metafiction," that
is, experimental writing in which fiction imitates other fiction.
Critics chided Vargas Llosa for turning his back on social concerns
in this novel. Such criticism, however, was probably the result not
so much of his narrative interests in an esoteric theme like metafiction as it was for his growing influence as an intellectual and
highly visible public figure. By the late 1970s he was seen in Peru
as a supporter of anachronistic liberal progressive tendencies that
sought to return to outmoded forms of moralistic bourgeoise democracy. The humor in his most recent novels was said to be the
product of a writer who had succumbed to the lucrative enticement
of literary supply and demand and who had become a commercial
interpreter of the preferences dictated by his novels' consumers (O'-
Hara 1980, 41).

Overseas, however, Vargas Llosa's stature continued to flourish.
His speech "Social Commitment and the Latin American Writer,"
presented at the 1977 University of Oklahoma conference in his
honor, synthesized the problematical nature of the writers' vocation
vis-à-vis the outrageous socioeconomic conditions in Latin America.
He makes a distinction between Latin American writers and writers
from Western Europe and the United States. Whereas the latter

need only assume a personal responsibility "to achieve in the most rigorous and authentic way a work which, for its artistic values and originality, enriches the language and culture of one's country," the former must "assume a social responsibility: at the same time that you develop a personal literary work, you should serve, as an active participant in the solution of economic, political and cultural problems of your society." For "to be a writer, to discover this vocation and to choose to practice it," he adds, "pushes one inevitably, in our countries, to discover all the handicaps and miseries of underdevelopment" (6). This situation is unique, says Vargas Llosa, because it "confers on the writer, as a citizen, a kind of moral and spiritual leadership, and he must try, during his life as a writer, to act accordingly to this image of the role he is expected to play" (8).

A challenging response to this situation resulted in Vargas Llosa's seventh novel, *La guerra del fin del mundo* (*The War of the End of the World,* 1981), a notable artistic achievement. It is another voluminous novel, similar to his novels of the sixties for its depiction of violence, brutality, and human chaos. In this case, however, it re-creates, modifies, reinterprets, and submits to the realm of the imagination a nineteenth-century Brazilian historical incident that serves, in effect, to underscore Vargas Llosa's long-standing thematic obsession with ideological fanaticism. Vargas Llosa had spent 1979–80 in working on *The War of the End of the World* as writer-in-residence at the Smithsonian Institution in Washington. He also traveled in Japan, lecturing on the biographical elements in his novels. At that time he also won the Spanish Godó Llallana award for his commitment to intellectual and artistic freedom.

In summary, 1981 was an outstanding year for the mature Vargas Llosa. In addition to *The War of the End of the World,* he published the highly acclaimed two-act play *La señorita de Tacna,* which opened in Buenos Aires and Lima, winning Argentina's Premio Anual de la Crítica. It has since been staged in Mexico City, Madrid, New York, and elsewhere. The volume of essays, *Entre Sartre y Camus,* was published in Puerto Rico. While in Lima he continued to direct and to host the popular weekly-events television program "La Torre de Babel" (Tower of Babel). In 1982 he received the Premio Iila of the Instituto Italo Latinoamericano in Italy.

In late 1983 Vargas Llosa published *Contra viento y marea* (Against all odds), a second edition of his literary and political essays. This edition swelled to over sixty articles, originally published between

1962 and 1982. Together the articles reveal the writer's staunch commitment to intellectual, cultural, and literary freedom. The last article of the book, "El elefante y la cultura" (The elephant and culture), for example, questions the concept of nationalism and its effects on culture. Vargas Llosa states categorically that when a particular country views its own culture in absolute and unquestionable terms, while attributing lesser importance to any other culture, the spiritual personality of that nation is threatened and impoverished. To practice "cultural nationalism" as a means of isolating oneself from the corrupting agents of foreign imperialism and universal cosmopolitanism is to err in the gravest sense. Ignorance and demagoguery prevent the development of healthy cultural values and must be fought with great tenacity. By the late 1970s the significance of Mario Vargas Llosa's position on the writer's vocation was more easily understood: it seemed quite similar in fact to the stance of British novelist John Fowles, who said that "increasingly human freedom lives in human art and we cannot tolerate—it is the one and only thing we must never tolerate—any outer-imposed restriction on the artistic methods and aims" (Fowles 1972, 188).

Vargas Llosa's interest in theater continued to grow. His play *Kathie y el hipopótamo,* published in 1983, carries certain theoretical concerns about the relationship of reality and imagination to new planes of significance and it generates contradictory interpretations. Vargas Llosa's absorbing chronicle "Inquest in the Andes" (subtitled "A Latin American Writer Explores the Political Lessons of a Peruvian Massacre"), published in the *New York Times Magazine* (1984), is significant; it is concerned with the gruesome events that led to the mass murder of several newspaper journalists by members of an Indian community in the Andes mountains. Vargas Llosa presided over a governmental investigative commission to report to the nation what had essentially transpired. The chronical is a highly readable combination of journalism, artistic creation, and the writer's vocation; it is typical of Vargas Llosa's exciting narrative capabilities and his commitment to the creation of a plurality of viewpoints and the possible interpretations of a tragic and unresolved human event. He is very adept at situating within the chronicle his personal views as to why the event occurred. The interpenetration of these perspectives produces certain ambiguities of interpretation, which coincides with the knowledge of what actually took place.

For Vargas Llosa, however, there is only one possible answer to why Latin American societies are afflicted with chaos and violence. It is a problem of communication among the citizens of those societies. The lack of information, the prejudices, and the tyrannical ideologies all create barriers to the resolution of economic, political, and cultural imperfections in society: "It is difficult for people to defend a free press, elections and representative institutions when their circumstances do not allow them to understand, much less to benefit from, the achievements of democracy" (56).

Vargas Llosa's position in this narrative chronicle appears clear enough in all its facets, literary, vocational, and political. Whether or not one agrees with his strong position about the writer's vocational commitment to reality, most readers cannot help but admire his independent spirit and expression, as well as his uncompromising position regarding the freedom to meditate, comment, and agree or disagree in literary and other contexts. To snatch freedom from the clutches of tyrannical power is the creative writer's moral responsibility as well as a physical necessity for him. Mario Vargas Llosa firmly believes that freedom is an essential requirement for the writer's vocation and for his life. The writer represents the pure expression of intellectual freedom that cannot and will not compromise with external interests but only with what is substantial: the writer himself.

## Chapter Two

# The Short Stories: Narrative Beginnings, Thematic Generators

The initial stage of Mario Vargas Llosa's literary career culminates in 1959 with the publication of his only book of short stories, *Los jefes*. After the first edition in Spanish was published in Barcelona in 1959, Vargas Llosa added one story to subsequent editions and changed the titles of two stories. The English translation by Gregory Kolovakos and Ronald Christ reflects these changes. Together the six stories are concerned with adolescence, machismo, and violence, themes that reappear more fully developed with remarkable aesthetic dimensions in Vargas Llosa's later novels. Three of the best stories—"Los jefes" ("The Leaders"), "El desafío" ("The Challenge"), and "Día domingo" ("On Sunday")—create an adolescent perspective of an adult world in which violence, both latent and actual, plays a major role. In fact, the reader comes to view violence as an integral part of Peruvian society. In effect, Vargas Llosa believes that it is at the heart of all human relationships, even those of friendship and family (Harss and Dohmann 1967, 352). He adds that "there is no possibility of dialogue, discussion, debate—no channeling. . . . I think in a country like mine violence is at the root of all human relations. It's ever present at all moments of an individual's life" (352). His characters struggle for survival and, in some cases, face possible death; much depends on their ability to adapt to strong cultural determinants, such as the cruel male ethic of machismo. In these stories, individuals are forced to submit to pervasive group pressures that pit the weak against the strong and the young against the old, foment class hatred, and demand of everyone a sense of loyalty to the dominant collective social and cultural values.

The other three stories—"El hermano menor" ("The Younger Brother"), "Un visitante" ("A Visitor"), and "El abuelo" ("The

Grandfather")—present further manifestations of violence that form an unfortunate common bond among members of society: corruption, hate, betrayal, and terror. Hence, in these stories, violence lurks and continually erupts; and the reader feels a strong sense of frustration when individuals are forced to confront inhuman social forces, which require an almost total submission if one is to survive. The presence of violence, even in these early pieces, corroborates the literary theories that Vargas Llosa began to develop concerning the most significant elements necessary to render reality adequately in fiction. In his literary study *La orgía perpetua: Flaubert y "Madame Bovary"* Vargas Llosa states that the basic ingredients are rebellion, violence, melodrama, and sex (20). He talks of the physical and spiritual violence that stems for example, from egotism, cowardice, exploitation, and stupidity. The effects to be obtained through the portrayal of violence in literature are of crucial importance to Vargas Llosa; he believes that readers' spirits are not necessarily lifted, nor are hearts made more ecstatic, by reading only happy stories containing optimistic moral messages (26). The focus on violence in these narratives substantiates, in part, Vargas Llosa's theories about the function of literature in society.

By 1957 Vargas Llosa's stories began to appear in journals and in newspapers. "The Leaders" was published in *Mercurio peruano,* and "The Grandfather" in *El Comercio.* "The Challenge" won the *Revue française* short-story competition in 1958, and Vargas Llosa was awarded a free trip to France, where he received his first taste of European cultural and literary life. In 1959 the collection won Barcelona's Leopoldo Alas award. Literary critics agree that "even in *Los jefes,* Vargas Llosa's initial work, one can recognize his ability to create dramatic scenes, his acute sense of economy, and his ability to develop tension" (Aldrich, 1971, 31).

In discussing the period of his life when the stories were written, Vargas Llosa states that they

are a handful of survivors out of many I wrote and tore up between 1953 and 1957, while I was still a student in Lima. I have a certain fondness for them because they remind me of those difficult years, when, even though literature mattered more to me than anything else in the world, it never entered my mind one day I would be a writer—in the real sense of the word. I had married early and my life was smothered by jobs to earn a living as well as by classes at the university. But more than the

stories I wrote on the run, what I remember from those years are the
authors I discovered, the beloved books I read with voracity that char-
acterizes one's addiction to literature at the age of eighteen. ("Author's
Preface," *The Cubs,* xiii).

He had begun to read Dostoyevski, Miller, Faulkner, Hemingway,
and others: "Those readings saturate my first book. It's easy for me
to recognize them in it now, but that wasn't the case when I wrote
the stories. The earliest of them, 'The Leaders,' ostensibly recreates
a strike that we, the graduating students at the San Miguel Academy
in Piura, attempted and deservedly failed at. But it's an out-of-time
echo of Malraux's novel *Man's Hope,* which I was reading while I
wrote the story" (xiv).

## "The Leaders"

"The Leaders" is based on an experience in which Vargas Llosa,
as a high-school student in the northern provincial city of Piura,
participated in a move to halt all classes, with the students at-
tempting to force the school director to set the examination sched-
ules. The essence of the story depends not on the outcome of the
confrontation between the school and the students (for the strike
fails), but on the rivalry between two students who struggle to gain
student recognition as the strike's leader; meanwhile, on a parallel
level, the two rivals decide to settle an old personal grudge. The
story focuses on the process of resolving the antagonisms between
the two students: the narrator-protagonist describes his adversary,
Lou, as a lower-class bruiser. On the surface the story seems to
revolve around their attempts to dominate each other as a way of
proving their leadership to their fellow gang members; on another
level, however, it is a question of personal vengeance and ill will.

The problem goes back to a time when the narrator was ousted
as the gang leader by Lou. The narrator devises a way to precipitate
the student strike, and Lou uses physical violence to keep some of
the younger students out of the classroom. The two confront each
other at the end and prepare for a last fight, which is narrowly
averted when another friend tells them not to waste their time: "We
have to be united" (*The Cubs,* 67). The narrator demands that Lou
explain why he used physical violence on the students. The story
ends as the two reach a tacit understanding of their differences:
"Apparently sorry, Lou raised his face and looked at me. When I

felt his hand in mine, I realized that it was soft and delicate, and that this was the first time we'd greeted each other this way" (67). With Lou's apparent defeat and humiliation comes the narrator's acceptance of him more as a human being than as an adversary. The conciliatory tone of the last scene suggests the need among human beings for sympathy and understanding. The story is saying perhaps that, in the face of oppressive social institutions, individuals must work together in order to solve their problems. Since Vargas Llosa believes that violence is a determinant of individual human action in society, and although the new friendship between the narrator and Lou may seem genuine, it is probably only a momentary settlement, soon to revert back to other forms of violence. For some readers brutality could function as a means to conduct violence to a higher state of comprehension and consciousness as a means for converting an adolescent into an authentic man.

## "The Challenge"

In "The Challenge" Vargas Llosa is once again concerned with the theme of violence. Two young men, Justo and the Gimp, are lower-class Piurans who must prove or lose their manliness by confronting each other in a deadly knife fight. In this story, the first-person narrator, Julián, functions differently: he does not participate directly in the action but observes and alters the action as it builds slowly to the fatal confrontation between the two members of rival neighborhood gangs.

The story begins in a bar where old man Leonidas tells one gang that he wants them to be at "the raft" that evening where Justo will fight the Gimp. Julián retrieves his switchblade from home and goes out. At this point, still early in the story, the reader already feels the presence of death. Day is over, and night is fast approaching. The city band has just finished playing in the park, and the crowd is dispersing. As Julián is leaving the house his wife arrives carrying their sleeping baby in her arms, giving him the impression that his son is dead. Julián then goes to another bar, where he discusses the impending fight with the owner. The Gimp is described as a mean and diabolical figure; Justo, as his name implies, is seen as an innocent child, a sacrificial lamb. Justo tells Julián about his encounter with the Gimp. Then the gang proceeds to the spot designated for the fight.

As the time for the fight draws near, an uncanny sense of death begins to invade the environment. The reader feels confronted by an obscure, vague mixture of life and death, of the seen and the unseen. It is nighttime, when it is difficult to see anything clearly; the sky has clouded over, and on the outskirts of town "the sand was lukewarm and our feet sank in as if we were walking on a sea of cotton" (115). More important, the place of the fight is described in legendary terms; it is situated in a dry river bed, where a large tree trunk—"the raft"—is known to move downriver a few yards during the spring floods each year. Hence, nothing seems permanent; everything is constantly shifting. In this context, magical and irreversible forces seem to be working to bring about the tragic encounter between Justo and the Gimp.

The final scene of the story presents the actual fight—described not as Julián might faithfully report it (for the night is too dark to permit clear sight), but as he imagines an affair of honor might be conducted as a clash of arms between primitive forces in a sacred ritual. The scene is transformed into a modern-day version of the age-old Roman spectacle in which two gladiators perform a symbolic dance of death. The movement of the two figures—advancing, crouching, and sidestepping a gleaming blade thrust into the darkness—is magnificently communicated through Julián's creative imagination: "I wasn't able to see their faces, but I closed my eyes and saw them better than if I'd been in their midst: The Gimp sweating, his mouth shut, his little pig eyes aflame and blazing behind his eyelids, his skin throbbing, the wings of his flattened nose and the slit of his mouth shaken by an inconceivable quivering; and Justo, with his usual sneering mask intensified by anger and his lips moist with rage and fatigue. I opened my eyes just in time to see Justo pounce madly, blindly on the other man, giving him every advantage, offering his face, foolishly exposing his body" (121). The tension continues to mount, and the fight transcends its immediate significance: "But even without distinguishing who was who, without knowing whose arm delivered which blows, whose throat offered up those roars that followed one another like echoes, we repeatedly saw the naked knife blades in the air, quivering toward the heavens or in the midst of the darkness, down at their sides, swift, blazing, in and out of sight, hidden or brandished in the night as in some magician's spectacular show" (122).

As fast as it began, the fight is over. But in the moment before Justo falls dead on the sand, the Gimp yells to the old man to stop the fight before Justo is killed. But Leonidas screams in reply to keep fighting to the end. Afterwards, as his friends carry Justo's body back to town, one of them tells the old man not to cry: "I've never known anyone brave as your son. I really mean that" (124). A fact has remained hidden from the reader from the beginning: the old man is Justo's father. This suppressed piece of information, revealed at the very end, suggests additional implications for the meaning of the story. The role of the father, who determines whether his son lives or dies, provides a new twist to the theme of machismo and violence, for the reader is led to realize that the real tragedy does not lie simply in Justo's death, understood in terms of a personal grudge with the Gimp; rather, the tragedy is revealed more in the character's obligation to live by the brutal male code, which is the same one that Justo's father must adhere to and that he subsequently forces upon his son. Not only is the reader confronted with the fact that adolescents mimic social values forced upon them by adult behavioral codes; the reader is also brought face to face with the actuality that all the characters are victims of oppressive social values. Expressions of compassion and understanding are nullified by stupid gestures of manliness. The reader comes to realize that the characters' lives are based on appearances, deceit, and fatalism. From the very beginning, a sense of defeat is pervasive. One character says that "if they had to fight, better that way, according to the rules." Leonidas, in resigning himself to this fact, responds: "Maybe it's better like that" (111). There arise opportunities to thwart the fatal encounter, but no one is capable of going against the code. Before the fight, a bartender says, "I feel sorry for Justo, but really, he's been asking for it for some time" (112). In the scene in which Justo meets up with the Gimp at a bar, a priest pulls them apart, calls them animals, but does nothing when he hears the Gimp shout: "At 'the raft' tonight, then?" (114). Another remote possibility of stopping the fight occurs when they discover that without moonlight it is too dark to see:

"We'll light bonfires," Justo said.
"Are you crazy?" I said. "You want the police to come?"
"It can be arranged," Briceño said without conviction.

"It could be put off till tomorrow. They're not going to fight in the dark."

Nobody answered and Briceño didn't persist. (115)

The last opportunity to stop the fight comes when the Gimp tells the adversaries to call it off just before he kills Justo:

"Leonidas!" he shouted again in a furious, imploring tone. "Tell him to give up."

"Shut up and fight!" Leonidas bellowed without hesitating. (123)

The characters' fates are sealed within a system that is determined by those unfortunate human values of injustice, deceit, hypocrisy, and stupidity—all of which lead to violence.

"The Challenge" is a conventional but well-crafted short story. Here Vargas Llosa develops a special mythic environment of primitive ritual, which includes the dance of death and final sacrifice. The build-up of tension through the different scenes, in which attempts to stop the fight are thwarted, culminates in the macabre dance of the flashing switchblades. And, finally, the discovery of Leonidas's identity at the very end of the story forces the reader to reconsider the story's ultimate significance. The concealed relationship between father and son, whose revelation at the story's end resembles the denouement of a typical detective story, shows the extent to which the social codes control even the most basic human relationships.

## "On Sunday"

In "On Sunday," two middle-class Lima bourgeois adolescents, Miguel and Rubén, challenge each other to absurd contests of physical prowess in order to prove their worth to Flora, the neighborhood sweetheart and prize for the boy who can dominate the other. A subtle combination of an exterior third-person omniscient narration and the interiorized point of view of Miguel provides the principal narrative focus of the story. From the beginning the reader becomes aware of Miguel's most private thoughts, fears, and insecurities in an adolescent world of first love. The story begins with his attempts to find the courage to tell Flora he loves her and to tell Rubén how much he hates him.

Although shy, Miguel does tell Flora one day that he loves her. She blushes and turns down his invitation to go to the movies, because she is spending the day with Rubén's sister. Miguel sees this as a ploy so that Rubén can be alone with Flora. He decides to take action to foil Rubén's plan. Miguel goes to look for his neighborhood friends, who call themselves the Hawks, at a bar where he eventually thwarts Rubén's early departure by challenging him to see who can drink the most beer: "Miguel turned toward the others, spreading his arms wide. 'Hawks, I'm making a challenge.' Delighted, he proved that the old formula still had the same force as before. In the midst of the happy commotion he had stirred up, he saw Rubén sit down, pale" (95). The drinking bout ends in a tie, and although both adolescents are thoroughly drunk by the end, Rubén reciprocates by challenging Miguel to a swimming race in the wintery cold Pacific waters at one of Lima's beaches. As both swim out to a jetty and begin their return, Rubén suffers stomach cramps and pleads for help, and Miguel rescues him.

Accordingly, the apparent physical superiority that Rubén enjoys over Miguel dissipates. Upon their return to shore where the rest of the gang is waiting, Rubén begs Miguel not to tell them how Miguel saved his life, but only that he won the race. Although it is understood that Flora now belongs to Miguel, he is denied the pleasure of being praised and congratulated for having saved a friend, a heroic deed by any standard and a sincere act of friendship. On one level, then, Miguel's decision to comply with the machismo code of not revealing Rubén's physical weakness (by almost drowning under absurd circumstances) indicates how both adolescents acquiesce to the system and accept deceit and hypocrisy in order to keep their manliness and the social code intact; they are impostors, fakes—or, as Miguel keeps telling Rubén when they get drunk, "You're just a phony" (97). On another level, however, Miguel's successful conquest, while much more than a demonstration of his superiority over Rubén, is a sign of having put his adolescence behind him and acquired the courage, honor, and confidence necessary to become a real man.

In this way, the last lines of the story can be interpreted according to the two levels that the narrator employs to describe Miguel's illusions: "Smiling, he thought how that same night he would go to Salazar Park. All Miraflores would soon know, thanks to Melanés, that he had won the heroic contest and Flora would be waiting for

him with glowing eyes. A golden future was opening before him"
(109). On the outside, Miguel complies with the social code, and
Flora becomes his trophy; on the inside, Miguel passes a courageous
test of true manhood that allows him to find personal meaning
through a modern-day process of initiation. The story can also be
viewed through Rubén's defeat by his own false sense of pride, not
to mention Miguel's determination to block Rubén's plan because
of Miguel's passion for Flora. Although it is Miguel's sense of human
solidarity that saves Rubén, their new friendship is tenuous at best.

## "The Younger Brother"

The fourth story, entitled "The Younger Brother," opens with
two brothers, David and Juan, combing the countryside on horse-
back and hunting for an Indian who their sister Leonor claims has
raped her. The family honor is at stake and must be avenged. Juan,
the younger brother, has just returned to the family hacienda from
the city where he has been living. Now, he feels out of place and
insecure in the new environment. Night sets in as they approach
the fugitive's hiding spot near a waterfall. While they rest, Juan
contemplates his situation, finding it difficult to make much sense
of what is happening:

He lit another cigarette. When he had returned to the ranch three months
ago, it had been two years since he had seen his brother and sister. David
was the same person he had hated and admired ever since childhood, but
Leonor had changed: she was no longer the little girl who used to throw
stones at the imprisoned Indians, but a tall woman with primitive gestures,
and her beauty, like the countryside around her, had something brutal
about it. An intense brilliance had appeared in her eyes. Juan felt a sickness
that blurred his sight, an emptiness in his stomach as after a jab of anger
every time he associated the image of the man they were hunting with
the memory of his sister. Still, at dawn of that day when he saw Camilo
cross the clearing separating the ranch house from the stables to get the
horses ready, he had hesitated. (128)

Later they approach the Indian, who is facing a campfire as David
leaps upon him: "Juan closed his eyes and imagined the Indian:
squatting, his hands stretched out toward the flames, his eyes ir-
ritated by the sputtering of the campfire. Suddenly something fell
on him, and he had guessed it was some animal, when he felt two

violent hands closing around his neck and he understood. He must have experienced infinite terror at this unexpected attack coming out of the darkness" (130). As David and the Indian roll on the ground, locked in a deadly clench, Juan fires his pistol into the darkness. After a long silence, David finally speaks, cursing his brother for nearly killing him instead of the Indian. On the way back, Juan informs David that he is going to return to the city immediately. David wants to know what is wrong, and Juan blurts out: "What's wrong with me? Do you realize what you're saying? Have you forgotten that guy at the waterfall? If I stay at the ranch I'm going to end up thinking it's normal to do things like that" (133). David responds by saying, "He was a sick dog . . . your scruples are foolish. Maybe you've forgotten what he did to your sister?" (133).

Back at the ranch, the two brothers find Leonor emotionally out of control. She knows that they had gone to hunt down the Indian; and she tells them now that there was no rape, it was a lie. Suddenly Juan cannot contain himself: a whole gamut of feelings—guilt, self-reproach, hatred—well up inside him, and like a volcano, erupt. He charges outside the house, climbs on a wild horse, and in a short time, brutally tames it. Afterward he knocks down the door of a hut, thereby freeing some of the ranch's Indians who are being punished: "After that he came back to the house walking slowly. David was waiting for him at the door. Juan seemed calm; he was drenched in sweat and his eyes showed his pride. David came up to him and brought him inside; his arm around Juan's shoulder" (139).

By taming the horse, Juan is initiated into a strange, primitive, and brutal environment in which violence dominates life in the country. Beginning with the initial scene of the story—when Juan's brother shoots a frog off a rock on the side of the road—Juan is repulsed by so much violence. The hapless death of the Indian is the result of gratuitous violence, and ironically, Juan is responsible for killing him. Yet Juan avenges this impetuous deed by releasing the imprisoned Indians. These acts seem to compensate for the original acts; in an abnormal and almost barbaric society, Juan proves his virility by demonstrating his capacity to force his will upon others, that is, to tame the horse. In remembering the moment when Juan closed his eyes and imagined the Indian, the reader realizes that Juan is capable of feeling the force of the cruelty, injustice, and indifference that dominate his brother and sister's lives on the ranch. In addition, Juan mitigates his strong passions of condemnation by turning violence against itself. Rather than become another victim of evil social forces that are determined by aberrant codes of behavior, Juan seemingly liberates himself through the discovery of an intense sense of inner peace.

## "A Visitor"

The setting of this story is a small mud shack situated along a trail in a desolate rural area outside Piura, where travelers stop to buy supplies. The owner doña Mercedes, is drowsing when a gaunt black man unexpectedly appears at the door. Neither of them is surprised to see the other, for they have met before. He demands food and forces her to drink several beers. He asks where her man Numa is hiding. Then he ties her up and tickles her feet. Time passes, and evening approaches. Suddenly, soldiers arrive. The arrogant black man literally commands the officer in charge to hide his men and horses in the nearby brush. Doña Mercedes tells the black man that he is a double-crosser for having led the police to where Numa, a fugitive, can be captured. He was sure to show up because the black man had spread stories around the area that he was going after Numa's woman, Mercedes. When Numa arrives with his men, he is quickly taken prisoner. The black man has won his freedom in exchange for betraying Numa and assisting the police. When he realizes the police are going to leave him there, the black man pleads with the lieutenant to take him along. But the officer pushes him away and gets revenge for the black man's insolent behavior toward him earlier. Doña Mercedes begins to laugh hard, knowing that the black man faces grave danger if he remains behind, for Numa's men are hiding nearby, waiting to avenge their leader's fate by pouncing on the black man when the police leave. In effect, the story ends as "out of the woods comes the sound of snapping branches and dry leaves" (86).

Once again, violence is the theme. But in this story the reader experiences a different type of violence. Action is held to a minimum, while the tension is acute. Although violent acts do not occur, the potential for violence reveals the essence of the story from the beginning. The reader experiences two tension-filled, emotionally charged scenes in which violent acts are implied rather than presented: one, in the first part of the story, where it is suggested that the black man, after forcing doña Mercedes to drink beer, rapes her; and the other, at the end of the story, where Numa's men approach the hut intending to kill the black man.

The reader does not witness either of these two events, but the motives behind the brutal and violent acts are clearly revealed as betrayal, revenge, rancor, vindictiveness, fear, hatred, and cruelty. Moreover, the story is narrated in the present tense, which captures the feeling of immediacy, nearness, and convergence. The black man abuses doña Mercedes, and she is victimized; he betrays Numa in order to save his own skin; the officer deceives the black man in order to teach him a lesson about impertinence; and Numa's men avenge the fate of their leader. The betrayal by the black man breaks the code and turns the system against himself. In the first part of the story (the insinuated rape) the black man is the victimizer; in the end he is the victim. This story portrays violence among men and women not only as the potential but also the inevitable result of unseen evil and malicious forces that become a part of human nature in a system of corrupt social values.

## "The Grandfather"

In Vargas Llosa's last story the theme of violence is carried beyond the potential for physical violence and into the realm of mental terror and cruelty that don Eulogio inflicts upon the grandson whom he dislikes. An aura of fantasy, black magic, and morbidity pervade this story. Basically, the grandfather dislikes his grandson's regular visits to his house in an upper-class section of Lima. The child represents an invasion of the old man's private and solitary world centering around his garden; thus, the story begins: "Each time a twig cracked or a frog croaked or the window panes rattled in the kitchen at the back of the garden, the old man jumped spryly from his improvised seat on a flat rock and spied anxiously through the foliage. But the boy still had not appeared" (68). The first part of the story centers around the old man's childlike pleasure of planning something that strikes the reader as mysterious, odd, and evil. First the old man finds a skull on the roadside, and then he buys a candle. Tension mounts as the old man paces the floor, contemplating his secret: "He seldom lifted his head: it might be said that he was examining with profound devotion and some terror the bloody and

magical figures in the middle circle of the carpet, but he did not
even see them" (71). On the next day he tries to clean the skull,
without success. Using olive oil as a remedy, he turns the scene
into a form of ritual: "Leaping to his feet suddenly, he stared in
wonder at the skull he held up over his head: clean, radiant, mo-
tionless, with several little drops like sweat on the rolling surface
of the cheekbones" (72–73). The ritual becomes an offering to the
youth that he once possessed but which is no longer his.

Returning home through the back garden gate, he hears the voices
of his son, daughter-in-law, and grandson coming from inside the
house. Deciding then and there to carry out his plan, he sets the
skull with a candle inside on the garden path; he intends not only
to startle the young lad but, moreover, to terrify, haunt, and in-
timidate him. In the moment of black magic and sinister ritual, he
lights the candle, but the whole skull (still soaked in olive oil)
unexpectedly bursts into flames sending fire shooting out of the eye
sockets, the cranium, the nose, and the mouth. The boy appears
from nowhere and experiences the scene firsthand. He screams, starts
to tremble, and is frightened out of his wits: "His grandson could
not see anything but that flaming head. His eyes were fixed, with
a deep, everlasting terror painted in them. Everything had been
simultaneous: the sudden blaze, the howl, the vision of that figure
in short pants suddenly possessed by terror. Enthusiastically he was
thinking that things had turned out even more perfectly than he
had planned." (75).

This story reveals an ever-expanding concept of violence. The
grandfather menaces the boy by preying on his mind, inflicting
mental cruelty upon the child. Vargas Llosa has been careful not to
expose directly the motives behind such a heinous act but rather he
places the reader inside the distorted mind of the old man, where
the reader may experience the enigmatic nature of the conflict between the old man and his environment. Although the reader is
never sure why the flaming ritual becomes a kind of catharsis or
purification of his emotions, the old man's fascination with the skull
is morbid. Only once does he consider abandoning his plan; one
day he spots the empty, lifeless birdhouse outside the window and
remembers how it was once full of birds and bursting with life.
Other visions he experiences seem to indicate that wherever there
is life he is bent on destroying it. Violence rears its head through
the invisible forms of punishment that are inflicted on human beings.

In the old man's case, his punishment may be old age and isolation. At one point in the story, before the climax, the young boy is heard telling his father in the house that his punishment was to end that same day and that the next day he was not going back to his grandfather's house (supposedly). Ironically, one punishment ends and another begins (with the flaming skull). Violence in this story takes on the form of mental cruelty whereby don Eulogio's solitary, alienated, and closed world of old age is transmitted to the young boy who experiences the death of his own adolescence when he participates in the ritual of the burning skull.

## Conclusion

The six stories possess common themes: the major theme of violence is created by implicit and explicit combinations of machismo, perversion, alienation, betrayal, treason, exploitation, deceit, injustice, hypocrisy, and hatred; while other themes include the rite of initiation, the loss of innocence, and the distortion of reality by appearances and imagination. The characters are required to react to a shifting, ambiguous, unknown, and threatening environment. The brutal code of machismo and the characters' submission to it—in "The Leaders," "On Sunday," "The Challenge," and "The Younger Brother"—are probably the most detrimental force working on the individuals in these stories. Human beings learn from an early age that by submitting to the rules of the game they may possibly survive; however, they may adopt evil ways in order to do so. If a person reveals basic feelings of solidarity, love, and cohesion—which are in turn deemed typical of a weak and vulnerable person—he or she is apt to die (as in "The Challenge"), or to suffer mental anguish (as in "The Grandfather"). Between these extremes lie the unfortunate hypocritical individuals who live by false social codes, such as machismo, and deny themselves the right to truly fulfilling lives. Despite the usual tragic results of violence in the majority of these stories, some of them—"The Leaders," "The Younger Brother," and "On Sunday"—end in such a way as to communicate feelings of hopefulness and reassurance that individuals can overcome the destructive nature of oppressive values held by the society at large.

Beyond the common themes, the action and settings in the stories possess certain similarities. Usually two people are pitted against each other in a basic conflict that triggers a set of reactions resulting in violence. Through narrative point of view the reader is situated closer to one adversary and more distant from the other. The new perspective forces the reader to assume a moral stance with regard to the issues. The action, however, usually takes place at dusk, at night, or on cloudy, rainy, hazy days, and the absence of light and color, which obscures vision, creates shifting, changing, and threatening environments. As a result, the description of the surroundings in the stories adds to the feeling of uncertainty that the reader must deal with when reacting to moral and emotional interpretations of the stories.

# Chapter Three
# The Time of the Hero:
# Lost Innocence

The Chilean novelist José Donoso states that the spectacular artistic growth, internationalization, and economic success of the contemporary Spanish American novel is composed of three principal phases. The first centers around the publication in 1959 of Carlos Fuentes's novel *Where the Air Is Clear,* and Donoso says, "Mario Vargas Llosa embodies the second phase of the Boom: the great explosion was produced in 1962, when, still a twenty-four-year-old, he received the Biblioteca Breve Prize from the Barcelona publishing house of Seix Barral. With that prize and a great deal of hoopla, his name— and, incidentally, that of Seix Barral Publishers—suddenly became popular in the entire Spanish-speaking world. *The Time of the Hero* caused the whole continent to talk" (Donoso 1977, 60–61). The third phase revolves around the publication of García Márquez's *One Hundred Years of Solitude* in 1967.

## Plot: Banal Events, Moral Struggles

The impact of Vargas Llosa's novel was indeed great; it was acclaimed as one of the best novels written in Spanish during the past three decades. A felicitous combination of theme, style, and technique in the novel produced widespread surprise, bedazzlement, and admiration. It has been said that *The Time of the Hero* breaks with mimetic, regional *criollista* fiction and makes an alliance with other art forms such as film. It actively incorporates slang and taboo vocabulary into the text, captures the mannerisms of people from marginalized social sectors that are uncommon in Hispanic-American literature, and brings into play the subjective, emotional, and fantasized worlds of its characters. Moreover, Vargas Llosa's narrative strategies include the complex juxtaposition of multiple character points of view and the chronological disjunction of time. In this respect, the form and style of the novel call attention to themselves, for the action, which involves the theme of adolescent initiation into society, revolves around the familiar and even trite daily activities of military school cadets.

A literal translation of the Spanish title *La ciudad y los perros* reads "the city and the dogs." The action takes place in Lima, the capital city of Peru, and "dogs" is a derogatory name given to first-year cadets at the military school that provides the setting for a major part of the novel's action. Vargas Llosa initially entitled the novel "Los impostores" (The impostors) and provisionally used another title "La morada del héroe" (The abode of the hero), which is close to the English version. The translation produces an irony that does not exist in the Spanish title, for the characters in the novel are anything but heroes; they are in fact antiheroes.

On the surface, the story might appear to be totally mundane and anything but profound. A thumbnail sketch of the novel's action does not reveal its overall complexity: (1) the theft of an exam at a military school is followed by the collective punishment of the suspension of weekend leaves; (2) one cadet squeals on another and is mysteriously shot while on military maneuvers; (3) another cadet accuses the suspected executioner; (4) an investigation ensues and the incident is ruled an accident. Yet John Brushwood is correct in stating that "although it is completely 'modern' in technique, plot development is the basis of the experience of this work. That is to say, Vargas Llosa creates a world, presents a problem, develops interesting characters, and works out a climax and denouement that hold his readers in suspense" (Brushwood 1975b, 253–54). Like Brushwood, Jorge Lafforgue and others see *The Time of the Hero* as a moral novel in which personal and social behavioral attitudes are at odds.

The present of the novel is a two-month period in the final year of high school of five young student cadets at Leoncio Prado Military School in Lima. Approximately half the novel's action takes place in the past, providing a contrapuntal structure between past and present. Organizational patterns based on the concept of duality begin to emerge early in the novel. The opposition between the city and the school is indicated in the title, of course, and the contrast between present and past provides another organizing strategy for the development of the novel's plot.

The author's penchant for action and an immediate and heightened sense of growing tension in the present time of the plot is found in the opening lines. It begins in medias res:

"Four," the Jaguar said.
Their faces relaxed in the uncertain glow which the bulb cast through the few clean pieces of glass. There was no danger for anyone now except Porfirio Cava. The dice had stopped rolling. A three and a one. Their whiteness stood out against the dirty tiles.
"Four," the Jaguar repeated. "Who is it?"
"Me," Cava muttered. "I said four."
"Get going, then. You know which one, the second on the left." (7)

Four cadets—Alberto Fernández, alias Poet; Porfirio Cava; Boa; and Jaguar—who belong to an "in" group called The Circle, are throwing dice in the barracks bathroom after curfew to see who will steal a chemistry examination locked up in a classroom. When the adolescents were first-year cadets, they formed The Circle to protect themselves from the savage initiation rites of the older cadets.

Cava loses the throw, and during the theft he breaks a window. The crime is discovered by the school officials, and the cadets who were on guard duty that evening are confined to the barracks. Early in the novel, tension mounts because there are intercalated moments from the past, particularly from the lives of Alberto, Jaguar, and another cadet, Ricardo Arana, who is nicknamed Slave because of his weak and cowardly nature. When other illegal activites in the barracks are discovered, weekend furloughs are cancelled. Unable to cope with the punishment, Arana reveals Porfirio Cava's name to the school officials in order to get an afternoon off to visit a girl named Teresa. Cava is suspended, and Jaguar, The Circle's leader, pledges revenge. While the cadets are performing military exercises in the country, Ricardo is shot in the head from behind and dies. The circumstances surrounding his death are never revealed, nor is the guilty party ever brought to justice.

In this sense, the plot contains the flavor of a detective story; pieces of important information are withheld from the reader (Vargas Llosa's use of the *dato escondido,* or hidden fact), making the plot strikingly similar to a riddle or a puzzle. Rilda L. Baker states that "Vargas Llosa refracts, even multiplies, the puzzle format until it not only contributes to the structural frame of the work but also affects the conceptual apprehension and ultimate interpretation of the novel" (Baker 1977, 7–8).

Each of the two parts and the epilogue of the novel are prefaced by epigraphs. Part One's epigraph is from Jean-Paul Sartre: "We play the part of heroes because we're cowards, the part of saints because we're wicked: we play the killer's role because we're dying to murder our fellow man: we play at being because we're liars from the moment we're born." The aptness of this quotation is made patent by the author's perspective on adolescents growing up in a corrupt adult world in which they are obligated to play tragic games in order to survive.

The narrative content of the second half of the novel revolves around the attempt to discover Arana's killer. When the preliminary investigation reveals nothing substantial, the school officials declare the death accidental. The school's reputation is at stake, and if a scandal were to break out the school officials would be subject to reprimands. Arana's only friend, Alberto, knows that Jaguar is the murderer. Alberto decides finally to tell Lieutenant Gamboa his version of the incident and to turn in Jaguar. He also tells Gamboa of the illicit cadet activities in the barracks—the commonplace thefts, fights, and escapes from the school. The lieutenant feels morally obligated to pursue the accusations, and he urges the school officials to investigate the incident further. A shakedown in the barracks takes place. But the school officials prefer to let the death of Arana go unsolved rather than precipitate a scandal. Hence, Gamboa's request goes unheeded, and he is even reprimanded for wishing to discover the truth.

Alberto is blackmailed by the school officials. After discovering incriminating evidence in Alberto's locker—he writes pornographic stories and love letters for his classmates in return for cigarettes—the school officials threaten to expel him. He and Jaguar are forced to share the same jail cell, and they fight bitterly. When they return to the barracks, the other cadets think that Jaguar is responsible for causing the shakedown. He does nothing to admit or to deny his guilt. Jaguar's code of honor does not allow a person to snitch on another person. The epigraph that prefaces this part, from Paul Nizan, indicates Vargas Llosa's highly critical stance and harsh, even bitter, attitude toward the adolescent initiation into society: "I'm twenty years old. Don't let anyone tell me it is the most beautiful period of life."

In the epilogue three events are narrated. First, Jaguar admits to Lieutenant Gamboa that he did shoot Arana; by then, however, it is too late. The officer, reassigned to a lonely outpost, is too disillusioned to pursue the incident any further: " 'The Arana case is closed,' Gamboa said. 'The army doesn't want to hear another word about it. It would be easier to bring Arana back to life than to convince the army it's made an error.' " (387). Second, by dropping his accusations, Alberto is permitted to graduate and to return to civilian life. The reader feels the author's sarcasm and his highly critical stance toward the hypocrisy of the military in a scene in which an army colonel who is as much a caricature as a character congratulates Alberto for his capitulation to blackmail: " 'In the army,' the colonel said, 'justice always triumphs sooner or later. It's something inherent in the military system, and you've had opportunity to observe for yourself. Just consider, Cadet Fernández: you were on the verge of ruining your life, of soiling an honorable name, an illustrious family tradition. But the army gave you a last opportunity to mend your ways' " (395). Third, Jaguar also goes free, marries his old boyhood sweetheart, Tere, and becomes a lowly bank clerk.

The epilogue's epigraph is a verse by Peruvian poet Carlos Germán Belli: ". . . in each lineage / deterioration exercises its dominion." Here part of the irony is directed at the outcome of the different characters' lives. Alberto, for example, rejoins his group of middle-class friends and dreams about becoming rich and living the easy life. He tells his new girlfriend that he is going to the United States to study. "Alberto thought, I'll study hard and be a good engineer. When I come back, I'll work with my father, and I'll have a convertible and a big house with a swimming pool. I'll marry Marcela and be a Don Juan. I'll go to the Grill Bolívar every Saturday for the dancing, and I'll do a lot of traveling. After a few years I won't even remember I was in the Leoncio Prado" (398–99). The epigraph suggests that in this case, even though Alberto has learned about a part of Peruvian society that he had never experienced as a spoiled child from a well-to-do suburb of Lima, he has forfeited his opportunity to become aware of Peru's social problems by returning to his insipid social class and shutting the door to his painful but possibly socially and culturally enriching past.

Beyond the events that reach a climax with Arana's death in the first part of the novel, the attempts to discover the truth about his death in the second part, and the revelation of hidden information in the epilogue, approximately half of the novel's content alternates with the present moment of action to narrate the past lives of Poet, Slave, and Jaguar. Basically, two time periods in the lives of the cadets become apparent: events covering the three-year span of cadet life in the military school preceding the action of the present two-month period (the immediate past), and childhood experiences (the remote past) up to the period immediately prior to entering the military school. The juxtaposition of such diverse material creates a temporal and spatial montage effect. But although the plot structure seems at first disturbingly fragmented and lacking relevant connections and significant relationships among the parts, the reader finds that the chapter segments set in the past decrease progressively as the novel advances into the second part, which deals with the enigmatic nature of the Slave's death. The structure of the novel is organized to place more emphasis on the past lives of the characters in the first part, while the second part delves into the interior conflicts of the characters, who must face the moral dilemmas of deciding between right and wrong and between their consciences and certain social codes, that is, between personal honor and machismo.

## Structure and Point of View

The organization of the novel is a series of contrasting and parallel elements primarily recognizable through the fragmented presentation of multiple points of view. The external structure provides the first hint of the novel's overall complexity and ambiguity. Each of its two parts is divided into eight chapters, and each chapter is broken down into short segments. The Epilogue contains three scenes. Taken together, eighty-two segments make up the novel; and they alternate between the past and the present, between the school and the city, between the cadets and the neighborhood friends, between the school's military codes and the social norms of society at large, between victims and victimizers, and among several different types of narrators. Rilda L. Baker states that "through this contrapuntal rhythm the stress is placed on simultaneity, on the shifting center of the fictive present and the confounding effects of such movement. The ultimate result is the blurring of temporal and spatial categories, the interpenetration of time and space" (Baker 1978, 7).

A brief description of the events in the first segments of the novel indicates the juxtaposition of vastly different kinds of narrative material. The lead segment deals with the theft of the exam and reveals certain stylistic and descriptive aspects that are at work throughout the novel. The action takes place at night, making it difficult to discern clearly what is happening. Everything dissolves into shadows, silhouettes, and vague forms. Through Cava, the reader, who does not see much, learns about the events through other sensorial means: sound, smell, and touch.

The implication here is that the characters are unable to perceive reality intellectually or in such a way that they can make clear judgments about the conflicts they are facing. Cava cannot recognize voices, and the drifting fog erases any recognizable outlines of the environment; these circumstances reflect his mood: "In a confused way he wanted to lose his will and imagination and just carry out the plan like a blind machine. Sometimes he could go for several days following a routine that made all the decisions for him gently nudging him into actions he hardly noted. This was different. What was happening tonight had been forced on him. He felt unusually clearheaded and he knew perfectly well what he was doing" (9). The clarity refers more to Cava's recognition of the "in" group's code, which he must obey without question. The burden of the moral significance of the theft of the exam is left to the reader. This initial segment also underscores the relativist perspective with which the author requires the reader to perceive the reality of the novel, for Cava's point of view remains largely undeveloped throughout and serves only to introduce the problematic world of illusion.

The highly volatile racial, geographical, and social differences among the cadets also permeate the first segment, which sets the stage for the rest of the novel. The cadets are depicted as savage animals, while the school's mascot, an Andean vicuña, resembles a human being more than an animal. Cava is from the mountains of Peru; other characters come from the coastal regions. The school contains a racial mixture of whites, blacks, Indians and mestizos; prejudices are rampant throughout the institution.

The next segment narrates a moment in the remote childhood past of Ricardo Arana, when he and his mother move from a pro-

vincial northern city to Lima. There "Richi" meets his father for
the first time and finds the encounter unbearable. The new family
relationship marks for Arana the end of a period of innocence and
happiness. The intercalated segments concerning this character's
past always begin with the phrase, "He has forgotten . . . ," which
alerts the reader to the segment's content and establishes an elegaic
tone.

The third segment of the first chapter begins with an interiorized
first-person narration by Alberto, who is standing guard duty on
the night of the theft. He is thinking of what he will do with his
time off on the following Saturday. He imagines writing love letters
and lurid stories for other cadets in exchange for money or cigarettes,
and he mentally re-creates the things he must do: steal some shoe
laces for inspection the next day, borrow money from friends, try
to visit a brothel in town, and pay for the answers on the stolen
exam. While on duty he interrupts a barracks card game and jokingly
threatens to call the captain. Then he meets Ricardo Arana, who is
also on guard duty. "The Slave" has been forced to take the Jaguar's
place. The two cadets carry on a conversation about Ricardo's vulnerability. Alberto asks him why he lets everyone treat him like a
slave. Arana says he does what he wants. Alberto declares that he
is a weakling because he has never proven himself in a fight at the
school:

"That's why you're screwed," Alberto said. "Everybody knows you're
scared. You've got to slug somebody once in a while if you want them to
respect you. If you don't, they walk all over you."
"I'm not going to be a soldier."
"Neither am I. But you're a soldier here whether you like it or not.
And the big thing in the army is to be real tough, to have guts, see what
I mean? Screw them first before they screw you. There isn't any other
way. I don't like to be screwed." (23)

This is one of the major themes of the novel. The young boys must
learn the law of the jungle by applying the theory of the survival
of the fittest. The rite of initiation for the young men involves their
apprenticeship to the adult world, where everyone must abide by
harsh social norms. Ricardo notices that Alberto manages to take
care of himself without having to fight, and Alberto responds that
"I make believe I'm crazy. I mean I play stupid. You could do that
too, so they wouldn't walk all over you. If you don't defend yourself

tooth and claw they jump on you. That's the law of the jungle"
(24).

The fourth segment narrates, in the present tense, a period in
Alberto's past when his family moves from one Lima neighborhood
to another. In the new neighborhood he makes friends with the
boys who live on the same street. But his parents' marital problems
make the new period in his life more difficult. The apparently
unrelated segments, which are so abruptly juxtaposed to one another,
create violent contrasts throughout the novel. These relationships
also create parallels that reinforce the novel's thematic elements.
From the beginning, a parallel is established between the disruptive
pasts of Ricardo and Alberto. The unhappy family environments of
both Alberto and Ricardo, which are narrated in the first segments
of the novel, reinforce the destructive effect that this period has on
the lives of these characters.

The fifth and last segment of the first chapter is narrated from
the collective point of view of several cadets who are involved in
sexual activities with animals; however, the telegraphic and indirect
narrational dialogue of isolated moments among a group of unidentified cadets deflects the intensity of these incidents.

In general, the reader begins to appreciate the diversity of the
narrative material presented through the multiple points of view,
divergent narrative voices that range from third-person omniscience
to first-person singular and include interior monologue, a free indirect style, and anonymous singular and collective voices speaking
in dialogue. The complex nature of the narrative point of view in
*The Time of the Hero* can be understood more easily by concentrating
on the four principal narrators: Alberto, Ricardo, Jaguar, and Boa.
In each case, there are stylistic, linguistic, lexical, and rhythmic
differences that enable the reader to distinguish one voice from
another. Although each narrational point of view is continually
interrupted and fragmented by the other points of view, a sense of
chronological continuity is discerned within each point of view; that
is, the stories of each character develop chronologically, beginning
with early moments in their lives in the first part and ending with
the most recent events in the epilogue—particularly in the case of
Alberto and Jaguar, whose lives are projected into the future in the
novel's final scenes.

Each narrational point of view, however, is internally complex
and serves a particular function in the novel. While the viewpoints

of Alberto and Jaguar provide the novel's backbone and thematic substance, other narrative voices serve different purposes. For example, the reader is confronted with Boa's innermost thoughts through an almost pure form of interior monologue. A strange, intimate, and at times sexually perverse yet strangely human relationship develops between Boa and Skimpy, a stray dog living in the barracks. These narrative segments present the cadet's most secret emotions and capture crude feelings of passion, sex, and violence. In this way, Boa's point of view serves as a sensorial register of reality in the military school. His monologue is a vehicle for the emotional perceptions and highly charged impressions of the cadet's activities, such as sodomy, rape, and masturbation. The presentation of sexual violence through Boa's interiorized point of view deflects aesthetically the impact of this material, dangerously close to pornography. Vargas Llosa presents these activities as forms of interpersonal violence that is an ethical correlative of specific social pressures and corruptions.

In striking contrast to Boa's narrative mode is the one used to capture the Slave's perspective. Rather than utilize a first-person interior monologue, Vargas Llosa employs a seemingly objective third-person omniscient narrator voice to present Slave's point of view. The technique is strikingly similar to Henry James's use of the omniscient narrator to capture the interiorized perspective of a character. As a result, the reader approaches but never directly participates in Arana's pathetic and lonely situation. But it is this particular point of view that evokes in the reader the feelings that Ricardo experiences as an outsider unable to survive in a dog-eat-dog world.

In parallel fashion, as we shall see, Alberto's story is presented by means of a special subjective omniscience similar to Ricardo Arana's narrational point of view. But Jaguar's story is, like Boa's, narrated by means of a subjective monologue and is constructed of remote and recent moments in his life, and as with Alberto and Ricardo, the reader also learns about him in the present time of the novel's action. In addition, the epilogue takes Jaguar's life beyond the present and projects it into the future.

As it turns out, the control of distance between characters and reader is of the utmost thematic importance in the novel. Major differences, for example, exist between Jaguar's narrative voice and the points of view employed by the other characters. Whereas Boa narrates a constant, unrestrained flow of sensorial perceptions and instinctual reactions to his surroundings (which are similar to a typical Faulknerian monologue), Jaguar tells his story in another form of first-person monologue. It is carefully thought out and so highly structured that an implied listener perceives a completely different type of subjectivity. It is simple, clear, and direct; for these reasons, it produces the feeling of innocence and goodness on the part of the narrator. In one passage, for example, Jaguar narrates his boyhood relationship with Tere, the girl next door with whom he would study every afternoon: "Sometimes I'd meet her coming back from school and anybody could tell she was different from the rest of the girls, her hair was never mussed up and she never had ink spots on her fingers. What I liked best about her was her face. Her legs were too thin and you still couldn't see her breasts, or maybe you could, but I don't believe I ever thought about her legs or even her breasts, only about her face. If I was playing with myself at night in bed and I suddenly thought about her, I felt ashamed of myself and went to the toilet to piss. But I thought all the time about kissing her. When I closed my eyes and pictured her, I could see both of us already grown up and married. We used to study together every afternoon for at least two hours, sometimes longer, and I always lied, I said, 'I've still got lots to do,' so we could stay in the kitchen a little longer" (64).

Despite its straightforward style and uncomplicated plot, this story acquires an enigmatic presence in the novel: the reader does not learn the identity of the story's narrator—Jaguar—until the epilogue; upon leaving the military academy he meets up with an old friend and describes the moment when after several years of not seeing her, he appears unexpectedly at Tere's door hoping to become reacquainted. For the first time Jaguar's name is associated with the story of the unidentified narrator.

Vargas Llosa's use of the narrative strategy of *dato escondido,* which hides Jaguar's identity as narrator from the reader until the very end of the novel, produces varying but pronounced effects in the interpretation of the character's behavior and his adaptability to exterior social circumstances. The problem lies in the fact that Jaguar's character in the past is not at all compatible with the image that the reader acquires of him as a military cadet in the present of the narration. As he grows up, he is portrayed as an innocent and unassuming lower-middle-class youth drawn into circles of bad in-

fluence where he learns a moral code diametrically opposed to those
values he had idealized as a youth—that is, study hard, get a job,
save money, and marry the girl next door. As the leader of The
Circle in the military school, Jaguar personifies the thug who depends on a macho image to dominate others; he is feared by some,
despised by others, and respected by all.

The incongruous relation between Jaguar's past and present goes
far toward explaining Vargas Llosa's attitude toward reality: it is
totally complex, contradictory, and enigmatic in nature. Jaguar's
conflicting behavioral patterns also serve as the indictment of a
society that requires people to asume conflicting and undesirable
roles in order to survive. Jaguar appears to beat the system by
adopting a macho front; but in killing Ricardo Arana in order to
gain revenge, Jaguar has committed a serious crime. The novel
reveals how certain institutions contribute to this situation through
encouraging hypocrisy and self-interest. Moreover, Vargas Llosa is
telling the reader that Jaguar's limited perception of the circumstances prevents him from comprehending Arana's actions as simply
another response or form of rebellion—perhaps just as valid as his
own—against the same hostile environment that Jaguar has learned
to dominate. Jaguar erroneously believes that society is organized
around concepts of loyalty (to the group), of the refusal to turn
informer, and of the need to perform acts of revenge as necessary
countermeasures to punish deviants from this social code.

All along Jaguar believes that Arana was wrong to squeal on Cava
in order to get a pass. In the final moments of the novel, the two
strong men, Lieutenant Gamboa and Jaguar—both of whom represent outwardly different but morally similar codes of honor—meet
before going their separate ways. Jaguar, rejecting the code, admits
his error but becomes its victim when the other cadets decide that
he has turned informer on them, causing a shakedown and general
punishment for everyone. Their mistake infuriates him, and he sees
them as traitors. Jaguar is unable to reveal that it was Alberto who
had turned informer because his reasons for betraying Jaguar were
different—more noble—than the other cadets' betrayal of Jaguar's
leadership. When Gamboa asks Jaguar why he does not tell the
cadets that Alberto was to blame, Jaguar becomes very disturbed:
" 'But his case is different,' he said hoarsely, forcing out the words.
'It isn't the same at all, Sir. The others betrayed me out of plain
cowardice. He [Alberto] wanted revenge for the Slave. He's a squealer

and that's the worst thing you can be, but he did it to get revenge for a friend. Don't you see the difference, Sir?' " (385).

Hence, the ambiguous and contradictory relation of Jaguar's past and present allows this character to make judgments about his actions and to admit finally that he is wrong. At the end he states that he now understands Slave's actions better: "To him, we weren't his friends, we were his enemies. Haven't I told you I didn't know what it was like to have everybody against you? We all bullied him, so much we sometimes got tired of it—and I was the worst of all. I can't forget his face, Sir. I swear to you, I don't know in my heart how I came to do it. I'd been thinking of beating him up, of giving him a scare. But that morning I saw him right in front of me, with his head up, so I aimed and fired. I wanted to get revenge for the section, Sir. How could I know the rest were worse than he was?" (386). In these final passages, the present-future time period of Jaguar's life, the reader becomes aware of a narrative style and tone that is strikingly similar to the first-person monologue narrated by the unidentified voice (of Jaguar) about his childhood. That period is recognized as one of innocence, moral goodness, and sincerity. Jaguar's confession to the military officer represents a kind of cleansing of his sins, a recognition of his past, a form of exoneration and vindication. The lesson that Jaguar may or may not have learned is inconsequential to the experience of the novel; more important is the fact that the reader is confronted with the moral dilemma of judging human behavior.

The fourth and final major point of view—Alberto's—is completely different from the others. Basically, his narrative stance in the novel involves a combination of the points of view that are employed by Ricardo, Boa, and Jaguar. The narrative points of view include: (1) an exterior, third-person omniscient narrator; (2) a third-person omniscient stance, but one that identifies with the character (similar to Ricardo's narrative point of view); (3) a first-person interior monologue (as in Jaguar's presentation); and (4) a completely interiorized point of view (Boa's "stream of consciousness" perspective).

On one plane, the juxtaposition of these different narrative techniques reveals the diversity of Alberto's thoughts, feelings, and reactions to his civilian and military lives; on another level, it produces ambiguous, conflicting, contradictory, and deceiving attitudes on the part of Alberto. Flashbacks are also employed in the

creation of Alberto's perspective, and their juxtaposition to other
material helps to intensify the same effects. Most readers naturally
find Alberto to be the most complex and possibly the most fully
developed character in *The Time of the Hero*.

There is a constant feeling of tension among the different aspects
of Alberto's life, and the contradictory psychological dualities of his
behavior bare his true nature and not what he seems to be. Finally,
the diversity of points of view in Alberto's case, as in the case of
each of the other characters, reveals how much he is determined by
society in conforming to a life of self-deceit. Alberto's weaknesses
are exposed through the frequently paradoxical juxtaposition of exterior description, dialogue, interior monologue, and flashback. Alberto, for example, outwardly demonstrates his masculinity not by
using physical force, as in the case of Jaguar, but by manipulating
society's sex roles and using his apparent dominance over women.
Even though he has never been sexually involved with a woman,
he gains the admiration of the other cadets by writing love letters
and titillating pornography for them; he only dreams of visiting a
whore that everyone knows as Golden Toes. When Alberto takes a
letter to Ricardo's new acquaintance, Teresa, he begins to go out
with her behind Ricardo's back—the relationship, however, is anything but secret, mysterious, or racy; rather, it is dull, predictable,
and a failure. His upper-class macho snobbery requires that he view
her as his inferior; yet he perceives something substantial in her
that he never discovers. Another girl turns him down; Helena says,
"I'm not in love with you. I've thought it all over, and I'm not."
" 'Oh,' Alberto said. 'Well, all right, then' " (228). At the end of
the novel, when Alberto finally returns to civilian life, he can only
dream or imagine a satisfying life with one of the local neighborhood
girls, like Helena, whom he will marry someday; the ultimate irony
of his fantasies becomes evident when he says that, like his father
before him, he will become a Don Juan.

Alberto's soft and misguided middle-class morality is underscored
in minute detail throughout the novel. His saving grace may lie in
his decision to turn informant and to reveal Jaguar's culpability in
Ricardo's death. Even within Jaguar's dog-eat-dog world, in which
to squeal on another is a serious violation of the "in" group's code,
Jaguar understands that Alberto broke the code because of his friendship for Ricardo (and Jaguar, in finally understanding the importance of friendship, does not seek revenge). In the novel, however,

the critical scene, in which Alberto contemplates his situation and finally decides to tell Lieutenant Gamboa how Ricardo died is riddled with irony and sarcasm. The structural juxtaposition of contradictory material in the scene makes a caricature of Alberto's seemingly profound moral decision. Alberto finds himself walking the streets for three hours one evening, trying to sort out everything in his mind: the Academy, Teresa, Ricardo (now dead), his father's carousing, Jaguar. He walks past a bar and decides to go in and call Gamboa:

The noise battered him from every direction, and the glare hurt his eyes and made him blink. He managed to get to the bar, squeezing through men who reeked of tobacco and alcohol. . . . The noise upset him, it kept him from concentrating on the name he was looking for. At last he found it. He picked up the receiver quickly, but when he reached out to dial the number, his finger stopped a fraction of an inch away. There was a harsh buzz in his ear. He glanced toward the bar and saw a white jacket with wrinkled lapels. He dialed the number and listened to it ring: silence, a ring, silence, a ring. He looked around him. Someone at a corner table was making a toast, roaring out a woman's name. The others held up their glasses and repeated it. The telephone went on ringing. Then a voice said, "Hello." He was speechless for a moment, he felt as if there were a lump of ice in his throat. The white shadow in front of him moved, came toward him. "I'd like to speak with Lt. Gamboa, please," Alberto said. "American whisky is shit," the white jacket said, "English whisky is good whisky." "Just a moment," the voice said, "I'll call him." The man who had made the toast was now making a speech. "Her name's Leticia and I'm not ashamed to tell you I'm in love with her. Marriage is a serious business, but I love her and I'm going to marry my half-breed." "Whisky," the shadow said. "Scotch. Good whisky. Scotch, English, doesn't matter. Not American. Scotch or English." "Hello," he heard another voice say. He felt himself shivering, and took the receiver a few inches away from his ear. "Hello," Lt. Gamboa said, "who's calling?" "I'm off the booze for good. I've got to behave myself from now on. Got to earn lots of money to keep my half-breed happy." "Lt. Gamboa?" Alberto asked. "Montesierpe pisco," the shadow said, "that's bad pisco. Motocachi pisco, that's good pisco." "Yes, speaking. Who is it?" "So here's to my half-breed and here's to my friends." "A cadet," Alberto said, "a cadet from the Fifth Year." "In my personal opinion," the shadow said, "it's the best pisco in the world," but then he qualified his statement: "Or *one* of the best, gentlemen, *one* of the best. Motocachi." "Your name," Gamboa said. "We'll have ten kids, all of them boys, and I'll name every one of them

after my friends. Not one of them after myself, just after my friends."
"They killed Arana," Alberto said. "I know who it was." (281–83)

The contrapuntal effect of the barroom noises and voices colors the
cadet's decision to reveal the truth. Woven finely into this scene
(as into others) is the presence of the social world of sex and of the
adult hypocritical attitudes toward men and women that reaches to
the image Alberto possesses of his cavorting father and suffering
mother. Also apparent is the way in which Alberto's unfortunate
situation is determined by the pathetic role models that family
members, in particular, and society, in general, force upon adolescents in a world of distorted social values. Alberto's heroic moment
of applied justice—which is based on his decision to call Gamboa
and to risk ruining his relationship with the other cadets, not to
mention his school career—is reduced to an insignificant act that
simultaneously threatens the established order of things. Even though
he finds himself despising his father and wanting to rebel against
what he represents, Alberto chooses to follow the same corrupt path.

In addition to the specific narrational styles mentioned above—
each of which is used to communicate the point of view of individually distinct characters—an objective omniscient perspective
presented in the third person describes the environment of the novel
and the action that occurs within it. Yet the sweeping overviews
of the narrative situation in the novel are told through a subjective
and omniscient voice that portrays in a negative and condemning
fashion the habits, customs, and rules that the characters must
embody in order to survive. For the most part, the routines and
practices of the school system and of society's values generally are
viewed as omnipotent forces over which individuals have no control.
In the novel this narrator's viewpoint is always ironical and, much
of the time, incisively sarcastic:

Mass was said on Sunday mornings after breakfast. The chaplain of the
Academy was a blond, cheerful priest who delivered patriotic sermons in
which he spoke of the immaculate lives of the great and their love for God
and Peru, and sang the praises of discipline and order, and compared the
military with the missionaries, the heroes with the martyrs, and the army
with the church. The cadets admired the chaplain because they considered
him an honest man: they had often seen him in street clothes barging
around in the worst parts of Callao with alcohol on his breath and a lewd
look in his eyes. (119)

Similarly, this narrative stance presents the detailed and selective description of the novel's action. Specific references to time are inconsequential; large blocks are purposely skipped over in order to identify isolated moments of crisis. The language used by the subjective omniscient narrator in most of the passages describing the environment becomes visibly symbolic in its relationship to the conflicts among the characters. As a matter of fact, Joel Hancock states that the "basic thesis of *La ciudad y los perros,* that Peruvian society is a jungle of animals fighting for existence, is borne out by the descriptive language of the novel" (Hancock 1975, 38). Vargas Llosa refers to many animals in the novel in order to create comparisons with the characters, and Hancock states that

"it is no coincidence that many of the characters have nicknames suggesting animals: Jaguar, Boa, Piraña, Gallo [Rooster], Mono [Monkey], Rata, Burro, to name some. This is more than just an animal label, however, as the characters are described as physically resembling the creatures. What is more, the behavior, activities, and general condition of the characters are clearly likened to those of the more primitive beings. There are no limits to the species employed in the elaboration of the graphic descriptions: birds, mammals, reptiles, insects, all serve as raw material for the pictorial representations. Understandably, dogs are used most frequently in the comparisons." (Hancock 1975, 38)

Of equal symbolic importance are the descriptions of the novel's settings. In the same study, Joel Hancock (as José Miguel Oviedo before him) analyzes Vargas Llosa's marked inclination toward the use of light and darkness in order to underscore the novel's themes. Throughout the novel, tension-filled, highly dramatized scenes of conflict are created in part by skillfully contrasting not only strident oppositions between extremes of light and darkness, but also by situating the characters within settings in which they are prevented from fully seeing or comprehending reality; ambiguity distorts the scene. The description, on one level, represents the characters' faulty understanding of reality. On another level, it underscores the thematic impact of the novel. The narrator creates an ominous mood, for example, when describing the school's chapel where Ricardo Arana's funeral is held: "It was worse than if the chapel had been completely dark. The shifting half-light exaggerated every movement, cast weird shadows on the walls or the stone floor, and showed everyone's face so dimly, so gloomily, that it almost made them look hostile or even sinister" (257). The ambiguity that evokes the presence of death and subsequently produces a mood of hostility and evil pervades the scene. Symbolically, the description of the setting is an indictment of "they"—Arana's parents, his schoolmates, society—who are responsible for his death. In general, the opposition between extremes of light and darkness and the creation of opaque and obtuse images, in which only silhouettes and shadows can be perceived, do nothing but blind the characters and, on a symbolic level, deprive them of their powers of reason. Reality becomes ambiguous and enigmatic. The characters are unable to distinguish between their real worlds and their fantasized worlds, that is, between truth and falsehood.

## Conclusion:
## The Moral Implications of Ambiguity

The moral issues that the novel poses and the way in which certain characters deal with them invite the reader's participation in the overall experience of *The Time of the Hero*. John Brushwood (1975b) states, in effect, that "the dynamic factor in *La ciudad y los perros* is involvement of the reader in these moral questions through sustained interest in the plot. The author captures the reader by allowing the characters to react in ways that repeatedly complicate an issue" (256). The shifting relationships among the characters vis-à-vis their particular worlds are, on the whole, negative; like the ambiguity created in the description of the novel's settings, they prevent a proper understanding of the character's circumstances and of how to react adequately to such situations. As a result, the void is filled with thwarted love, deadly hatred, unremitting indifference, and savage violence.

It is in the epilogue, however, that the reader must confront the novel's moral issues as well as the narrative strategies that Vargas Llosa perfects in his later novels. This final part adds little to the action of the present in the military school; instead, it presents brief moments in the lives of Jaguar and of Alberto subsequent to their graduation from the school. Basically, three scenes comprise the epilogue: in the first, Jaguar confesses to Lieutenant Gamboa and explains his concept of morality; in the second, Alberto returns to his old neighborhood friends and picks up where he left off before entering the military school; and finally, Jaguar encounters an old friend and talks about his marriage to his childhood sweetheart.

These scenes serve to highlight the changes that the two young men have undergone. Both Jaguar and Alberto undergo substantial transformations in character. Jaguar rejects the hollowness of the group and finds, in the authenticity of his own individuality, the strength to repent for the murder of Ricardo Arana. If the novel's ambiguity seems to mitigate somewhat Jaguar's culpability for Arana's death, the novel also seems to force the reader to question the role that Arana's family life and the hostility he feels toward his father play in these moral issues. Because Alberto capitulates to the threats of the school officials by retracting his accusations, the issue of whether he is morally wrong for not bringing Ricardo's killer to justice must also be confronted by the reader.

This issue is compounded at the end, when in the scene with his friends Alberto makes every attempt to erase from his memory his recent experiences at the military school. In the process, he becomes trapped in a world of degrading social values and lax moral codes. Different levels of time in Alberto's past are presented through monologue and flashback to highlight his sense of entrapment. In an essay demonstrating how form complements content in *The Time of the Hero,* George R. McMurray (1973) states that in a series of time shifts within the segment in the epilogue dealing with Alberto's return to middle-class complacency the young man's mind deprograms itself in making the adjustment; and here, once again, descriptive aspects of the setting symbolize the dissolution of his past. Alberto receives a fancy watch from his father for graduation, and its shockproof and waterproof resistance "symbolizes the materialism, physical toughness and moral insensitivity that have molded Alberto's character and prepared him for adult life in a corrupt society" (584).

These and other moral considerations—such as the position that Lieutenant Gamboa is finally forced to accept with regard to the incident—underscore Vargas Llosa's deep concerns about the ambiguous nature of reality; the relative nature of truth; and the effects of falsehood, error, and misconduct. As it turns out, Alberto, Ricardo, and Jaguar all know the same girl—Teresita, Teresa, Tere—and many readers find this implausible. In the novel, however, improbability is not at issue; more important is the way in which each cadet relates to the same girl. She is a female archetype representing permanence, and each one of the young men treats her according to the dictates of his social class.

Of greater import is the reader's acceptance or rejection of the characters in the context of the development of the plot; how a character is led astray from his or her true identity is carefully manipulated by the author. A significant result of the novel's structure and its multiple point of view is that while the reader has condemned Jaguar all along only at the end do we fully realize that Jaguar is the only person capable of recognizing his guilt. Equally disconcerting is the fact that the reader sympathizes throughout with Alberto and his problems, only to discover finally that his motives and consequent acts are not laudable; hence, we learn a lesson about the impossibility of formulating any permanent or steadfast truths about human reality.

The multiple points of view that are employed in the novel prevent the reader from reaching any final decision as to what actually happens; yet judgment has already been passed on the characters' previous acts as we reach the end of the novel. Given the enigmatic parameters of *The Time of the Hero,* the interpretations of the novel vary. In general, however, the theme of the individual as the victim of a corrupt society, which frustrates humanity's aspirations for a happy future, is the key to understanding the basic experience of Vargas Llosa's first novel.

## Chapter Four

# *The Green House:* Formal Invention, Greater Realism

In June 1967—the same year in which *La casa verde (The Green House)* was published—Mario Vargas Llosa wrote a review of the translated version of Joào Guimaràes Rosa's seminal novel *Grande sertão: Veredas*. In noting that the novel possessed all the fascinating ingredients of the medieval romance, the narrative of the romantic musketeers, and the Far West adventure, Vargas Llosa said that the Brazilian writer "has constructed a novel that is ambiguous, multiple, destined to last, difficult to capture in its totality, deceptive and fascinating like everyday life, profound and fathomless like reality itself. A creative writer could not be more worthy of high praise" ("Epopeya del sertão," 70). For Vargas Llosa there could be no other goal for the fiction writer. Most literary critics and general readers alike would agree that this description also fits *The Green House* perfectly.

The significance that Vargas Llosa attaches, in his review, to the key phenomena of multiplicity, intensity, ambiguity, and totality is of fundamental importance with respect to *The Green House*. These qualities are applicable to the nature of the technical apparatus he uses to construct the framework of his novel, and they are also descriptive of its theme. In fact, the ambiguity created through the use of multiple narrative forms and intricate narrative strategems produces a sense of totality and of an aggregate world vision.

Reader reaction to *The Green House* surpassed the positive response to *The Time of the Hero*. Literary prizes and international recognition were bestowed on the thirty-year-old Peruvian writer. Vargas Llosa received the Premio de Crítica Española a second time for *The Green House,* which was also awarded the Peruvian Premio Nacional de Novela. Above all, he won the $22,000 Rómulo Gallegos award for the best novel written in Spanish during the previous five years, the highest honor bestowed on a writer in Latin America.

The action of *The Green House* is developed through five different plot lines and takes place simultaneously in two Peruvian settings: Piura, a northern desert provincial city, where Vargas Llosa spent part of his childhood; and Santa María de Nieva in the Peruvian jungle, where a religious order of nuns still operates a Catholic mission. A key element of the setting, from which the novel gets its title, is the probable existence of a brothel, painted green, on the outskirts of Piura. As a ten-year-old boy, Vargas Llosa would spy on such a place with his friends. Nestled alone among the shifting sand dunes, this single-story structure possessed a somewhat diabolical attraction for the young boys. Vargas Llosa says that the green house conjured for them all sorts of weird feelings; in fact, it acquired mythical proportions (*Antología mínima,* 14–15). When the author returned to Piura five years later, then old enough to visit the brothel, he got his first glimpse of its interior. He described it as a strange one-room building with several doors leading to the outside. An old harp player, a singer-guitarist, and a drummer made up the orchestra. The prostitutes would take their clients outside to make love among the sand dunes because it never rained there. Overall, the green house inspired Vargas Llosa to write a story that was both poetic and terrible. In 1972, Vargas Llosa published *Historia secreta de una novela,* an analytical study of how *The Green House* had come into being.

Another key element of the setting is a popular lower-class neighborhood district in Piura, "La Mangachería," located on the outskirts of the town and bordering the desert. The proletarian district is made up of straw and mud houses and local bars. Vargas Llosa says that it reminded him of certain popular areas of Paris that the novelist Alexander Dumas captured in his works; it had its own personality, its picturesque aspects, and yet it was all very strange. "La Mangachería" was a haven for delinquents and drunks, and somehow its people took pride in representing a semifascist political party that legend had created; they were, in effect, fanatic supporters of the political extreme right.

The novel gains complexity from fictional elements found in the other locale, the jungle region of Peru. Vargas Llosa traveled on two occasions to the upper Marañón River region, where he learned firsthand the meaning of culture shock. He wrote a chronicle in *Cultura peruana* about his first jungle experience in 1958. Returning from abroad in 1963, Vargas Llosa made a brief visit to the same area in order to update the information that he had written about five years earlier. In addition, he had read extensively on the jungle area, where he discovered the devastating effects of economic and human exploitation on vastly different cultures that meet head-on in an atmosphere of mistrust, fear, skepticism, and hatred. Outside economic and social forces continued to abuse and enslave primitive Indian tribes, who exchanged their rubber crops for trinkets and tools. Religious indoctrination was imposed in a cruel and disruptive manner, producing alienation. The green house becomes the pivotal force of Vargas Llosa's narrative world. It may be seen, on the one hand, as a legendary house of ill repute, and, on the other, as symbol of the vast expanse of lusciously green yet deceptive and discordant Amazon region to the east.

## Plot: Five Stories, One Paralyzed Society

The presentational technique employed in *The Green House*'s five stories is, at best, bewildering—at least in the beginning. The stories are juxtaposed, and the reader jumps back and forth among them, picking up stories that were left behind and leaving others temporarily in the midst of their development. In addition, characters cross over from one story to another and acquire new names in the process. Events are presented in such a way that they seem to be part of the past when, in reality, they are later understood to have foreshadowed future events.

The breakdown of linear structure and the simultaneous juxtaposition of distinct temporal planes in *The Green House* stress Vargas Llosa's overall view of the human condition, that is, his insight into the circumstances that most affect human beings at any one moment in their lives. Specific and isolated actions, reactions, events, or periods in a single human life are never rationally or chronologically connected but rather cruelly severed from each other. In a chronological causality, they might reveal significant relationships among each other and even capture the essence of the human spirit; but as in the novel, these moments or fragments of life gain importance only in terms of their singular and isolated immediacy. The reader of *The Green House* feels caught up in the hazy and chaotic twilight zone of continuous experience, of an eternal present. Yet the five major plots and their numerous subplots of Vargas Llosa's novel are intricately interrelated and of equal importance.

The lack of character development has been a major criticism levelled at the novel, but the plots are in fact inseparable from character development. Hence, the bulk of the novel's content can be summarized in a brief account of several characters' lives:

1. Bonifacia, a young Aguaruna Indian girl from the jungle, is snatched from tribal life and taken to live at the mission run by nuns in Santa María de Nieva, a government outpost. At the mission her indoctrination inflicts upon her a new set of cultural values; but she responds to her latent rebellious nature and without premeditation frees a group of newly recruited girls. As a consequence, she is expelled from the mission. The river guide Adrián Nieves and his wife Lalita (an important secondary character) take her in and provide for her. Police sergeant Lituma seduces her, later marries her, and takes her back to Piura, his hometown, after his tour of duty is over. A senseless game of Russian roulette with a local landowner leads to the latter's death and a ten-year jail term for Lituma. While he is away, she is seduced by Lituma's neighborhood friend Josefino, who is one of the Inconquistables (Champs); she aborts a child and becomes a prostitute in the Green House.

Along the way Bonifacia acquires the nickname La Selvática, (Wildflower). The name change signals a new stage in her life, just as in the jungle Lituma's altered condition is indicated when he is called Sergeant. Although the beginning of this particular story is presented in a relatively chronological fashion, vital questions with regard to Bonifacia's past are withheld until later. If any one of the stories in the novel could be seen as reaching beyond its own point of reference and touching a major portion of the novel's plethora of characters, conflicts, and geographical regions, it would be Bonifacia/La Selvática's story. She is taken from her parents as a child, dispossessed of her cultural roots as an adolescent, displaced like a refugee in Piura after she married Lituma, and exiled as a prostitute to the Green House at the end of the novel. In effect, Bonifacia's story forms the novel's backbone, to which other stories and subplots are tightly or loosely, directly or indirectly, explicitly or implicitly anchored. In addition, her story might be seen as diametrically opposed to the sense of hope and continuity that is communicated through Lalita's story.

2. Fushía, a Japanese-Brazilian man jailed for a crime he said he never committed, escapes from jail and flees to Iquitos, Peru, where he works for Julio Reátegui, a shady politician, crooked

businessman, and affluent landowner. Fushía learns corruption first-hand, steals money from Reátegui, and flees once again to the jungle interior with Lalita (who later leaves him for Nieves). Monomaniacally, he bends his efforts to using the system, turning his unfortunate past into a golden future. He dreams of building a wealthy empire by creating an island kingdom on the Santiago River near the border of Ecuador. From there he will strike out with his small army of Indian renegades into the outlying areas, where he will plunder Indian villages for all the rubber, food, and women they can find. Fushía evades Reátegui and sells the rubber as contraband.

During his trips to the jungle, Vargas Llosa learned about the historical existence of a person like Fushía. According to local legend, this man became a regional warlord reigning over his territorial possessions and the master of a harem of captured Indian girls. In Vargas Llosa's novel, Fushía's plan goes awry: he is stricken with a fatal disease, Lalita leaves him, and he dies in a leper colony near Iquitos. This story is retold in the novel by Fushía himself, who is now old, sick, and at the end of his life. As Fushía and Aquilino, a longtime friend, journey downriver on a month-long trip from the island of destroyed illusions to the San Pablo leper colony, fragments of dialogue between the two friends reveal part of the story; the rest is told through flashbacks of dialogues between Fushía and others. Despite the fragmentary nature of its presentation, the quest adventure lends an archetypal tone to Fushía's existential anguish as he tries to find meaning in the absurd attempt to make reality conform to his distorted dreams. Vargas Llosa discovered that the real-life Fushía had written letters to the mission in Santa María de Nieva, in which he told of his repentance and fear of being condemned to hell. In compensation for his crimes, he offered to marry (by mail if necessary) one of the young girls of his entourage. For Vargas Llosa this story represented nothing but pathos and tragedy.

3. The novel alludes to the business deals that Julio Reátegui had made with the Axis powers during the 1940s, which is one period of the twenty-five-year span encompassed by the novel's action. Jum, an Aguaruna Indian chieftain from Urakrusa, had tried to create a cooperative that would bypass Reátegui's organization of intermediaries who traded tools, cloth, and food to the Indians for their rubber. For rebelling against the rubber trade monopoly, Jum had been brought to his knees and then shamelessly tortured.

As governor of the region, Reátegui took police action: tribal villages were burned, Indian women were raped, and Jum was taken to the garrison where he was made a public spectacle. When his hair was cut, a symbolic act of regicide, he lost his role as tribal leader. He was hung by his arms between two trees and tortured.

In the novel this story functions to corroborate the shocking cultural and racial-historical disparities that exist among the social groups of present-day Peru. In fact Jum's story is based on a person Vargas Llosa met in his jungle travels. When Vargas Llosa returned to the area in the 1960s to see if any social changes had taken place after Reátegui's consolidation of power he found that Jum had pathetically resigned himself to failure. Jum felt deeply responsible for what had happened to his people, the events described in the novel. Worse yet, he believed that Reátegui was a good man, who, after all, had provided them with machetes and tools throughout those years. In short, nothing had changed except that economic exploitation had achieved an even greater level of human degradation.

4. Anselmo, who suddenly and mysteriously appears out of thin air in Piura's main plaza one day after trekking across the desert (his origin is never directly revealed in the novel), begins to ingratiate himself with the seemingly uninteresting northern desert townspeople. He envisions the possibility of not only making Piura his permanent home but also of bringing "civilization" to the city and lifting the secret veil of repressed feelings and sexual inhibitions among its people. Anselmo dies there, an old man, some fifty years later. His scandalous yet attractive decision to build a brothel amid the shifting sand dunes on the edge of town is paralleled by the townspeople's fascination with his determination and incongruous activities.

Anselmo's downfall, however, is his erotic desire and his almost parental affection for the vulnerable deaf-mute Antonia. She mysteriously disappears from the plaza one day, only to turn up unexpectedly months later in Anselmo's tower sanctuary of the Green House, where she gives birth to his child. A public uproar ensues. The firebrand Father García leads a throng of outraged women into the desert to protest, and the Green House is razed by fire. The relationship between Anselmo and Antonia undergoes a lyrical metamorphosis in the novel. Like the brothel itself, their love is a source of subjectivity, deep-seated, titillating, unsatisfied fantasy and unrepented lust. However, it is also a fountainhead of passion and tenderness that arouses pity and even causes Anselmo (and the reader) to feel human again. Anselmo ends his days strumming a green harp with other musicians in a bar and brothel run by his grown daughter, Chunga. This second Green House rises in phoenixlike fashion not only from the ashes of the first house (although even its actual existence is questionable until the very end of the novel), but from the emotionally charged memories of those whose desires and fears are constantly reinforced by the ritual quality of local legend and myth.

Through Anselmo's story the reader learns of the rich creative capacity of the townspeople: gossip, down-home stories, legend, and even cultural myths. In this way, the Piurans modify and reshape events, episodes, and incidents that lie somewhere between fable and falsehood. At issue is not the veracity of the events but the accurate portrayal and re-creation of a society's collective powers of imagination, self-deception, and even social immobilization. Within this process, Anselmo's story plays a key role. From the beginning, the series of fragmented episodes, the characters, and events dealing with Piura and Anselmo's life are concealed in an aura of "once upon a time": "One hot December dawn, a man arrived in Piura. On a mule that was slowly dragging itself along, he rose up suddenly out of the dunes to the south: a silhouette beneath a broad-brimmed hat, wrapped in a light poncho" (43). Later, Anselmo rides a white charger in a blinding sandstorm on the outskirts of Piura, searching for the site of his future brothel. Carlos Rojas, whose blurry vision barely makes out the figure of Anselmo, narrates the event later to his friends, enveloping it in mystery and fable.

The enigmatic quality of Anselmo's story, which arises from the description of the scenes by the narrator and from the version of what happened that is created by the characters in the novel, mirrors the collective subconscious quality of ritual performance in a society. In effect, the reader learns that "small myths grew up about him: when they reached his ears, Anselmo would celebrate them with a great laugh and would neither confirm nor deny them" (46). Sprinkled throughout the narration of incidents making up Anselmo's story are other references to how his presence in Piura comes to be only partially understood: "Carlos Rojas' story had the city intrigued and it was the subject of conversation for days" (67). The reader then learns that "when people stopped talking about that excursion, there was an even more surprising piece of news. Don Anselmo had bought a piece of land from the city" (67). Anselmo's activities in Piura become the talk of the town: "When the house was finished Don Anselmo had it painted green all over. Even the children laughed hard on seeing those walls covered with an emerald skin where the sun sparkled and made fleeting reflections. Old and young, rich and poor, men and women made merry jokes about Don Anselmo's whim to daub his house like that. They immediately christened it 'the Green House' " (84). It is significant to correlate the outrageous color of the house with the fact that *verde* in Spanish is not a neutral color term but, in fact, even suggests obscenity. The new structure titillates people's minds: "a kind of effervescence grew up all over the city, a noisy and agitated curiosity" (84). The true significance of the Green House is felt implicitly by the townspeople: "Suspicions grew. From house to house, from parlor to parlor, the church biddies were whispering, ladies looked at their husbands with mistrust, people would exchange mischievous smiles" (84). Not long afterwards, "new myths about Don Anselmo arose in Piura. According to some, he was only the front man for a business group that had the Chief of Police, the Mayor, and several ranchers among its members. In popular fantasy, Don Anselmo's past became enriched, sublime or bloody deeds were daily added to his biography" (90).

The transfiguration and canonization of Don Anselmo confirm the obscure and inscrutable nature of reality. His life conforms to the concept of the archetypal hero. Here, as Michael Moody (1977) points out, "the process by which the past and reality are reconstructed by others reaches its ultimate condition. What may appear to be primarily a problem of narrative reliability in characterization becomes a formative principle with bold implications in the story of Don Anselmo. Through the collective memory and imagination of the people, the portrayal of Don Anselmo's life loses meaningful contact with objective reality. His individuality has no real extension; it is only a circumstantial phenomenon which eventually dissolves in the generic world of myth" (188). In effect, the elaboration of a higher state of awareness concerning man and his reality is ultimately thwarted. Whereas Bonifacia's story is a serious condemnation of corrupt social forces, Fushía's tale a tragic re-creation of the way economic imperialism ruthlessly exploits man and nature, and Jum's biography the eternal tragedy of the rebel who, in this case, faces formidable cultural, racial, and historical odds, Don

Anselmo's story delves into the farthest reaches of the collective unconscious to touch the very process by which man's capacity to distinguish between the unknown and the known diminishes as his need to respond to contradiction and ambiguity grow, thus creating multiple perspectives of reality.

5. Los Inconquistables are a gang of four unemployed free-loaders who spend most of their time in bars, particularly at Chunga's place in the Mangachería slum of Piura: "The Champs came in as always: opening the door with a kick and singing their theme song: They were the champs, work wasn't for them, they lived off the rest, they emptied their glasses, and now they were ready to wiggle their asses" (204). Most of the scenes in this plot deal mainly with brief moments in the lives of the Champs—José, Monk, Lituma, and Josefino (the son of Carlos Rojas, who, decades before, had seen Anselmo ride a horse into a blinding sandstorm). Other characters connected to the Mangachería underworld include Anselmo (now old and blind, called simply "the harp player"); La Selvática, a prostitute at Chunga's; Father García (the aging ex-firebrand); and the moderate Doctor Zevallos (who attends at Antonia's death, Chunga's birth, and much later, La Selvática's abortion). Nearly half the scenes involving the Champs narrate Lituma's return to Piura after his jail term ends in Lima. Josefino, José, and Monk meet Lituma at his house, where, drinking heavily, they relive old times. Lituma is anxious to see Bonifacia (now called La Selvática), who, he has heard, works at Chunga's. At first they talk him out of going, because Bonifacia/La Selvática is a prostitute. Eventually, they all go there anyway. Lituma, after learning that Josefino had seduced her and set her up at the brothel in order to support him, seeks revenge. The other members of the gang trick Josefino into going outside, where all of them, including La Selvática, pulverize him. Nonetheless, Lituma understands that his machismo has been diminished and that in the eyes of the others his personal honor has been invaded; yet one of his buddies tells him to stop crying and to forget the past.

Also part of this story is the Russian roulette challenge between the landowner and Lituma. While part of it is presented in the form of a flashback, the rest is retold by several characters who were witnesses to the scene. The harp player, two other musicians, and Chunga reconstruct the incident. Coming after the aforementioned scene of inglorious revenge, this scene is, in reality, the origin of the past that Lituma is told to forget. The juxtaposition of the two scenes reverses the order of causality. The reader learns the effects of Lituma's past before he learns its cause, and therefore any attempts on the reader's part to make clear-cut judgments, to take a moral stance, or, finally, to place blame are ultimately thwarted.

Another fascinating structural device at work in these scenes is also found in other stories. As the roulette scene is reconstructed at the bar through memories, gossip, and exaggeration, it serves as the framework for another conversation that takes place when the first scene is building to a climax (the fatal shot in the Russian roulette scene). The interpolated nature of these segments reveals how Vargas Llosa's *vasos comunicantes* (the narrative art of emptying one level of the story into another) works: events occurring in different times and places are juxtaposed in one narrative segment of the plot, producing the illusion of simultaneity; in addition, events that occur in one narrative story serve to clarify others that take place in different ones:

Seminario [the landowner] had gone back to his table, and the champs too, without any signs of the jollity of a moment before: let him get drunk and he'd see, but no, he had a gun on, better let it go for another time, and why not set fire to his pickup truck?, it was just outside, next to the Club Grau.

"Maybe we should leave and lock him up here and set the Green House on fire," Josefino said. "All it takes is a couple of matches and a can of kerosene. The way Father García did."

"I was five years old when the fire happened," Josefino said. "Do you guys remember anything?"

.....................................................................

"Let's have the old man tell us about it," Monk said. "We'll buy him some beers."

"Were they lying?" Wildflower asked. "Or were they talking about the other fire?"

"Piuran ways, girl," the harp player said. "Never believe anything they say when they talk about that. Nothing but lies." (208)

Several characters here are trying to piece together the real story of the first Green House, which by now has become a legend among the Champs. The remaining scenes of the story also present a period temporally located between the roulette incident and Lituma's return to Piura, that is, during the years after Josefino seduces Bonifacia, moves in with her, and forces her to abort Lituma's child. Finally, the last scene of this plot pulls together all its characters when Anselmo, the harp player, dies.

The five basic stories indicate that there is no one single most important plot in *The Green House*. The symmetrical nature of the exterior division of the novel and the consequent presentation of the novel's action are rigorously controlled, and yet the reader cannot discern any logical explanation with regard to why things happen the way they do; the discovery of new phenomena only leads, in turn, to new suppositions about the seemingly infinite and complex movement of the diverse characters through the novel. The result is highly ambiguous and extremely disconcerting, relegating each character's infinitesimally small role in the larger picture to one of frightening alienation and the need to create some kind of response—a myth, perhaps—that would provide him or her with a reason to live.

## Structure and Technique:
## The Pressure to Cope, Collate, and Condense

The worldview of *The Green House* is fragmented, complex, confusing, and alienating. The reader's initial feeling is one of bewilderment and even frustration. Ultimately, however, the novel makes a significant comment on the nature of reality as perceived by contemporary humanity—it is chaotic and complex. Bent on avoiding the outmoded and "primitive" process of representational realism characteristic of some earlier Latin American novels, Vargas Llosa has erected an elaborate conceptual framework around his narrative material to create—as Marianne Hirsch has characterized other novels—"an instrument of knowledge about the structure of external reality" (Hirsch 1981, 4).

The reader's natural tendency is to reconstruct sequences and to create in the narrative a sense of causality; but out of the fragmented time relationships only arises the insecure feeling of ambiguity. The notion of chronology is destroyed, and the discontinuous nature of events produces the illusion of their simultaneity. As a consequence, human events are relegated to a repetitious, cyclical, and almost timeless flow of isolated and senseless present moments. The process effaces human individuality. Hence, Vargas Llosa seems to be trying to tell us that contemporary man has little hope of giving any meaning to one's life. In Vargas Llosa's worldview, the multiple relationships that normally give meaning, coherence, and stability to one's life now snare and immobilize man within the larger configuration of countless and complex human events and the many possibly meaningful but frustrated links that exist among them.

The five stories that make up the novel's plot do not, individually, transcend their own parameters of action. Hence, the effects created by techniques of multiplicity, disjunction, simultaneity, and ambiguity are central to an overall understanding and appreciation of *The Green House*. Vargas Llosa has reworked his material with superb control of a provocative set of narrative techniques. The techniques of interpolation and concealment are those that most affect plot sequence in the novel; in this way, Vargas Llosa focuses, as Marianne Hirsch (1981) has said about other writers, "not so much on the discovery of the real but more as a careful scrutiny of fictional methods and skills that might enable us to embark on such a discovery" (5).

Structurally, the novel is divided into four parts and an epilogue. Parts 1 and 3, and the epilogue contain four chapters each; parts 2 and 4 contain three chapters each. The beginning of each part and of the epilogue is an unnumbered, independent chapter that functions like the aperture of a camera; it provides an opening to the narrative world and to the thematic structure of each part. In a similarly geometrical fashion, each chapter is divided into short segments of varying but usually short length (from three to five pages each). The four chapters of part 1 and the three chapters of part 2 are broken down into five narrative segments each. In alternating symmetrical uniformity, each segment presents one of the five stories already summarized. The chapters of parts 3 and 4, however, contain only four narrative segments, suggesting the disappearance of one repeated narrative segment. The epilogue, finally, contains four chapters with no internal segmentation. The pattern that emerges suggests variation within repetition, disjunction within continuity, and mobility within permanence.

Variation occurs as pieces of each of the five stories alternate within the separate chapter segments; repetition comes into play, for example, when the first segment of each chapter focuses consistently on events that take place in and around Santa María de Nieva and the nuns' mission. In the second segment of each chapter we hear the conversation between Fushía and Aquilino as they travel downriver, complete with flashbacks initiated when Aquilino's continual barrage of questions about Fushía's past touches a nerve and sends Fushía explosively, nostalgically, and probingly back to earlier periods of his life. The third segment concentrates on the life in Piura, Anselmo's arrival there, the creation of the first Green House, and Antonia's story. The fourth segment (which disappears as a separate narrative and then reappears as a part of Fushía's story) centers generally on the problems of the jungle Indians and in particular on Jum's story. The fifth segment is located in Piura again and focuses on the Mangachería barrio, the Champs, Lituma's return from jail, the second Green House, and speculation about the existence of the first one.

The structure of the epilogue deviates from the schematic nature of the four parts. The concealment of information and the creation of speculation and ambiguity in the main body of the novel yields to partial revelation in the epilogue. The first chapter of the epilogue portrays Fushía's impending death as he slowly rots away in the leper colony. In the second chapter events surrounding Anselmo's heart attack are narrated as well as La Selvática's search for a priest and a doctor to attend him. The third chapter brings Lalita's story to a close as she travels with her third husband to Iquitos for her son's wedding. Finally, chapter 4 follows Father García and Doctor Zevallos as they leave Anselmo's deathbed and have breakfast at a local bar. In the conversation that ensues at the end, heretofore undisclosed facts are revealed: two different moments in the history of Piura, two generations, two distinct Green Houses, and two deaths are all fused to complete the pattern of disjunction and continuity. Doctor Zevallos recaptures Antonia's death, which occurred during the period of the first Green House; and the story of La Selvática's abortion (set during the period of the second Green House) is interpolated into Zevallos's memories.

By itself the epilogue possesses a certain internal symmetry. The events in chapters 1 and 3 are similar both geographically and temporally: Fushía spends his last days at the colony near Iquitos while Lalita is returning to her hometown, which is also Iquitos. Both stories close the circle of life that began there decades before and portray the process of mobility within permanence. Similarly, chapters 2 and 4 are linked by Anselmo's death, which creates a sense of closure in the novel's events; on another level, however, the process of concealment, speculation, ambiguity, and revelation comes full circle, leaving the future to be determined for the reader by the disjointed and deceptive moments of the past. Yet the future is determined for the characters by the agitated, shifting, and displaced action of the present time. Hence, in the epilogue, the lives of Anselmo and Fushía are played out to their end. They both die, and with them, a legend dies; and yet from those legends myths are born and embodied in those who survive. While the first Green House begins to fade in the memory of the priest and the doctor, it becomes an essential part of the Champs' living cultural history.

Further structural symmetry is evident in the series of unnumbered chapters that precede each part and the epilogue; here, a camera-eye perspective opens up the narrative worlds of the novel while providing certain common unifying traits. The action of these narratives takes place only in the jungle areas, not in Piura. Together, they constitute a kind of informative sociological narrative of life in that area. The reader learns how the nuns' mission recruits its pupils; how rampant the exploitation of the Indians is; how corruption has infiltrated the state bureaucracy; how the uncontrolled expanses of the Amazon region foster lawlessness and banditry; and, in general, how Indians, missionaries, military personnel and others suffer from the hardships imposed by the primitive region. In addition, these narratives communicate symbolic meaning that is relevant to the previous discussion of the fragmented and disjointed nature of the structure. Luis A. Díez says that the action in each of these five narratives opens "with an arrival [of someone] and convey[s] a feeling of transcendence: lives, and destinies, propelled by uncontrollable outside forces. It is as though the huge, uncharted Amazon rivers in their timeless flow, were joining and separating the destinies of a group of people, sometimes bringing moments of happiness that will soon turn into sorrow" (Díez 1970, 2/23).

The structural relationships among the different parts, chapters, segments, opening narratives, and the epilogue of *The Green House* may be complex and totally puzzling, but they do create specific effects and communicate significant themes: changeableness, uncertainty, insecurity, anxiety, betrayal, duplicity, enslavement, oppression, and alienation. If we can accept the observation that people everywhere today consider the world as anomalous, fragmented, and hostile, then the narrative structure of this novel and of other contemporary novels reveals a purpose. Appropriately, Marianne Hirsch (1981) states that this type of "fiction thus becomes a means not only of ordering the chaos but of understanding it without appropriating, taming, or falsifying it" (5). Hence, this seemingly bizarre narrative structure places reality in a new perspective, laying bare heretofore covert links and networks, and forces reality within it.

Although many readers agree that Vargas Llosa's early novels are full of frustration, pessimism, and resignation—that their characters' futures are determined by a fall of the cards—the Peruvian writer does give credence to man's capacity to shuffle those cards and to continue to live within an otherwise hopeless situation. In this respect, Vargas Llosa is counting on literature to influence society. His stance, in effect, is a declaration of the writer's vocation, that is, to throw light on the hidden truths about man and reality. Structural elements, then, determine the reader's understanding of the novel. The author has reduced the characters' perspectives on reality to conjecture, speculation, and fabrication; and in the process the reader's ability to make moral judgments based on the characters' acts of perception becomes equally challenging. At the same time, reader participation is indispensable in giving shape and meaning to a novel that might otherwise remain ambiguous and open-ended. With the disappearance of narrative omniscience, the reader plays a significant role in creating meaning.

Vargas Llosa's master plan for eliminating fictional authority, acquiring objectivity, and transferring creative responsibilities to the reader is based on his idea of the "total" novel. Frank Dauster (1970a) was among the first to point to the significance of this concept in Vargas Llosa's novels:

> Not only is it ludicrous to attempt to abstract information from the plots while ignoring the fact that these plots form part of a work of art; such a procedure overlooks the fact that in the form, too, there is meaning. Vargas Llosa's predilection for the chivalric novel is little short of notorious. This is not only simply a matter of pardonable aberrant criticism, but a vital link in his creative process. His fascination is rooted in the effort to capture the whole of reality. (276)

Vargas Llosa bases his ideas of totality on the premise that there is a direct correspondence between the level of diversity in the work and the expansive nature of its scope and the truth of its content.

Hence, Vargas Llosa works and reworks a narrative scene in order
to explore fully its implications for reality. In the novels of chivalry,
for example, he has uncovered fantastic, historical, military, social,
erotic, and psychological planes of reality. But he has reduced the
concept of total reality to a manageable number of interpolated
levels. These different levels can be further reduced to an opposition
between two planes of experience: objectivity and subjectivity, that
is, action and dreams, reason and wonderment. The objective stance
taken by Flaubert and the subjectivity emanating, say, from Faulkner's primary mode of narration illustrate the two intersecting planes
of reality at work in Vargas Llosa's novels.

The objective level is based on the novel's action. It describes
human conduct and behavioral patterns that transcend positivist
mimeticism to reveal invisible and almost psychological secrets about
the characters. Hence, the planes begin to intersect immediately.
Characterization on this level is achieved in a radically different way.
The character's course of action is determined by a series of external
stimuli, his way of proceeding becomes important only in relation
to the problems he must confront on a moment-to-moment basis.
Yet an analysis of a character's actions does not, in itself, complete
the picture. A statement about social problems is also presented,
and a graphic account of physical reality is rendered as well.

In *The Green House* the reader learns that the anecdotal nature of
a character's point of view is always circumscribed by conjecture
and speculation. Social ills are exposed in the opening narratives of
each chapter, and the delineation of exterior reality embodies the
difficulties the characters face in obtaining a clear perspective on
reality. In *The Time of the Hero* Alberto is constantly diverted from
reaching the truth by an entire set of social circumstances. The fog,
mist, and darkness of the environment, or the blinding light in
another scene, represent these circumstances and prevent him from
seeing reality clearly. His perspective, like that of so many characters
in *The Green House,* is confined to an ever-changing, erratic, and
vacillating vantage point; it is similar to the problem of Carlos
Rojas, who, immersed in the deceptive shifting sands of the Piura
desert one day, stretches his imagination, strains to make sense of
the bursts of laughter, tries to visually capture the mysterious nature
of the white charger galloping across the desert, and is almost struck
dead when suddenly he sees Anselmo grinning down at him from
the saddle. The reality of the scene is reduced to conjecture and

speculation, thereby adding to the unusual nature of Anselmo's presence in Piura. Certain facts become known, but their motivations and psychological background remain a mystery. Yet the presentation of social problems within the objective level of reality plays a significant role in the overall creation of the novel. The opening narratives provide the key to this role, and the hardships Bonifacia faces throughout her life—enslavement, exploitation, victimization—are given graphic relief through them.

The second level of reality is the realm of subjectivity. It manifests itself in the wide range of characters' memories, fantasies, and dreams, including magic and myth, that represent momentary aspects of a previously real or imagined reality. By going beyond the interior monologue (a mechanism employed for creating subjective narrative material) Vargas Llosa astutely subverts the notion of regularly narrated dialogue and replaces it with a process of interpolation, offering "interpolating dialogues," that is, fluid, dynamic, and introverted glimpses of reality that begin as speculation, easily turn into fantasy, and even become myth. The concepts of past, present, and future are, on another plane, converted into memories, imagination, and anticipation. Past and future, that is, memory and anticipation, collapse into the single force that propels the present, providing strength to the string of elusive visual perceptions. The continual flow of imagery, or responses to exterior reality, frees the subconscious from reason and works to deceive the characters' imagination with regard to their hopes, fears, dreams, and frustrations. In this way, characters not only interact among themselves and relate to reality through regular dialogue, interior monologue, and narration, but they also communicate through the mechanism of interpolating dialogues. Vargas Llosa has developed this technique to provide the reader with a sense of history regarding the characters' lives. Curiously, Vargas Llosa's process of creating history occurs less on the objective level of reality and more on the subjective plane.

The technique of interpolating dialogues complements, strikingly, Vargas Llosa's strategic organizational principles of narrative, the "communicating vessels" and the "Chinese boxes." Events occurring in one plot are juxtaposed to events that occur in different times and places in another plot. The interpolative nature of the relationship comes into play as each episode or plot segment throws light on another, continually providing more information and further clarifying various situations. The dispersed segments change each other reciprocally and mutually give meaning to their presence in the novel. Since dialogue is the predominant narrative element of Vargas Llosa's novels, it is not surprising to see how he has seized dialogue to make it an instrument that goes far beyond its usual function. Fushía's story, for example, is completely built around the interpolation of multiple dialogues. The conversation between Fushía and Aquilino as they travel downriver to the leper colony provides the overall narrative frame for his story; however, it quickly begins to dilate and fill out in such a way that, by the novel's end, Fushía has exposed and pondered his entire life. The following example of interpolated dialogues begins, as usual, with a question from Aquilino, which sets off the process. The moment in question picks up Fushía's life just after he has robbed Reátegui and fled into the jungle:

"Haven't you ever felt sorry, Fushía?" Aquilino said. "I've been asking you that question for quite a few years now."

"For robbing that bastard Reátegui?" Fushía asked. "That guy is rich because he stole more than I did, old man. But he had something to begin with and I didn't have anything. That was always my bad luck, I always had to start from scratch."

"And what's your head for, then?" Julio Reátegui asked. "How come it didn't ever occur to you to ask to see his papers, Don Fabio?"

But he has asked to see them and his passport looked brand new; how could he have known that it was forged, Don Julio? And besides he was dressed so well when he arrived and he spoke in such a convincing way. He even said that as soon as Señor Reátegui got back from Santa María de Nieva, I would introduce him and they would do a lot of business together. A person can get careless, Don Julio.

"And what are you carrying in that suitcase, then, Fushía?" Aquilino asked.

"Maps of the Amazon Region, Señor Reátegui," Don Fabio said. "Great big ones like they have in the barracks. He put them on the wall in his room and he said it was so he could know where we would get the wood from. He had drawn some arrows and notes in Brazilian, it was very strange."

"There's nothing strange about it at all, Don Fabio," Fushía said. "Besides wood, I'm interested in trading too. And sometimes it's useful to have contacts with the Indians. That's why I wrote down the names of the tribes."

"Even the ones on the Marañón and the ones from Ucayali, Don Julio," Don Fabio said, "and I thought what an enterprising man; he'd make a good partner for Señor Reátegui."

"Do you remember how we burned your maps?" Aquilino asked. "Nothing but junk. People who make maps don't know that the Amazon is like a hot woman, she's never the same. Everything is on the move here, the rivers, the animals, the trees. What a crazy land we've got for ourselves, Fushía." (40–41)

Basically, three sets of dialogue are intercalated, with each one capturing a different moment and place in Fushía's life: (1) Aquilino–Fushía (present time); (2) Don Fabio–Don Reátegui (immediate past); and (3) Fushía–Don Fabio (remote past). The segment begins and ends on a wishful note, with Fushía saying, "I don't like feeling useless, Aquilino. I wish it was the way it was before," and at the end: "And look at us now; take a good look. I've sacrificed myself more than anyone ever could, no one has taken the chances I have. Is it fair to end up like this, Aquilino?" (39–43). The radically altered time continuum at work in this short segment catapults memory and anticipation into the realm of imagination, that is, a world of desires, dreams, and frustrations filled with a sense of tragic fatalism. In Piura an anonymous voice that captures the strange relationship between Anselmo and Antonia says it all: "things are the way they are, reality and desire become mingled" (323).

Once Fushía's story is finally told, no objective reality remains to which the reader can effectively relate. Subjective reality, then, conforms to the characters' memory, imagination, and anticipation; this, in turn, runs parallel to the process of speculation and fantasy. As a result, clarity disappears, and all absolute or unequivocal aspects of reality are lost. The dialogue technique or the conversational format of the novel produces confusion and ambiguity about what is true. The reader is faced with the characters' self-deception, half-truths, and even lies.

Lacking a complete or truthful picture of reality, the reader is lured into the story to attempt to decipher reality, like the characters themselves. A natural consequence of the presentation of information through a dialogue or through conversations that are interpolated in the narration is the partial and one-sided nature of the revelation or disclosure of information to the reader. By intentionally suppressing certain facts, the story acquires a heightened sense of the ambiguous nature of life itself. Reasons that things happen the way they do and what lies behind people's motivations are never fully comprehended. It is as if reality were somehow changed and made dubious by an act of magic; common, everyday occurrences are somehow infused with surprise, incredulity, and even fable.

Reality, then, is perceived but never fully understood. Through the conversations themselves, suppositions and conjecture lead to gossip, gossip creates stories, stories grow into tales, tales turn into legend, and legend becomes myth. The complexity of the reality that Vargas Llosa deals with in *The Green House* may be compared to the description in which the shifting and evasive Amazon river becomes indistinguishable from the ever-changing and wind-flung desert surrounding Piura. Aquilino says the Amazon is never the same: "Everything is on the move here, the rivers, the animals, the trees" (41). The mysterious and unidentifiable collective voice of the narrative segments dealing with Anselmo and Piura describe the desert as "unstable, soft. The dunes change their location every night, the wind creates them, does away with them, and moves them at will" (61). The menacing common mutability of these seemingly different environments reflects the volatile, erratic, and kaleidoscopic nature of the characters, whose lives are defined by the capricious circumstances in which they exist.

If the substance of Fushía's story allows it to dominate the others that take place in the jungle, there is no doubt that Anselmo's story generates the other stories that take place in Piura. Moreover, the subjective level of Vargas Llosa's "totalization" process has its crowning touch in Anselmo's story, for the series of narrative segments devoted to Piura are imbued throughout with fabulous and mythical resonances. Several narrative elements coincide here to create simultaneously an adventure, a confession, a fable, a legend, and a myth. Anselmo's life fits the classic pattern of the archetypal hero: his origin is unknown; he faces great odds; he undergoes a symbolic death and rebirth; and his story is narrated by a collective, anonymous voice. In referring to the attractive, spellbinding, and magic nature of certain events that occur in the novel, Luis A. Díez (1978b) says that "this happy encounter of the desert dunes and the jungle undergrowth, of *inconquistables* and *selváticos*, of 'the green house' and the mission, of Fushía and Don Anselmo, of Chunga and Bonifacia, turned this novel into a jewel of imagination and narrative craft. But if I were forced to make a choice, I fancy that it would be Piura that would come to the rescue of the jungle and win the day. It is the Piuran stories that add the yeast of poetic sensibility to the dazzling techniques so arduously wrought to chart the quavering Amazonian chaos" (50).

Finally, time (and, by extension, space) is perhaps the most significant organizational concept that governs form, content, and meaning in *The Green House*. The temporal aspect envelops practically all other structural and technical devices used by Vargas Llosa. The general plot—in this case, the numerous stories, dozens of characters, and their illimitable relationships and conflicts—is atomized, and a sense of chronology is reduced to a continual string of senseless moments of action in the present. The mass of disconnected temporal segments—there are seventy-three in the novel—forces the reader to attempt to rearrange them. While Flaubert, Proust, Joyce, Dos Passos, Faulkner, and Borges had already reworked chronological time to conform to new perspectives of reality, the primacy that Vargas Llosa gives to the breakup of causality is equally remarkable. Yet the Peruvian's concept of time is, in reality, only superficially distinct from time's conventionally accepted chronological nature. The duration of events within the novel seems to depend on the nature of the action and on how much it affects or alters the characters' lives rather than on a sense of continuity. Yet this phenomenon is an illusion.

In fact, two temporal patterns emerge that are more important than time's velocity or the changes that it precipitates; for when time is subject to a cyclical and repetitive configuration, it is transformed into some form of rational organization that can be arranged, understood, and even predicted. The other possibility allows for time to be organized in a linear, unremitting, and infinite way. The molecularized progression of even the most fundamental events in a character's life makes them disconnected, irrational, and completely meaningless. At the same time, these two types of temporal configurations imply two orders of character transformation, one dealing with the metamorphosis of the individual and the other with social change. In the first type, the character's life is affected by a regular process that begins with birth and ends with death. This transformation is seen as regular, predictable, and universal in nature, and it corresponds to the cyclical configuration of time. The second type of character transformation is imposed from outside the self, that is, by society, and it conforms to the linear arrangement of time. Situated within the flux and unstable nature of multiple relationships among people in society, each character must react and respond to the clash between his or her inner dictates and the imperatives of society's norms and the force of collective values.

It seems possible to discern the presence of both temporal directions in *The Green House.* On the one hand, the cyclical configuration of time corresponds to the universal nature of the text, that is, the text created, for example, by the use of myth as motif and by the structure or pattern of the imagery in which Anselmo's life is immortalized; on the other hand, the linear arrangement of time demands a more aesthetic interpretation of the text, an act in which the reader plays a significant role. The nature of Bonifacia's story, for example, makes such a demand on the reader. The clash between individual choices and the external demands of society transcends the immediacy of her story, through which society is viewed as an infinite number of just or unjust relations. The name changes that the characters undergo in the novel reflect the changes to which their lives are subjected as they pass from one stage of life to another. The linear nature of the changes in Bonifacia's life reveals, on one level, the lack of connection among the stages of her life, and on the other, the process of her victimization and assimilation into society.

The conceptual framework of this dual temporal sequencing drives home the major thematic concerns in *The Green House.* As the individual and society are reduced to the roles of victims and victimizer, the question of individual destiny comes to the forefront. The cyclical nature of time seems to impose a deterministic interpretation on man's destiny; yet the novel's linear configuration allows for the movement of free will, which precipitates violent decisions with respect to the future of each character. In both cases, however, a sense of fatalism pervades the characters' lives and produces frustration. Vargas Llosa might view frustration as a form of dynamic personal initiative that leads, in turn, to a sense of hope. Even though the process of victimization subverts hope and causes frustration to repeat itself, Vargas Llosa has singled out the need for an individual and moral rebellion against the problems of society.

# Chapter Five
# The Cubs:
# Societal Immolation

*The Cubs* (1967), published one year after *The Green House* and two years before the gargantuan, two-volume *Conversation in The Cathedral,* gave Mario Vargas Llosa the opportunity to experiment with another narrative genre, the short novel. Yet in only forty-three pages (of the English version), Vargas Llosa delves once again into his own past, re-creating parochial school life in Lima during the 1950s, describing the adolescent years of a group of young people growing up in a middle-class neighborhood, and fashioning the story around a newspaper account that he had read years before of a young child emasculated by a dog.

The challenge to transpose *The Cubs* into experiences that the author had enjoyed as a child, had braved as an adolescent, and had known as a young adult stimulated him to go beyond the technical mastery that he had achieved in his two previous novels to produce once again a multifaceted reality in which certain thematic obsessions are revealed through a dazzling array of contemporary narrative strategies. Although the novelette has taken a back seat to Vargas Llosa's longer narratives and, therefore is not well known, many Vargas Llosa fans agree that *The Cubs* achieves a notable balance between form and content, that is, between technique and theme. In fact, Vargas Llosa could be said to have achieved a much more striking equilibrium between style and substance in this novel than in any other works. Luis A. Díez (1970) states that *"thematique* and technique are so harmoniously balanced that nowhere in the book does the technique overshadow the themes of the story" (4/2). Eminent writers such as Mario Benedetti, José Miguel Oviedo, and José Emilio Pacheco agree that *The Cubs* is nothing short of a masterpiece.

## The Plot: P. P. Cuéllar's Misadventures

As is customary in Vargas Llosa's fiction—and aside from the technical complexity of each work, including this one—the events that constitute the action of *The Cubs* are relatively simple. After entering a private school in Lima and struggling hard to become part of the in-group because he is an outsider—that is, he is physically smaller and weaker, but more intelligent and well-to-do than the other students—a third-grader whose last name is Cuéllar makes the school soccer team. One day, in the shower room after practice, he is attacked and emasculated by the school's guard dog, a Great Dane named Judas. Most of the novel develops around the fact that this act of castration not only cripples him sexually but, more significantly, paralyzes him socially. His unfortunate physical deformity prevents Cuéllar from adapting to the norms of society, and he becomes more and more alienated until he dies in his early thirties in a suicidal auto crash.

The opening section of the story reveals not only a glimpse at the kind of technical experimentation that the reader must confront throughout the novelette; it also evokes the sudden feeling of tension surrounding that unfortunate period in the young man's life: "They were still wearing short pants that year, we weren't smoking yet, they preferred soccer to all the other sports and we were learning to surf, to dive from the high board at the Terrace Club, and they were devilish, smooth-cheeked, curious, very agile, voracious. That year, when Cuéllar enrolled in the Champagnat Academy" (1). In effect, the narrative personae *they* and *we* alternate in seesaw fashion four times in the first sentence, which creates its own tension because the reader immediately begins to wonder about the identity (or identities) of the narrator(s). The second sentence only heightens the reader's curiosity, for its grammatical shorthand increases the ambiguity; and, above all, the laconic and ominous reference to "that year" foreshadows the central incident, while evoking all sorts of questions at the story's beginning.

*The Cubs* is divided into six chapters, each one narrating in chronological order a different period (usually a time of crisis) in the life of Cuéllar. The first chapter describes his acceptance into the group, the castration incident, and a brief period in the hospital. The second narrates a period immediately following the scene in which the school officials and Cuéllar's parents give him preferential treatment—the former because the boy's father threatens to take action against the school, and the latter because they know he has been damaged for life. At about the same time, someone gives Cuéllar the nickname of P. P. (a reference to the male sex organ), which hurts Cuéllar deeply, although he does not quite understand why. His father, whose manly pride and family name are at stake, tells his son to fight back tooth and nail; but the more Cuéllar fights it, the faster the name spreads through the school. His four "buddies"—Choto, Chingolo, Manny, and Lalo—go by their nicknames, they explain; but, of course, theirs do not seem as cruel. One of them tells him that "it [is] a nickname like any other and finally don't you call lame Pérez Gimpy and cross-eyed Rodríguez Pock Face or Evil Eye and the deaf-mute Rivera Golden Tongue? And didn't they call him Choto and him Chingolo and him Manny and him Lalo? Don't get mad, brother, keep on playing, c'mon, it's your turn" (11). By the time he reaches sixth grade he is resigned to the nickname, and "he even put[s] out his hand to new friends saying how do you do, P. P. Cuéllar, glad to meet you" (11–12).

The end of the second chapter narrates the period in the boys' lives when their interests turn from sports to girls. Together, they spend their Sundays learning how to dance, and it is not long before they try smoking, going to bars, and crashing Saturday-night parties. Logically, then, the next chapter concentrates on the period in their lives when each boy acquires his first girlfriend. Cuéllar, however, fails to find a female companion, and he becomes shy, fickle, and emotionally agitated; he grows very defensive and begins to perform crazy stunts in order to gain everyone's attention. By his senior year in high school, only Cuéllar has no steady girlfriend: "Silent, sulky, hunched over in his corner chair, Cuéllar downed shot after shot, stop pulling that long face, man, now it was his turn. He should pick out some chick and she'd fall for him, we told him, we'll do the spadework for you, we would help him and our girlfriends would too. Sure, sure, I'll pick soon, shot after shot, and suddenly, bye, he stood up: he was tired, I'm going home to bed" (19).

At one point Cuéllar becomes a recluse, then he is suddenly transformed into a daring surfboard hotshot at the beach; but, in pendulum fashion, "as the days passed, Cuéllar became more standoffish with the girls, more tight-lipped and distant. Crazier too: he ruined Kitty's birthday party throwing a string of firecrackers through the window, she burst into tears and Manny got mad, went to find him, they slugged each other, P. P. nailed him" (23). When the school graduation dance comes around, Cuéllar does not go.

Chapter 4 narrates the group's university years, and when a new girl moves into the neighborhood Cuéllar's outwardly kaleidoscopic personality changes again. Seemingly, he comes to life and tries to impress Teresa, but he does not have it in him to ask her to go steady. Everyone teases and embarrasses him. Even the girls join in sarcastically by singing lines from popular songs, such as "You're wasting your time, thinking, thinking." As though they were passing sentence on him, Cuéllar's buddies correctly predict: "They're making his life impossible, we said, he'll end up a drunk, outlaw, madman" (33). While this is going on, Cuéllar's hopes are dashed that his father will be able to locate a foreign surgeon who can return P. P. to normal. To make things even worse, a newcomer to the group claims Teresa as his girlfriend, and everyone reacts by declaring that P. P. deserved to lose her. Cuéllar's stuttering, an outward manifestation of his inner anxiety, grows worse.

The fifth chapter documents Cuéllar's growing mental anguish, insecurity, and sense of panic. He reverts to vanity and exhibitionism by committing even crazier acts than before, such as driving full speed with his hands tied to the steering wheel and a blindfold over his eyes. His destiny seems certain, however, even though he works during the day at his father's factory, he spends his nights "getting drunk in the worst dives, where he could pawn his Parker pen, his Omega watch, his gold bracelet (bars in Surquillo or Porvenir), and some mornings he turned up scratched, a black eye, a bandaged hand: he was washed up, we said, and the girls his poor mom and the guys do you know now he hangs out with queers, pimps and junkies?" (37).

The process of ostracism, which prevents Cuéllar from leading even a "seminormal" life with the guys, in particular, or with society, in general—reaches an ironical climax in a scene outside a brothel one night. There his buddies find Cuéllar slumped over the steering wheel of his car, crying. No one dares to discuss his problem; everyone knows what it is. At this truly pathetic final stage in his downward spiral toward total destruction, Cuéllar tries to find solace in condemning human vice, in not offending God, and summoning pity for prostitutes and the world's poor, blind, and crippled humanity. Like the alternating points of view between *they* and *we* and between *they* and *I* that coalesce to form a single wretched state of human corruptibility and condemnation, he is one of those pitiful souls; and he is all of them: an outsider, condemned to suffer.

The sixth and last chapter jumps ahead in time; we learn that one of Cuéllar's buddies is getting married and that two others are graduating from engineering school. As if to seal further his fate, his parents condemn his reckless, devil-may-care driving: "You're going to kill yourself, sweetheart, don't do crazy things and his old man that was the last straw, boy, how much longer before he changed, out of line once more and he wouldn't give him another cent" (40). While the others gradually move into adulthood, Cuéllar recoils into markedly infantile activities. He separates himself from the group and hangs around with teenage rock 'n' rollers, homosexuals, and drug pushers. He dresses like James Dean, acts the part, and becomes a race-car driver. Finally, he dies one day in a car accident: "in a crack-up, where? on those treacherous curves at Pasamayo, poor guy, what a life he had, but this finish is something he had in store for him" (43).

The last paragraph of *The Cubs* is significant for the basic experience of the novel. Syntactically and grammatically, it is a single long sentence—similar, in fact, to the initial paragraph of the novelette—with the reader once again switching back and forth between the third-person plural and the first-person plural narrators: "They were mature and settled men by now and we all had a wife, car, children who studied at Champagnat, Immaculate Conception or St. Mary's, and they were building themselves a little summer-house in Ancon, St. Rose or the beaches in the south, and we began to get fat and to have grey hair, potbellies, soft bodies, to wear reading glasses, to feel uneasy after eating and drinking and age spots already showed up on their skin as well as certain wrinkles" (43). The run-on sentence creates the feeling of continual movement and change, but the tone is one of inflexibility, entrenchment, and indestructibility, connoting a sense of death and rigor mortis. This paragraph also reminds us that the focus all along has been less on Cuéllar and more on his four buddies and their girlfriends, the group, which represents society's mores and determines P. P.'s life. Society becomes collectively responsible (Forgues 1976, 47).

## A Modern Parable

The novel elicits diverse interpretations. Vargas Llosa has created a fine example of a fictitious reality that is all-encompassing in scope, yet paradoxical and highly ambiguous. In fact, *The Cubs* could be considered one of Vargas Llosa's most symbolic pieces of fiction. Vargas Llosa's biographer José Miguel Oviedo (1982) states that most readers prefer to read it as an allegory (196); some literary critics look to the novel's metaphorical implications (Ortega 1972, 265–73), while still others see it as a parable (Díez 1970, 4/20). The interpretive possibilities are indeed great; in general, however, the meaning of the insignificant but grotesque castration incident that leads to Cuéllar's death transcends the immediate, individual, and physical parameters of his reality to reach a level in which the spiritual castration of a generation of youth or of an entire social class in conveyed. P. P. Cuéllar is an insignificant victim of an omnipotent, destructive force: middle-class mediocrity and its false-hood and deception. As the last paragraph of the novel suggests, the group continues to live in a world devoid of human values, a sense of spiritual emptiness prevails. At the heart of the problem, perhaps, is the author's own ambiguous stance toward the reality he creates in *The Cubs*. Vargas Llosa has been involved in a marked love-hate relationship with his childhood and with his adolescent experiences of growing up in Peruvian middle-class society. On the one hand, the barrio life of Miraflores provided him with crucial experiences, on the other, it gave him an awareness of just how frivolous, blind, and stupid the middle class is with regard to the rest of Peru's harsh, violent, and savage reality. In the author's preface to *The Cubs and Other Stories*, Vargas Llosa makes a comment about the short story "On Sunday" that is pertinent to this discussion. As youngsters in Miraflores who never ventured beyond their neighborhood block, Vargas Llosa states that

we boys and girls were condemned to our *barrio,* an extension of our home, a kingdom of friendship. The *barrio* in Miraflores was innocent: a parallel family, a mixed tribe where you learned to smoke, dance, play sports and open your hearts to girls. The concerns were not very elevated: they came down to enjoying yourself to the hilt every holiday and every summer. The great pleasures were surfing and playing soccer, dancing the mambo gracefully and switching couples after a while. I grant that we were rather silly, more uncultured than our older brothers and sisters—which is already saying a lot—and blind to what was going on in the immense country of hungry people that was ours. Later on we would discover all that, as well as what good fortune had been ours in having lived in Miraflores and having a *barrio!* And retroactively, at a given moment, we came to feel ashamed. That was silly too: one doesn't choose one's childhood. As for

me, my warmest memories are all linked to those *barrio* rites out of which—
nostalgia blended in—I wrote "On Sunday."

The *barrio* is also the theme of "The Cubs." Yet this story is no youthful
transgression but something I wrote as an adult in Paris in 1965. I say
"wrote" and I should say "rewrote," because I made at least a dozen versions
of the story which never worked out. It had been going through my mind
ever since I had read in a newspaper about a dog's emasculating a newborn
child in the Andes. From then on I dreamed of a story about this strange
wound that, in contrast to others, time would open rather than close.
Simultaneously, I was turning over in my mind the idea for a short novel
about a *barrio:* its character, its myths, its liturgy. (xvi–xvii)

The narrative world of *The Cubs* is certainly not new to the author.
In dealing with the story of a group of teenage adolescents growing
up in the Miraflores neighborhood of Lima, the action in *The Cubs*
is similar to parts of the narrative in *The Time of the Hero,* particularly
in the case of Alberto Fernández's past life. With each successive
work, the reader is able to detect with increasing ease Vargas Llosa's
love-hate relationship with the Peruvian bourgeoisie.

Wolfgang A. Luchting sees interpretive possibilities for *The Cubs*
as functioning on different levels. In one study, he uses an intertextual perspective, combining ideas from other works by Vargas
Llosa in order to decipher the novelette. To start with, Luchting
astutely discovers the importance that Vargas Llosa gives to the
person to whom the novelette is dedicated, Sebastián Salazar Bondy,
an important Peruvian writer who died in 1965; to Vargas Llosa,
this dedicated writer represents the person for whom writing is a
vocation and a serious full-time responsibility. Given the hostile or
even nonexistent reading public in Latin America that Vargas Llosa
talks about, the writer is rendered virtually powerless to change
society; in this sense, then, Luchting sees Cuéllar's emasculation as
a parable of the Latin American artist's destiny (Luchting 1968,
277).

In another study, Luchting delves much deeper into the novel to
discover intriguing psychoanalytic interpretations. He works from
the premise that one of Vargas Llosa's major thematic obsessions
throughout his fiction is social maladaptation or inadaptation in
which a sexual ingredient is constantly present. Indicating that the
"real concern [in *The Cubs*] was never meant to show easily," Luchting claims that the theme represents, in essence, a type of "exorcism
perpetrated upon himself by the author" (Luchting 1978, 54–55).

Two of the most provocative interpretations that emerge from his
study involve, on the one hand, a symbolic attempt on the part of
the author to assassinate his own alter ego, and on the other hand,
a unique relationship between writing and sex. In the first interpretation, Luchting looks at an existential paradox in Vargas Llosa's
works in which the act of writing and what is produced from it
reveal not only what the author is but also what he could have been:
"Had Vargas Llosa's schooling, especially that at the Leoncio Prado
in Lima, succeeded in making of him what his father envisioned in
sending him there, he might have become artistically and entele-
chially what Cuéllar becomes physically: unable to produce that
which he was previously potentially able to produce. He would have
remained 'unsatisfied' " (Luchting 1978, 61).

The love-hate syndrome is so powerful that Vargas Llosa is at
once attracted and repelled by a polar oscillation, as José Miguel
Oviedo (1974a) points out, between authority and freedom, orders
and acts, rules and violations, military and civil life, teachers and
pupils, fathers and sons, groups and individuals—and, here, Vargas
Llosa and Cuéllar (5). These debilitating relationships, based on a
hierarchical concept of "imposition" in the ordering of society, produce negativity and, hence, rebellion. In the second interpretation,
Luchting sees sex as a metaphor for writing or writing as a replace-
ment for sex. He wonders, at bottom, "whether the novella is not
ultimately a long allegory for or 'surrogation' of Vargas Llosa's most
intimate doubts about his 'vocation' " (Luchting 1978, 62).

There is no doubt that *The Cubs* can stand up to a solid religious
interpretation as well. The reader is given an inkling of the Christ-
Cuéllar connection upon learning that the name of the vicious dog
that attacks P. P. is Judas. As in Christ's life, four friends tell his
story. Like Christ, Cuéllar demonstrates concern for oppressed and
destitute people. It is also true that both men die in their early
thirties. A scene in the novel, which is significant in its symbolic
potential, also highlights the religious interpretation of the work.

In an act of defiance and exhibitionism, Cuéllar foolishly goes
surfing during winter, when the Pacific Ocean's monstrous waves
pounding Lima's beaches are most unsuitable for surfing: "Why
would the water get so rough during Holy Week? Fina said, and
China in anger because the Jews killed Christ, and Choto had the
Jews killed him? he thought it was the Romans, how dumb" (35).
A sense of guilt is present in this interpretation of Christ's death,

in which the Jews are assigned the responsibility for having committed a deicide. This interpretation falsely lays blame on the Jews and seemingly absolves the Christians. Hence, the true meaning of his death is evaded obliquely, just as the society responsible for Cuéllar's death is not directly indicted for its crime (a similar ambiguous situation exists in the case of Ricardo Arana's death in *The Time of The Hero*). In this way, then, the novel does become a parable of social integration or of the lack of it.

These varying interpretations surprised Vargas Llosa. At the time he wrote the book, he says that he was completely absorbed by the technical problems involved in combining the life of a typical barrio with the newspaper story of emasculation. The possibilities are intriguing: "the parable of an impotent social class, castration of the artist in the underdeveloped world, a paraphrase of the aphasia among young people brought on by comic strip culture, a metaphor of my own ineptitude as a narrator. Why not? Any one of these may be correct. One thing I have learned from writing is that in this craft nothing is ever entirely clear: truth is a lie and the lie truth, and no one knows for whom it works. What's certain is that literature does not solve problems—instead, it creates them—and rather than happy, it makes people more apt to be unhappy. That's how it is and it's all part of my way of living and I wouldn't change it for any other" (*The Cubs* xviii).

## Technical Experimentation: Point of View, Language, and Structure

The success of *The Cubs*—as well as Vargas Llosa's other novels, is due to the author's narrative expertise in converting his convincing ideas on fiction writing into an actual text. And his admiration for the genre of the novel runs deep. "The novel is the supreme genre," he says, "because it's the genre that installs the reader at the very heart of the reality evoked in the book." At the same time, Vargas Llosa believes that "reality is chaotic. It has no order. But when translated into fictional terms it acquires one. The stricter the construction of a novel the better will be the understanding of the world it evokes." If his novels are to have any significance, he says, it is because "I think every method, every procedure must be conditioned by the fictional material at hand. The best novels are always those that exhaust their material, that don't throw a single light on reality,

but many. The points of view that can be brought to bear on reality
are infinite. It's impossible, of course, for any novel to exhaust all
of them. But a novel will be greater and vaster in proportion to the
number of levels of reality it presents" (Harss and Dohmann 1967,
358).

Vargas Llosa says that he confronted a major problem in *The Cubs*
when he decided to merge with the story of the barrio the newspaper
article: "Who was going to narrate the story of the mutilated boy?
The *barrio*. How to insure that the collective narrator didn't drown
out the various voices speaking for themselves? Bit by bit, filling
up my wastebasket with torn sheets of paper, that choral voice
gradually took shape, dissolving into individual voices and coming
together again in one that gives expression to the entire group. I
wanted 'The Cubs' to be a story more sung than told and, therefore,
each syllable was chosen as much for musical as for narrative reasons.
I don't know why, but I felt in this case that the verisimilitude
depended on the reader's having the impression of listening, not
reading, that the story should get to him through his ears" (xvii–
xviii).

Clearly, then, the Peruvian writer refers to two elements in *The
Cubs* that are responsible for creating a dynamic experience for the
reader. First, he mentions the importance of point of view, and,
second, he comments on the attention that he gives to language.
A third element, structure, is greatly determined by both point of
view and language. The combination of the novel's two narrative
voices—*they* and *we*—creates a multidimensional point of view that
encompasses the broad spectrum of reality, from an exteriorized
objective level to an interiorized subjective plane. Fluctuating within
and between each of these two points of view are dialogues among
characters, free and indirect speech patterns of narration, and narrative omniscience. At first, the ungrammatical nature of the text,
the elliptical structures of sentences and phrases, and the lack of
concordance, for example, between subject and verb and between
other parts of speech, may make the reader uneasy because of the
style's seeming incoherence (especially in the translated version).
The overall effect is audacious, however, for Vargas Llosa is able to
present the objective reality of action and the subjective world of
thought and dreams simultaneously with the unique juxtaposition
and fusion of the different points of view fusing into one dramatic
perspective.

In addition to the creation of a collective narrator or neighborhood "group" character—Choto, Chingolo, Lalo, Manny, Fina, China, Chabuca, and Kitty—who, in effect, not only tell Cuéllar's story but also become responsible for his demise, a curious temporal effect is also present. The third-person-plural narrator presents the action in the preterit tense; and the omniscient nature of this voice creates an exterior, formal, and detached perspective that judges the actions of the collective character. The first-person-plural narrator provides a different function. The action seems frozen in the present moment, and the subjective voice and its point of view emerge from the choral effect of the emotional, oral, colloquial, and infantile language.

The experimental nature of *The Cubs* plays havoc with the English translation. Jerome Charyn (1979) curses translations because readers "long for a writer's natural line, and we usually get a voice that sounds broken and silly. It may not even be the translator's fault. How do you render the 'music' of one language into another and still manage to hold on to the meaning of a word? And what if the prose has an unconventional 'music,' a rhythm that depends heavily on the exact placement of words? Such is the predicament of *The Cubs.*" Unfortunately, Vargas Llosa's desire to have the reader "hear" the story through a chorus of chants that relate Cuéllar's misadventures is not fully evident in the translated version; for, as Charyn states, "there are only a few moments in which the 'liturgy' of the prose survives" (12). This may not be completely true, however, because the juxtaposition of the points of view, the interpolative nature of the dialogues, and the relationship between the levels of reality and temporal planes stylize and dramatize the story in such a way as to involve the reader in its moral implications and, therefore, make him or her an accomplice to Cuéllar's demise.

Beyond the technical element of narrative point of view and its direct thematic implications for the reader, the language in *The Cubs* is extremely important as well. In order to create a composite, collective viewpoint that is basically immature, juvenile, and superficial, Vargas Llosa astutely utilizes a natural and telling characteristic of young people: their own language. By their nature, adolescents share an oral verbal reality. In the novel, certain highly successful syntactical applications of parataxis, enumeration, and listing (Hancock 1977, 16)—as well as linguistic devices such as onomatopoeia, graphic elements, interrogative forms, and colloquial language, including diminutives (Díez 1970, 4/10)—all play a significant structural role in the stylization of the physical death of Cuéllar and the spiritual death—mediocrity, superficiality, and moral laxity—of the group.

The paratactic nature of the text—the placing of related clauses in a series without the use of connecting words—effectively captures the oral and colloquial speech habits of adolescents (Frank 1981, 156–75). In addition, many other long sentences, which present multidimensional aspects and enumerate or list narrative material are joined by the conjunction "and," which is typical of children's speech. The use of onomatopoeia creates special effects throughout the text. For example, the "gr-r-r" sound of the dog that attacks young Cuéllar, provides two major functions; first, it creates a looming or threatening feeling in the scene, and second, the "gr-r-r" sound is the only bit of reality left for Cuéllar after the incident. Typically, Vargas Llosa utilizes an important narrative device found throughout his fiction, the retrospective account of a scene mediated through another person who may or may not have seen the action. In effect, Lalo describes the scene after it happens, leaving only the noises of the growling dog as a testament to the event. The scene is re-created around the questions fired at Lalo subsequent to its actual occurrence (which is similar, in fact, to the questions that Aquilino poses to Fushía), which provide another oral, colloquial, and inquisitive entrance into the narrative. In this way, the objectivity of the scene is diminished even more:

Sometimes they all showered, gr-r-r, but that day, gr-r-r gr-r-r, when Judas appeared in the doorway to the locker room, gr-r-r gr-r-r gr-r-r, only Lalo and Cuéllar were washing up: gr-r-r gr-r-r gr-r-r gr-r-r. Choto, Chingolo and Manny jumped out the windows, Lalo screamed he escaped look man and he managed to shut the shower door right on the Great Dane's snout. There, shrunk back, white tiles and trickles of water, trembling, he heard Judas's barking, Cuéllar's sobbing and only barking and a lot of water, I swear to you (but how much later, asked Chingolo, two minutes? longer man, and Choto five? longer much longer), Brother Luke's booming voice, Brother Leoncio's curses (in Spanish, Lalo? yeah, and in French too, did you understand him? no, but you could tell they were curses, stupid, from the anger in his voice). (5)

The novelette contains a plethora of onomatopoeic words that are graphically presented to create a piece of fiction totally oriented to acoustics. Luis A. Díez (1970) says that "more often, however, [these words] are used to lend an echo-like emphasis to certain actions" (3/11). José Miguel Oviedo (1982) states that a comic-book effect is also produced, capturing another well-known perspective of the world of adolescents (198). Similarly, the narrative achieves its aural and onomatopoeic quality when the narrator graphically captures Cuéllar's stuttering, which grows progressively worse throughout the narrative and represents his downward spiral toward delirium; for example, when his friends tell him that someone else will take Tere away from him if he does not ask her to be his girlfriend, this is his response: "and so what if he takes her way? and she doesn't matter to you anymore? and he wh-wh-why w-w-would it m-m-matter and they didn't like her anymore? wh-why-why w-w-would he l-l-like her" (34).

The use of colloquial language is rampant in the novel. It works to identify a particular social class and cultural attitudes. For example, Vargas Llosa relies heavily on the use of the diminutive to create certain effects in the characters' speech; most important is the feeling of childish, almost infantile aloofness and domesticity or snobbery. The diminutive, which can function either as a term of endearment or of scorn, reduces the importance of the object described and allows its describer, by seemingly becoming more important, to exercise dominion over it only in a false and superficial way, through imposition. Whereas the onomatopoeic quality of the language diminishes as the novel progresses—which probably represents the characters as growing up and shedding adolescent usages—the presence of the diminutive remains constant to the very end, suggesting that even though the characters pass from childhood into the adult world in terms of their age, they never really grow up and their relationship to reality is never truly established. As a matter of fact, the last paragraph (presented on p. 79 of this text) is glutted with diminutives, which are lost in the translation. Their importance, however, for the interpretation of the novelette is understandably great. Vargas Llosa makes admirable use of a linguistic-cultural phenomenon to give prominence to the novel's themes.

A brief look at the structural implications that arise from the novel's narrative point of view and its linguistic novelties reveals other acute relationships between form and content that have received high acclaim from readers and literary critics. Two examples will suffice. The essential effect of the sound "gr-r-r" in the emasculation scene has been described; however, the same sound has

another function that becomes significant for the structure of the
first chapter, which basically deals with Cuéllar's emasculation. The
dog's growling is heard at three different times in the first chapter:
once before, once during, and once after the attack. When it first
appears in the story's initial paragraphs, the caged dog is tormented
as he watches the young boys play soccer after school: "hurry up,
get to the goal before the others grab it, and in his cage Judas went
crazy, gr-r-r, his tail stood straight up, gr-r-r gr-r-r, he bared his
fangs, gr-r-r gr-r-r gr-r-r, he jumped in somersaults, gr-r-r- gr-r-r
gr-r-r gr-r-r, he shook the wire fence. Jeez, if he escapes one day,
Chingolo said, and Manny if he escapes you gotta stay quiet, Great
Danes only bite when they smell that you're scared of them" (2).

Since this scene is but one among several of equal or greater
importance, it is only the growling sounds of the dog that create
feelings of tension and fear in the reader; but nothing comes of it.
When the reader reaches the emasculation scene, with the growling
sounds repeated a few pages later, not much more needs to be
narrated in order to understand what will happen. Even the progressive nature in the string of "gr-r-r" sounds from the first to the
fourth "gr-r-r" is repeated in the first two scenes and left at a high
pitch at the end. The onomatopoeic effect is heard for the third
time at the end of the chapter, where a sense of internal symmetry
is created when Cuéllar's friends discuss the accident after school
one day and in revenge throw rocks at Judas: "poor Cuéllar, what
a lot of pain he must've been in, if a ball hits you there it'd knock
anybody out what would a bite be like and especially think about
Judas's fangs, pick up some stones, let's get out on the field, one,
two, three, gr-r-r gr-r-r gr-r-r gr-r-r, how'd you like that? bastard,
take that and that'll teach you" (7). Hence, the tripartite structuring
of the first chapter around the acoustic nature of the growling dog
serves as an aperture to the aural and violent world of *The Cubs.*

A second, randomly chosen example of intricately juxtaposed
elements of technique and theme appears in a symbolic scene in the
fourth chapter. Two complexly intertwined levels of narration, which
seem to clash at first sight, are juxtaposed to complement each
other; in this way, a multidimensional perspective is created to
transcend the immediate scene and to give deeper meaning to the
action. At the point where this scene occurs in the novel, Cuéllar
is on the brink of a total internal crisis, created (as I have tried to
show) by the forceful nature of the adolescent code, which requires

the teenagers at this point in their lives to pair up with girls. Cuéllar, of course, is not capable of asking Terry (Teresa) to go steady with him. One day, Cuéllar's buddies, all of whom have girlfriends, decide to play Cupid in order to get Cuéllar and Terry together. They want to find out if Terry really likes Cuéllar or if she is simply leading him on. They go to her house and talk to her outside while she sits on a balcony:

Cuéllar? sitting out on the balcony of her house, but you don't call him Cuéllar but some nasty swear word, rocking herself so the light from the streetlamp would hit her legs, he's dying for me? they weren't bad, how did we know? and Choto don't play dumb, she knew it and they did too and the girls and all Miraflores talked about it and she, all eyes, mouth, little nose, really? as if she were looking at a Martian: that's the first I've heard about it And Manny go on Terry, talk straight, out with it, didn't she realize how he looked at her? and she oh, oh, oh, clapping, little hands, teeth, tiny shoes, we should look, a butterfly! we should run, catch it bring it to her. He'd look at her, sure, but like a friend and, besides, how pretty, stroking its little wings, little fingers, nails, tiny voice, they killed it, poor thing, he never said anything to her. And they what a story, what a lie, he must've told you something, at least he'd have flirted with her and she no, honest, he'd dig a little hole in her garden and bury it, a little lock of hair, her neck, her little ears, never she swore to us. And Chingolo didn't she even realize how he was chasing after her? and Terry he follow her around as a friend, oh, oh, oh, tapping her shoes together, little fists, big doll eyes, it wasn't dead, the faker, it flew away, waist and small tits, well, if not, he'd at least held her hand, hadn't he, or tried to anyway, right? there you are, right there, we should run, or he had expressed his love, right? and again we should catch it, it's that he's shy, said Lalo, hold it but be careful, you're going to smudge, and he doesn't know whether you'll say yes, Terry, was she going to say yes? and she ahh, ahh, little wrinkles, little forehead, they killed it and mangled it, little dimples on her cheeks, little eyelashes, eyebrows, who? and we what do you mean who and she better get rid of it, the way it was, all mangled, why bother burying it: a little shrug. Cuéllar? (29–30)

Although the scene continues, this excerpt from the conversation between Terry and Cuéllar's buddies reveals the technical function of juxtaposed levels of dialogue and narration, which through the use of the *vasos comunicantes* envelop each other and richly alter the meaning of the scene. On one level, the reader learns through Terry's words and the description of her body (an open display of having reached puberty) that she is a complete coquette and extremely hypocritical. She plays the part of the innocent little girl (the ironic use of the diminutive is completely lost in the English translation), saying that she is unaware that Cuéllar has been pursuing after her for two months and feigning her inability to understand what Cuéllar's nickname means. As a result, the narrator's description of Terry's gestures in front of the boys communicates the artificial and fickle quality of her character.

The second level of narration that accompanies the description of Terry involves a tangential course of action in which the boys pursue a butterfly while they are talking to Terry. Their infantile nature is revealed as they chase after the butterfly, catch it, let it go, catch it again, and finally destroy it. Because of the confusion created when the two levels are interpolated, the reader cannot discern at certain points in the scene whether the girl and the boys are talking about the butterfly or about Cuéllar. The subtle arrangement of words at one point in the passage—in the moment they mutilate the butterfly—prevents the reader from knowing what or whom they are discussing. A disturbing relationship is established between the butterfly and Cuéllar, and the scene becomes a microscopic view of the action of the entire novel and of Cuéllar's fate. Just as the boys have the power to destroy the insect, society has the power to destroy individuals.

## Conclusion

The narrative achievements in *The Cubs* are impressive. Mexican novelist Gustavo Sainz (1968), who also feels at home working with the oral possibilities of language in his fiction, considers this short novel "the most radical experiment with language" (12). The multidimensional aspect of the novel—achieved through the combination of different points of view, the juxtaposition of different time levels, the interpolation of narrational materials (such as dialogue, narrated dialogue, monologue, and description), and the incorporation of highly diverse forms of language—is the direct result of Vargas Llosa's theoretical concepts concerning fiction writing and the purpose of fiction. The narrative strategy that he calls the "switch or qualitative leap," in which narrative reality is transformed through the accumulation of elements and tensions in crescendo fashion, becomes the cornerstone for the conversion of an objective reality into a fictitious one, in which the reader begins to make profound moral judgments about the newly created reality.

The temporal perspective that results from the plurality of narrative voices—particularly "they" and "we"—is significant in itself, as well as being important to the language in the novel. Whereas one of the narrators places the reader in direct contact with the action, as if he or she were participating in the events, the other narrator creates the feeling of the story being experienced almost mythically, as a series of unchanging events that predetermine the future of the characters. Since both narrators present different perspectives on the same reality, the reader is placed neither completely inside nor completely outside the reality of the plot, but on the periphery, where his or her point of view becomes exactly the same as Cuéllar's, one or alienation.

Yet the reader is drawn through the language into the world of the collective narrator, who, in representing the pressures that society imposes on individuals to make them conform to its rules, prevents persons from maturing and acquiring a sense of moral conscience. The group, Cuéllar's friends, and the neighborhood become collectively responsible not only for eliminating or destroying someone who rebels against the capricious nature of society but also for thereby enigmatically emasculating itself and preventing itself from growing up.

# Chapter Six

# *Conversation in The Cathedral:*
# Life as a Shipwreck

## Introduction: Historical Biography

The original, two-volume, 699-page novel *Conversación en La Catedral (Conversation in the Cathedral)*, published in 1969, was hailed at one point by Mario Vargas Llosa as his most significant work. In many ways, the novel marks a new level of artistic maturity for the author, and it certainly represents the culmination of a writing style that is by now easily recognizable as his own in its fragmented plot development; its complex character relationships; and its sophisticated narrative devices, which suggest the influence of Flaubert, Faulkner, Joyce, Dos Passos, and Hemingway. In fact, says Luis A. Díez, (1978c) "he has brought together all the techniques devised or insinuated in his previous works (*montaje dialogal*, plot fragmentation, juxtaposed narratives) and elevated them to a high plateau of unparalleled virtuosity" (63).

To make the novel coherent and meaningful, even greater demands are placed on the reader of *Conversation in The Cathedral*. For example, over 100 names of characters are presented at one point or another in the novel; and in one scene dealing with the activities surrounding a political rally, nineteen separate conversations in dialogue are juxtaposed in montage fashion, which creates the sense of movement, the intensity, and the inevitable clash that occurs between opposing political forces.

Whereas *The Time of the Hero* reveals the disastrous effects of an educational institution on adolescents, *The Green House* deals with the unfortunate yet abominable religious and economic effects on different social types, and *The Cubs* re-creates the destructive effects of rigid social-class norms on individuals, this novel offers basically a political orientation. It presents an overview of Peruvian society even greater in its sweep than the world of *The Green House*. Yet it provides—in a way that only Vargas Llosa can—an equally fascinating look at the interior of human lives from the singular and alienated perspective of different characters during a particular historical period. No doubt, readers will find the lines quoted from Balzac in the novel's epigraph—"the novel is the private history of nations"—a fitting description of *Conversation in The Cathedral*.

Suzanne Jill Levine (1975) declares that the novels written by Vargas Llosa during the 1960s—beginning with *The Time of the Hero* and culminating with *Conversation in The Cathedral*—are linked by common themes and structure and form "one of the largest narrative efforts in contemporary Latin American letters. With an ambition worthy of such masters of the 19th-century novel as Balzac, Dickens and Galdós, but with a technical skill that brings him closer to the heirs of Flaubert and Henry James, Mario Vargas Llosa has begun a complete inventory of the political, social, economic and cultural reality of Peru. This inventory is necessarily controversial" (7).

This novel shows how a Peruvian dictatorship in the 1950s not only determined but destroyed its citizens' lives. It is, in effect, an artistic reflection of a period in Vargas Llosa's life when an entire generation's hopes and desires for a better future were crushed. Specifically, *Conversation in The Cathedral* focuses on General Manuel Odría's dictatorship, which began in 1948 and lasted until 1956; however, that historical moment is recreated through a conversation—denoted in the novel's title—between two men in a seedy downtown Lima bar called The Cathedral, which occurs several years later, in 1963.

For Vargas Llosa, Odría's dictatorship left an indelible mark on his generation. During this period Vargas Llosa attended San Marcos University and participated in clandestine student political meetings to protest the Odría regime. Here he met people who later became characters in the novel. This was also a period in his life when he worked as a journalist for a Lima newspaper. As a city reporter he investigated crime cases that put him in direct contact with Lima's bohemian nightlife and Mafia underworld of vice. During this era, wrestling became a popular sport in Peru and Vargas Llosa discovered that professional wrestlers became political bodyguards for the privileged members of the dictatorship.

While these repressive regimes remain notorious for abrogating human rights and jeopardizing peoples' lives, Vargas Llosa tells José Miguel Oviedo that "Odría's dictatorship was quite different from others that were or are more violent. Its power was maintained through corruption, intrigue, compromise, and duplicity. . . . It was a dictatorship that robbed our generation. There were no heroes, nor did it produce any martyrs, only lots of failures" (Oviedo 1982, 247). Vargas Llosa's novel shows that every level of society—from the upper-class oligarchy to the downtrodden proletariat—is poisoned and debased by a corrupt, immoral, and evil system. Vargas Llosa renders the essence of this depraved society by juxtaposing the world of sex and crime with the political realm. The perverted sexual roles of several characters reveal the personalized, individual sense of degradation that matches the more impersonal and collective view of an immoral and dissolute political system. It is true, as Wolfgang Luchting (1975) states, that the reader of *Conversation in The Cathedral* "is confronted with sadism . . . , lesbianism, homosexuality, voyeurism, delirium tremens, hygenic procedures in a whorehouse, murder, tortures, blackmail, abortions, fraud; in short, if you. can name it, *Conversation* has got it. And pervading it all, pulsating in *everything,* even in the most perverse parts of the spectrum of Peru's 'quality of life,' peeping from actions and reflections, there is masochism" (12). In effect, virtually no one escapes the malignant and disgusting reality that is created in the novel.

As for the theme itself, Chilean novelist Jorge Edwards (1975) correctly states that "even though politics is the most visible aspect of this novel, it is not the central theme. Corruption as an instrument of power does not interest Vargas Llosa so much as the consequences for the individual living in a corrupt and corrupting environment; for politics, by affecting the conscience of the individual, can taint even the smallest details of ordinary life" (23). In calling the novel "a vortex of determinism," R. Z. Sheppard (1975) says that "if García Márquez is Latin America's Faulkner, Peru's Mario Vargas Llosa is aesthetically, if not stylistically, its Dreiser" (84). And most readers would agree with George R. McMurray's conviction that "more politically oriented than its predecessors, *Conversation* lacks the exotic fascination of *La casa verde* and, perhaps because of its length, the sustained intensity of *La ciudad y los perros.* It is nevertheless a powerful, dispassionate commentary on Peruvian—and Latin American—reality, a tour de force that will strengthen the opinion of many critics that Vargas Llosa is one of today's foremost writers of prose fiction" (McMurray 1971, 84).

## Plot: Conversation as (In)Action

As the title of the novel indicates, the plot develops around a conversation between Santiago Zavala, a rueful journalist and embittered son of a now deceased wealthy and influential businessman, and Ambrosio Pardo, a destitute black man from southern Peru who once worked as a chauffeur for Santiago's father (among others) during the Odría regime. Santiago, who has not seen Ambrosio in fifteen years, barely recognizes him in a chance encounter at the city dog pound. Here, where Santiago has gone to retrieve his pet, Ambrosio works part-time by clubbing dogs to death for a penny apiece. The fateful encounter between the two men at the pound that afternoon seems unlikely. In fact, the whole situation becomes ironic once the reader learns that Santiago has been recently writing editorials about the menace created in Lima by rabid stray dogs. Still, a sense of destiny pervades the initial pages of the text, making the encounter plausible if not predestined.

Both men are surprised to see each other after so many years, and Santiago invites Ambrosio to have a drink with him. Ambrosio suggests they go to La Catedral, where they spend the afternoon drowning their sorrows in beer and revive the past through sharing their memories. Their conversation gives way to other conversations that are spread loosely throughout the text and involve either Santiago or Ambrosio with other characters at different moments in the past. For Santiago, the chance meeting becomes a painful trip through the mind jail of the past in an attempt to solve the riddle of why his life has foundered, languished, and then plummeted to fathomless depths of estrangement and animosity. For Ambrosio, the conversation becomes a confession and indictment of the destruction of one man by a reprehensible period in Peruvian history.

From this conversation, then, the reader learns about the past lives of both men, who obviously represent opposite ends of a highly stigmatized social hierarchy in Peru. Other spinoff conversations lead, in turn, to diverse scenes and dialogues among many other characters at different times and places; and within the novel, what seems like a long series of flashbacks creates a feeling of discontinuity and simultaneity among the events. Complexly juxtaposed are an apparent multitude of plot narratives, which include the stories of dozens of characters—politicians, oligarchs, police, lackeys, servants, laborers, prostitutes, and many others—who represent different levels of social, racial, and economic degradation in Peruvian society. John Brushwood (1975a) describes how it works: "The novelist keeps us tied to the basic situation by maintaining a line of dialogue between Ambrosio and Santiago, but the narrative voice passes to other appropriate people. Scenes change and planes of time intermingle. However, the narrative plot is not hard to follow if you pay attention to the clues. There is a certain temptation to go back and reread, because it creates a very satisfying feeling that now you really understand what was going on. The story comes together the way a good mystery reveals itself" (8D).

In particular, Santiago Zavala is the most fully developed character in the novel. Through the conversation, the reader begins to pick up in chronological fashion snatches of his life, beginning with the year of his graduation from high school at the age of eighteen; continuing with his encounters with leftist politics as a university student; and ending in the present moment of the conversation with Ambrosio, when he is married, thirty years old, and employed as a newspaper journalist. At the same time, the conversation fans out to include other characters' pasts. In addition to Ambrosio and his life as chauffeur, bodyguard, and political thug during the Odría regime, other characters whose lives are rendered with great detail include Cayo Bermúdez, the Machiavellian minister of internal affairs, whose sadistic and corrupt secret police keep Odría in power; Santiago's father, Don Fermín Zavala, a rich and opportunistic businessman whose investments depend on the stability of the government; and Amalia, the Zavala family servant who, after a stormy life with Trinidad López (a plebeian textile worker who becomes involved in politics), marries Ambrosio and dies when she gives birth to his child. In addition, it is tempting to include, in a sliding scale of characters important to the novel, the life of Hortensia, alias The Muse, one of Cayo Bermúdez's prostitute concubines whose scandalous murder becomes a key incident in the plot that directly or indirectly involves the principal characters. In this way, the conventional plot device of the "whodunit" detective novel—which is important for the development of plot in *The Time of the Hero*—transports the reader to vastly divergent Peruvian social worlds, from influential oligarchic families to destitute rank-and-file proletarians. Through these worlds, the novel expresses the feelings of frustration and failure that a society experiences when a political regime foments widespread corruption in order to maintain order and power. The novel lays bare the tools of the dictator's trade: hypocrisy, subordination, humiliation, blackmail, and murder. Ricardo Cano Gaviria (1972) states that while the novel is a collective vilification of humanity, Vargas Llosa has probably gone too far in proposing the notion that human beings are ontologically condemned to failure, frustration, and unhappiness (98). In similar fashion, iniquitous forces at work in *The Green House* lead Michael Moody to draw the image of life for that novel's characters as a "web of defeat." Vargas Llosa's position with regard to these literary effects is just the opposite of their total results. In *La orgía perpetua: Flaubert y "Madame Bovary,"* he explains that the single redeeming quality of literature lies in its ability to portray characters confronting troubles in fiction that help readers to offset and even negate their own problems in life.

## Structure as Whirlwind

An overall sense of the novel's structural complexity, which includes the temporal fiction of its characters' lives and the strong presence of the historical moment in the text, can be appreciated through a key image provided by Santiago. Sitting in the midst of the noise and stench of The Cathedral, he retraces his past during the emotional four-hour conversation: "An inner whirlwind, an effervescence in the heart of his heart, a feeling of suspended time and bad breath" (15). The image of the whirlwind—as a current of air whirling violently in a spiral form around a more or less vertical axis and with a forward motion—helps the reader to visualize the way in which the novel's narrative materials are organized. The whirlwind as a form of violent or destructive action also calls to mind Santiago's life—whose movement forward in time contains no center—as well as the movement of the novel in general.

Other visual aspects of the natural "whirlwind" phenomenon are brought into focus when comparing it with the structure of *Conversation in The Cathedral,* particularly its circular nature and forward movement; its impenetrability; its interior vacuum; and in general, the perplexing nature of its energy, apparent invincibility, and dazzling form. Yet the organization of the plot is technically schematic, symmetrical, finished, and severe. This novel is the culmination of technical patterns that Vargas Llosa had mastered in his previous novels. Like a Dos Passos novel, the organization of this novel is based on the contrapuntal juxtaposition in montage fashion of narrative fragments and passages of dialogue that occur at different moments in time and places in Peru. Chronological linearity is not always readily apparent, however, and the reader must sort out mentally the fragments of the novel's content, thereby restoring order, logic, and meaning to the plot.

Yet if one were to reassemble all the fragments dealing with each individual story into a single uninterrupted narration, one would see that even though the plot threads are convoluted, cut, and separated from each other by other plot lines, each story develops in a basically chronological fashion. The first chapter of the novel is a framing device that sets the stage in the present moment and initiates the conversation between the two men (even the action leading up to the conversation, the conversation itself, and Santiago's return home afterward are presented in chronological fashion). The second chapter begins at some moment in the remote past, allowing the succeeding chapters to come forward in time, to pass through the immediate past, and to end near the present time of the conversation. A study of the narrative content of the chapters following the first chapter of part 1 reveals that outside the time frame of the Santiago-Ambrosio conversation, the second chapter jumps back in time to around 1950, starting with the period in Santiago's life when he finishes high school, tries with a friend to seduce the family maid, begins to show forms of adolescent rebellion and bourgeois frustration, and prepares for college. From that point, in Santiago's life and in the lives of other characters as well, the novel moves forward in time.

As early as the second chapter, however, the reader becomes disconcerted. Juxtaposed with the events in Santiago's life beginning in the second chapter are other conversations that invade the narration, disrupting the flow of things as if one were hearing strange voices or finding oneself in a nightmare. Name markers alert the reader to the interlocutors of the conversations that produce mysterious and disturbing echoes throughout the novel. They begin with the Santiago-Ambrosio dialogue in the bar, and include other conversations between Santiago and Carlitos, which take place after Santiago has become a journalist; between Fermín Zavala and Ambrosio during the time when Ambrosio was Fermín's chauffeur and was subjected to Fermín's sexual aberrations; and between Ambrosio and Queta (a lesbian friend of another prostitute, the Muse, whose brutal murder had become a social scandal years before), which takes place in a part of the past not too distant from the present moment of the Santiago-Ambrosio conversation. In addition, the narrative point of view—whether presented by the omniscient narrator who describes a scene or by a character who subjectively reacts to a particular situation—suggests a perspective that fuses different time levels into a continuous and subjective present moment that from beginning to end underscores Santiago's condition; although drunk after the conversation with Ambrosio, Santiago declares that his head is "spinning from thinking so much" (16). Without a doubt, the temporal organization of the different plot lines—all of which have been fragmented to create, on the one hand, a sense of discontinuity and, on the other, a feeling of simultaneity, the feeling of being caught in a vortex—forces the reader to take an active rather than passive role in discovering the novel's meaning and significance.

The novel is formally divided into four parts, which are almost evenly distributed throughout the book and provide an immediate sense of symmetry. The main focal points of interest in the development of the various characters are also parceled out evenly in the four parts of the novel. In the first part, for example, the reader learns about Santiago's adolescent years, his entrance into the university, his defiance with student communist activists, his time in jail due to Cayo Bermúdez's secret service activities, and his decision to leave home to find his own way in life. In effect, Santiago's story provides the axis around which the other characters' stories revolve; some of those stories expand in force and gain strength—as in the case of Cayo Bermúdez, who is first seen leaving a small provincial town for Lima where he becomes director of security for the Odría regime and surreptitiously uses blackmail to maintain control of the country—while others play out their designated roles and disappear as quickly as they appeared (for example, Santiago's university friends, Aída and Jacobo; factory worker Trinidad López, who lives with Amalia Cerda but who is tortured to death for his apparent political affiliations; and Ambrosio's father, Trifulcio, who was jailed for committing crimes).

The focal point in the second part of the novel is the life of Hortensia, alias the Muse, Bermúdez's prostitute-lesbian lover, whose relationship to the other characters is a mystery. Hortensia's life in this part of the novel becomes the pivot story for others that expand outward like concentric circles from her story: the period in Amalia's life when she works for Hortensia, whose house in a decent neighborhood is turned by Cayo Bermúdez into a den of sin for influential people (like Fermín Zavala); Bermúdez's upward spiral in his career as minister of internal affairs; the investigative work Santiago carries out as reporter for a newspaper; the lives of several bodyguards and hired gunmen who carry out orders to destroy people; the life of Ambrosio as chauffeur for Cayo Bermúdez; and the life of Queta, Hortensia's lesbian friend.

The third part of the novel revolves around the description of political developments at the time, the journalistic world of Santiago, the murder of Hortensia, and the revelation of a sexual relationship between Ambrosio and Fermín Zavala (the latter forces the former to engage in sex, suggesting the "black slave" motif in Arabic literature). The lives of other characters who are related directly or indirectly to these incidents are also presented in the third part: Amalia's life as a servant for Hortensia and her growing relationship with Ambrosio; Trifulcio's life after he leaves jail and becomes a political hit man until he dies in a political rally; and the lives of two of Santiago's journalist friends, Becerrita and Carlitos.

The fourth and last part of the novel portrays, in the case of Santiago, his continual downward plunge toward mediocrity as he marries a person below his family's social standing; the period in Ambrosio and Amalia's life when he takes her to the jungle, where she dies in childbirth; and Ambrosio's sexual encounters with Hortensia's friend, Queta. In the same part, however, the death of Fermín Zavala is presented; the end to Becerrita and Carlito's lives is narrated; and Queta's life history is recounted. One of the most important narrative effects of this structural scheme lies in its creation of anticipation. The denouement of the characters' lives is presented in the beginning, and the events that lead to each character's more or less tragic end are revealed afterward in other parts of the novel. The different conversations that echo throughout the novel communicate the results of earlier acts before they happen: Ambrosio's escape to the jungle, where Amalia dies; Fermín's death; the marriage of Santiago's sister; Hortensia's death; and Ambrosio's culpability in committing a serious crime. The narrative procedure that suggests anticipation forces the reader to consider not only the outcome of a succession of events in a person's life but the events themselves—the evil process at work. In other words, the reader comes to know the denouement of the characters' lives—fatalism, destruction, apathy, affliction, and death—through the events in their lives.

Even though a symmetrical balance between Santiago's life and the lives of several other characters—particularly Cayo Bermúdez— is brought to bear on the novel's structure throughout, other external factors might seem to undermine a complete sense of balance and harmony. For example, a lack of external symmetry becomes apparent in terms of the number of chapters in each part: ten, nine, four, and eight, respectively. But a parallel relationship exists between parts 1 and 3, and between parts 2 and 4, creating once again a sense of balance in the novel. The correspondence between the first pair of parts does not rest on the number of chapters in each part but on the kind of narrative patterns that evolve. Although the chapters of parts 1 and 2 may read like typical chapters of a novel, they are also complex, labyrinthine constructions of temporally and spatially diverse interpolated dialogues by numerous characters that weave in and around each other to form the narrative fabric of the chapters. Vargas Llosa achieves intriguing results that are similar to his previous works, for in a single narrative sequence multiple perspectives are created in rapid fashion. In a typical sequence several different levels of dialogue (identified with numbers) are compacted to create tension and irony; here, Santiago's decision to attend the state university instead of the private Catholic university causes concern:

(1)   "He doesn't want to go to the Catholic University but to San Marcos," Señora Zoila said. "That upset Fermín very much."

(2)   "I'll bring him to his senses, Zoila, don't you get involved," Don Fermín said. "He's at the foolish age, you have to know how to lead him. If you fight with him, he'll get all the more stubborn."

"If instead of advice you'd give him a couple of whacks, he'd pay more attention to you," said Señora Zoila. "The one who doesn't know how to raise him is you."

(3)   "She married that boy who used to come to the house," Santiago says. "Popeye Arévalo, Freckle Face Arévalo."

(4)   "Skinny doesn't get along with his old man because they don't have the same ideas," Popeye said.

"And what ideas does that snotnose still wet behind the ears have?" the senator laughed.

(5) "Study hard, get your law degree and you can dip your spoon into politics," Don Fermín said. "Right, Skinny?"

(6)   "Skinny gets mad because his old man backed Odría in his revolt against Bustamante," Popeye said. "He's against the military." (22–23)

The six different levels of narration involve dialogues between the following characters: (1) doña Zoila (Santiago's mother) and Popeye's mother; (2) don Fermín and his wife, doña Zoila; (3) Santiago and Ambrosio in the bar; (4) Popeye (friend of Santiago and boyfriend of Santiago's sister) and his father; (5) Santiago and don Fermín; and (6) Popeye and his father. As a result, different temporal planes are juxtaposed in such a way that, as John M. Lipski (1979) points out, "the textual continuity and coherence is effected not by chronological sequencing, but rather by an intricate series of verbal and pragmatic clues, which allow a temporally disconnected set of discourse to be interpreted as textually connected" (73). One noticeable effect produced in these narrative clashes is irony; the differences that exist between husband and wife, father and son, adolescents and adults, liberals and conservatives, and truth and hypocrisy begin to collide and set into motion the basic conflicts of the novel.

In the case of parts 2 and 4—which are equally dense, diffuse, and complex—the chapters are divided into marked segments (the nine chapters of part 2 contain a total of eighty-one segments, and the eight chapters of part 4 contain twenty-eight segments) and, as in Vargas Llosa's previous novels, the plot lines or narrative segments are presented in an orderly succession that repeats itself based on the following sequence: Amalia—Cayo Bermúdez—Santiago (or Amalia—Cayo Bermúdez—Ambrosio) in part 2, and Santiago—Queta—Ambrosio in part 4. Although the stories are in many ways radically different from each other, the sense of continuity that is created through the sequential alternation of each story blunts any distinctive aspects and suggests that everyone's destiny and the future of society is subject to the same evil and destructive process.

## Moral Implications: A Sadder and a Wiser Man

The first chapter of the novel sets the stage for the long conversation between Santiago and Ambrosio, which in the remainder of the text becomes its content. Moreover, the initial lines of the novel set the overall theme (lack of communication, failure, and alienation), the narrative perspective (basically, Santiago's), and the tone (doom) for the entire work. Philip Johnson (1976) correctly states that "the character of Santiago is complex and multifaceted. He is Vargas Llosa's most complete expression of defeat and represents the total pessimism the author feels for Peru" (205). The first scene describes Santiago as he leaves the newspaper building where he works, on his way home for lunch:

> From the doorway of *La Crónica* Santiago looks at the Avenida Tacna without love: cars, uneven and faded buildings, the gaudy skeletons of posters floating in the mist, the gray midday. At what precise moment had Peru fucked itself up? The newsboys weave in and out among the vehicles halted by the red light on Wilson, hawking the afternoon papers, and he starts to walk slowly toward Colmena. His hands in his pockets, head down, he goes along escorted by people who are also going the direction of the Plaza San Martín. He was like Peru, Zavalita was, he'd fucked himself up somewhere along the line. He thinks: when? Across from the Hotel Crillón a dog comes over to lick his feet: don't get your rabies on me, get away. Peru all fucked up, Carlitos all fucked up, everybody all fucked up. He thinks: there's no solution. (3)

Santiago's depressed point of view is created immediately through the description of the loathsome environment that reflects his downcast attitude toward life. He is trapped. A feeling of hopelessness is communicated through Santiago's introspective deduction that "there's no solution." Yet the reader is left with another question: To what is there no solution? The fact is that the reader has crossed paths with Santiago (or "Zavalita," as he addresses himself when he thinks) at a moment of crisis in his life. As it turns out, the conversation with Ambrosio later that afternoon is a frustrating, almost masochistic attempt by Santiago to give meaning to his past and find answers to the burning question that he poses at the outset. Although he deplores the upper-class luxury, superficiality, and mediocrity his father, his mother, Doña Zoila, his sister Teté, and his brother El Chispas represent, any change now at midlife seems beyond his reach.

On his way home for lunch that fateful day, he notices his bulging potbelly and thinks maybe sports is the answer. Then he ponders: "Maybe it would be worth putting out a little effort and getting a degree. He thinks: going backward" (6). In effect, the conversation with Ambrosio later drags him back into the past, preventing any chance of looking forward with optimism and hope. In addition,

the description of the bar presents a grotesque, hideous, and de-
caying society, which again reflects the unpalatable nature of reality
for Santiago:

It seemed impossible that little Santiago was drinking beer now, and
Ambrosio smiles, his strong greenish-yellow teeth exposed to the air: time
did fly, by golly. They go up the stairs, between the vacant lots on the
first block of Alfonso Ugarte there's a white Ford garage, and at the corner
on the left, faded by the inexorable grayness, the warehouses of the Central
Railroad appear. A truck loaded with crates hides the door of La Catedral.
Inside, under the zinc roof, crowded on rough benches and around crude
tables, a noisy voracious crowd. Two Chinese in shirtsleeves behind the
bar watch the copper faces, the angular features that are chewing and
drinking, and a frantic little man from the Andes in a shabby apron serves
steaming bowls of soup, bottles, platters of rice. Plenty of feeling, plenty
of kisses, plenty of love boom from a multicolored jukebox and in the
back, behind the smoke, the noise, the solid smell of food and liquor,
the dancing swarms of flies, there is a punctured wall—stones, shacks, a
strip of river, the leaden sky—and an ample woman bathed in sweat
manipulates pots and pans surrounded by the sputter of a grill. There's
an empty table beside the jukebox and among the scars on the wood one
can make out a heart pierced by an arrow, a woman's name: Saturnina.
(13).

This description is particularly important for the relationship that
is established between the way Peruvian reality is presented and
interpreted by the omniscient narrator and Santiago's point of view
and mental state; reality is an abscess—a hideous, grotesque, morally repulsive monster—and it is destroying everyone. As a matter
of fact, even the name Saturnina, which is carved into one of the
tables at the bar, takes on symbolic interpretations, once the mythical image of the female who devours her children is understood to
represent the Odría period in Peruvian politics that is destroying
Santiago's generation. Hence, Santiago's nihilistic attitude confirms
the narrator's negative description of the setting, and the impact
on the reader becomes doubly strong: not only does the description
of the environment reflect the character's sorry emotional state, but
taken together they make a strong, even depressing statement about
the nature of Peruvian reality during the 1950s and the dictatorship's
effect on the people.

    Although the drama and tension that is produced in *Conversation
in The Cathedral* may be due largely to the almost overpowering

presence of dialogue presented in the form of narration, there is much to be said for the importance placed upon scenic description. The special focus on the setting is created by the combination of Santiago's point of view and that of the omniscient narrator, and it is, indeed, important. In fact, Charles Bevelander (1975) points out that both Santiago and the reader perceive reality in the same way because of Vargas Llosa's repeated use of imagery that portrays the setting as viscous, fetid, slimy, and fecal. This perspective coincides with Sartre's observation that viscosity represents a feeling of entrapment and alienation. In this way, then, the description of the environment corresponds to Santiago's personal malaise (149–51).

To make his nihilistic attitude stronger, Santiago recognizes his own condemned state of affairs, and after the two men reach the bar, he says to himself: "You shouldn't have come, you shouldn't have spoken to him, Zavalita, you're not fucked up, you're crazy. He thinks: the nightmare will come back. It'll be your fault, Zavalita, poor papa, poor old man" (13). The reader is now faced with another enigma—namely, the role that Santiago's father plays in all of this. While no clear-cut, precise answers may be forthcoming, the author might contend that the attempt to find them becomes as significant as the answers themselves.

After posing the initial question in the opening scene as he leaves work, Santiago tries repeatedly to pinpoint introspectively (and literally, throughout the conversation) the moment when his downfall actually occurred in his life. Early in the conversation with Ambrosio, Santiago says that he would give anything to know when it happened. Each time after that moment, when the phrase "He thinks" and Santiago's subsequent reference to "there" (at that moment) are repeated, the reader is alerted to the crucial moments in Santiago's life. Through the repetition of this phrase, the decisions that he makes in life become linked in chainlike fashion, sealing his fate at every turn and leading to his present and permanent malady. These moments represent decisions that he made during the Odría years, and taken together they have produced his present condition as an outcast. The repeated phrase is also one of the necessary clues that maintain the reader in the present moment of the conversation between Santiago and Ambrosio, serving as a kind of homing device among other levels of narration in the novel.

The first period of his life that Santiago re-creates in his conversation with Ambrosio deals with his university years. He is exposed

to a new world of activities, friends, philosophies, and realities that
for a sheltered, young, rich, and upper-class person quickly becomes
intriguing, desirable (prohibitive), and complex. An incident earlier
in his life, in which he and his friend Popeye try to seduce the maid
Amalia (she subsequently loses her job, making Santiago feel bad),
suggests that he suddenly becomes aware of social differences that
exist in Peru; but it is at the state university (not at the private
Catholic university for Peru's "better" families) where young Santiago sees his country, his family, and himself in a new light. As
a result, he begins to doubt what he had always taken for granted,
that life was easy. To complicate matters, at this time in his life
he meets Aída, a liberal and lower-class student activist, with whom
he falls in love and experiences—for the first time—all the emotional ties to another person that are a part of a possibly serious love
relationship: infatuation, admiration, jealousy. He remembers their
passionate discussions about the Odría dictatorship, their desire to
study Marxism, and their challenges to each other to admit their
atheism—in short, their sharing of secrets, their growth as rebels,
and their demonstration of their defiance and independence. But
the bubble pops, and he finds himself back in the present, where
he faces the same question: "He thinks: did I fall in love then and
there?" (61).

Telling Ambrosio about his university years (re-created through
scenes reminiscent of flashbacks) during the conversation in the
present causes Santiago to recoil into an inner world of self-examination where the questions start to multiply. Aware of the social
differences that exist between his new working-class student friends
at San Marcos and the attitudes of superiority of his family's upper-
class environment, Santiago finds himself sympathizing with the
former and embarrassed by the latter:

Were you ashamed, Zavalita? he thinks: that Jacobo, Héctor, Solórzano
didn't visit your home and the people you lived with, didn't meet your
old lady and listen to your old man, that Aída didn't hear Teté's delightful
idiocies? He thinks: or that your old man and old lady shouldn't know
who you hung around with, that Sparky and Teté shouldn't see Martínez'
toothless half-breed face? That first day you began to kill off the old folks,
Popeye, Miraflores, he thinks. You were breaking away, Zavalita, entering
another world: was it then, was it then that you shut it off? He thinks:
breaking with what, entering what world? (68)

Although Santiago feels "tortured, exiled, betrayed" during this period in his life, he is also filled with the possibility of an open-ended, positive future: " 'Revolution, books, museums,' Santiago says. 'Do you see what it is to be pure?' " (72). This euphoria, however, is short-lived; for when he informs his family of his decision to attend San Marcos instead of the Catholic university—in a scene in which Santiago's family reveals its racial prejudice toward those who attend the state university—that sick feeling gnawing away at him is equally prevalent: "All the doors open, he thinks, at what moment and why did they begin to close?" (73). Throughout the novel, the dialogue of these family scenes, for example, is juxtaposed with his self-examination, thereby creating irony; when, in the present moment, he asks introspectively why the doors began to close on him, he hears his mother say in the juxtaposed scene that took place many years earlier, "You've had your own way, you got into San Marcos" (73).

Early in the novel the reader becomes aware of how Santiago's life is systematically undermined by doubt, which is produced by the contradiction between new and old alliances—friends and family, the lower and upper classes, mestizos and whites, and the poor and the rich. Placed in between, Santiago feels an attachment to all of them: he is personally, emotionally, and culturally tied to his family and social class; Santiago is at first intellectually tied to his friends, university life, and a sudden awareness of social inequality in Peru, but there are highly emotional links as well. In fact, life becomes markedly complex for him. Santiago's strong sense of the social, cultural, economic, and political injustices that exist among Peruvians is tempered and perhaps even undermined by his infatuation (first love) for Aída. Vargas Llosa views this process of Santiago's rebellion, doubt, and frustration as leading to a sense of crisis that is typical of growing numbers of young bourgeois nonconformists in modern-day societies everywhere.

Santiago, however, is unable to dissociate himself from the mores of his family's social class; nor is he able to fully accept the proletarian world of his new friends: "Had it been that first year, Zavalita, when you saw that San Marcos was a brothel and not the paradise you'd thought?" (90). After recalling all the problems that he had encountered there, and telling Ambrosio that "those were backward-looking criticisms" (90) because at the time he had liked San Marcos, Santiago once again punctures the bubble: "There, he thinks, did

I fuck myself up there?" (91). These particular moments of self-examination are significant because, on one level, the reader becomes involved in the personal problems of the novel's main protagonist. Ambrosio asks if Santiago's bitterness was not due to the fact that Santiago had become jealous of Aída. " 'I never saw her alone,' Santiago says. 'I wasn't bitter; a little worm in my stomach sometimes, nothing else' " (92). On another level, the reader is brought face to face with the serious problems confronting Peru:

The university reflected the country, Jacobo said, twenty years ago those professors were probably progressives and readers, then because they had to work at other things and because of the environment they became mediocre and bourgeois. . . . But if the university was a reflection of the country San Marcos would never be in good shape as long as Peru was so badly off, Santiago said, and Aída if what was wanted was to cure the disease at its roots there shouldn't be any talk of university reform but of revolution. But they were students and their field of action was the university, Jacobo said, by working for reform they would be working for the revolution: you had to go through stages and not be pessimistic. (92–93)

Santiago tells Ambrosio that at this time in his life his doubts about everything led to a loss of faith—the lack of power to believe in anything. Nothing was possible: idealism, agonisticism, Marxism. He recalls those conversations with his friends:

He thinks: you thought not, Zavalita. Closing your eyes, Marxism rests on science, clenching your fists, religion on ignorance, sinking your feet into the earth, God doesn't exist, grinding your teeth, the motive force of history was the class struggle, hardening your muscles, when it freed itself of bourgeois exploitation, breathing deeply, the proletariat would free humanity, and attacking: and set up a world without classes. You couldn't, Zavalita, he thinks. He thinks: you were, you are, you always will be, you'll die a petite bourgeois. Were nursing bottles, private school, family, neighborhood stronger? he thinks. You used to go to mass, to confession and communion on first Fridays, you prayed and even then a lie, I don't believe. (100–101)

In whirlwind fashion, Santiago's life begins to pass in front of his eyes in the same way that visual images on a screen flash in front of the viewer: " 'In prep school, at home, in the neighborhood, in the study group, in the party, at *La Crónica,*' Santiago says, 'My whole life spent doing things without believing, my whole life spent pretending' " (101). But then he asks himself, "Had it been a lack of faith, Zavalita, couldn't it have been timidity?" (101). The reader surmises that timidity may well have been the cause, for when Aída joins a different secret discussion group with Jacobo, Santiago (now in love with Aída and jealous of Jacobo) finds himself alone; and all of a sudden "it appeared, there it was, tiny and glacial, gelatinous. It would twist delicately at the mouth of his stomach, secrete that liquid that wet the palms of his hands, make his heart beat faster, and go away with a shudder" (103). The anxiety that he feels through the image of the worm gnawing away in his stomach finds part of its source in this frustrated relationship with Aída. When it comes time for a formal commitment to revolutionary ideology and action, Santiago holds back while Aída and Jacobo sign up formally to join the Communist party. A crucial moment occurs in the conversation when Santiago (in the present) talks directly about himself, Zavalita (in the past): " 'That's when it was shown that Zavalita wasn't pure anymore, Ambrosio,' Santiago says. 'That Jacobo and Aída were purer than Zavalita' " (138–39). And he wonders if he would have been better off if he had become something else.

Santiago's newspaper friend, Carlitos—with whom another conversation (dispersed throughout the novel) takes place during the period following Santiago's university years when he works as a journalist—puts the whole problem into perspective for Santiago when he says that "it wasn't horror over the dogma, it was the reflex of a two-bit anarchist child who doesn't like to take orders" (139). Moreover, Carlitos says, "underneath it all you were afraid of breaking with people who eat and dress and smell well" (139). It is true that the underhanded, behind-the-scenes dealings that go on between political parties leave a bad taste in Santiago's mouth. When a small group of students representing their political views must hold a secret meeting with a major political party in a billiard hall, Santiago once again becomes disillusioned with the process. The problem is serious for Santiago, "because, thanks to San Marcos, I fucked myself up, . . . and in this country a person who doesn't fuck himself up fucks up other people" (144). Through it all, Santiago suffers from remorse, jealousy, and embarrassment concerning who he is and what he represents in Peruvian society. As a consequence, when Santiago has become an anonymous and mediocre journalist, he tells his colleague: "every time I write something that's repugnant to me, I make the article as disgusting as I can. Suddenly, on the following day a boy reads it and feels like throwing up and, well, something's happened" (144).

In complete contrast to this morally commendable yet equally doomed stance is the opposite position that Cayo Bermúdez takes toward life. But their backgrounds are strikingly similar—they both rebel from patriarchal dominance and possess the malicious ill will that prompts an urge to hurt or to humiliate others. Santiago finds a masochistic comfort in seemingly throwing up a hypocritical barrier of moral goodness while Bermúdez openly and crassly uses evil power to obtain his ends because he understands the system all too well. Bermúdez is not only an immoral person, but a completely amoral one as well. Although it is impossible for the reader to feel much sympathy toward him, Cayo Bermúdez turns out to be almost as complex as Santiago. He is a person who reeks of evil, and the novel captures two aspects of his life: in one guise, he is a public figure—the blackmailing minister of internal affairs for Odría— while, as a private citizen, he is a sexually impotent, racially inferior, and culturally deprived Peruvian mestizo who knows he will always be barred from the country's elite classes. His ulterior motives are never directly revealed in the novel, but it becomes obvious that he is hateful, resentful, rancorous, and vindictive. Bermúdez is living proof of the system's destructive effect on a lower-middle-class person, while Santiago represents the same result for the elite and Ambrosio for the disadvantaged poor classes of Peru.

As other missing pieces of information begin to fall into place in the second half of the novel—revealing the role that Santiago's father and his chauffeur play in the sensational murder of Hortensia (the Muse)—Santiago's downward spiral seems to reach its nadir. While investigating the Muse's death for the newspaper, he learns that Hortensia had once been Cayo Bermúdez's mistress and that she had resorted to blackmailing Santiago's father, Fermín, also known as Golden Balls in Lima's sexual underworld. It is revealed that Fermín had carried on a relationship of sexual exploitation with Ambrosio, an affair that Bermúdez had initiated in order to blackmail the rich businessman. This relationship explains the third mysterious and unidentified conversation that takes place throughout the novel between Fermín and Ambrosio (in addition to the Santiago-Ambrosio and the Santiago-Carlitos dialogues).

In the primary dialogue, however, Ambrosio never divulges the vital information that Santiago wants to know about his father. Although Ambrosio's motives are never fully explained, it is suggested at one point in the novel (and almost determined near the end) that Ambrosio had killed the Muse in order to prevent her from further blackmailing Santiago's father simply for money that would enable her to leave the country and start over in Mexico. (This mysterious situation is similar to the death of Ricardo Arana in *The Time of the Hero,* for the murderer is never directly revealed but only indirectly mentioned through bits of information that the reader, in detective fashion, must piece together.) While recalling that climactic scene in which Santiago and several other reporters conduct interviews with other brothel prostitutes and discover the basic information that links his father to the grossly wicked world of sex and politics, he contemplates once again the significance of such knowledge and asks himself, "At that moment, Zavalita? He thinks: yes, there" (351). In a few brief pages, the past (the interview scene), a less distant moment afterward with Carlitos (in which Santiago breaks down and cries at a bar), and the present moment (the conversation with Ambrosio) merge into the image of the pain caused by the symbolic worm gnawing away at him: "at the entrance to his stomach the little worm growing, the snake, the knives, just like that time, he thinks, worse than that time. Oh Zavalita" (352). At the bottom of this social and moral abyss Santiago and the reader discover the underlying motive of Santiago's destruction; ironically, it is nothing more than his pride that has been deflated. In referring to the discovery about his father, he says to himself: "Not the moment when you found out, Zavalita, but there. He thinks: the moment I found out that everybody in Lima knew he was a fairy except me. Everybody on the [news]paper, Zavalita, except you" (355).

As a result, Santiago's path of destruction takes on a very strong tone of masochistic vindictiveness. As in the case of Santiago's marriage to Ana (a simple small-town nurse who represents the epitome of mediocrity and certainly occupies a place below his family on the social ladder), these responses to his situation are reprisals that Santiago inflicts on others and on himself in order to avenge the low blow he has been dealt in life and to strike back at the cruel system under which he lives. Near the end of the novel, after his father has died, Santiago's brother meets with him to discuss the settlement of the estate but Santiago rejects it all: "If you hadn't told Ana you probably would have avoided a lot of fights, he thinks. A hundred, Zavalita, two hundred. Had pride fucked you up? he thinks. He thinks: see how proud your husband is, love, he refused everything from them, love, he told them to go to hell with their stocks and their houses, love. Did you think she was going to admire you, Zavalita, did you want her to? She was going to throw it up to you, he thinks, she was going to reproach you every time they had to ask the Chinaman for credit or borrow from the German woman. Poor Anita, he thinks. He thinks: poor Zavalita" (592).

The scenes that describe these periods in Santiago's life—after he leaves the university and gets a job (one that he obtains through the help of an uncle)—are presented in conjunction with Santiago's introspective view of these critical moments in the past; as the reader views them in retrospect, these moments determine his condition in the present moment—that is, these conflicts in Santiago's past have led to his present situation as an insignificant, indifferent, and alienated journalist. However, as he sinks slowly into the quagmire of contemporary urban mediocrity and anonymity, Santiago seems to find solace in revealing the truth about such conditions; and by taking sadistic pleasure in the same process that is destroying him, he even discovers a way to affirm his existence. He is viewed as a person who freely chooses the most degrading option in life—failure. For this reason, Ricardo Cano Gaviria (1972) states that Santiago's choice "implies a certain dignity and even a secret greatness. He is a frustrated person because if one does not become [purposely] frustrated in the world in which one lives {here, Santiago's world}, one will be considered rotten and despicable, a truly ignoble person. . . . He has chosen mediocrity [of his own free will] in order to avoid mediocrity" (100).

The implications of Santiago's attitude place *Conversation in The Cathedral* squarely within the parameters of modernist literature. Santiago displays this modernist ideological stance, one in which he finds himself at odds with the dominant social and cultural order. By rejecting everything for which contemporary society stands, Santiago embodies the position of negation. Kingsley Widmer (1980) states that this modernist tendency in literature today subverts and even destroys true social culture because of the overpowering force of the "self-infinitizing spirit of the radical will" (42). The result and didactic function of modernist literature is to introduce anxiety into the conscience of contemporary man. Hence, the answer to the question that Santiago poses at the beginning of the novel is never fully revealed, and the question remains shrouded in a veil of mystery. For Santiago life is nauseatingly hopeless; there is no escape. The meaninglessness of life is compounded by the sordid description of the character's world, which helps to create the attitude of "why bother?" This attitude, which flows out of the novel's pages and repeatedly slaps the reader in the face, is based on the realization that life is cheap, even worthless. Ambrosio's story typifies the absurdity of an insensitive person who has unwittingly become the victim in a dog-eat-dog world. But Santiago's dramatized version of this perspective and the melodramatic conflicts in the novel that reverberate out into society and infiltrate all of its levels, attempts to encompass a philosophical position that allows the individual the freedom to choose his destiny. For Santiago, as well as for others in the novel, the result is disenchantment and cynicism, as the individual moves down from a socially privileged life to a prostrate, repugnant, abject, but freely chosen situation. In an "appealing contemporary fantasy," states Kinsley Widmer (1980), the "character [in the modernist novel] attains the moral limbo of totally alienated freedom" (64). While this type of existential modernism allows for a fuller cross-examination of the nature of truth, Widmer explains, it hardly provides the reader with a mythos by which to live: "Its insights may be considerable but remain alienated from a fuller sense of life, maintaining themselves only by endless self-purgings and demonic catharsis" (67). As a result, these negative heroics which are basically critical forms of the existential explorations of reality, demonstrate the limits of rebellion and defiance. In this sense, Vargas Llosa's scatological paroxysms—viewed through Santiago's aberrant attempt to demonstrate an intellectual albeit irrational awareness of a corrupt and frustrating world—are a fitting culmination of a modernist ideology that, according to Widmer, includes "Dostoyevsky's outrageous paradoxes, Conrad's nihilistic fears, Lawrence's apocalyptic yearnings, Hemingway's nada, Faulkner's puritan rages, Céline's deathly journeyings, Wright's black guilts, [and] West's surreal mockeries" (73).

## Chapter Seven
# Captain Pantoja and the Special Service: The Tragicomedy of a Madcap

With the publication of *Pantaleón y las visitadoras (Captain Pantoja and the Special Service)* in 1973, Mario Vargas Llosa utilizes comic farce to produce a humorous novel. Its mirth-provoking, jocular effect is uncommon in his earlier works. And the author's penchant for melodrama and the salient features of pulp fiction reaches new levels of significance.

### Parallel Plots: Rampant Fanaticism

Basically, the novel is a spoof on the manic organizational abilities of a Peruvian army captain who is given the dubious task of creating a squad of prostitutes for the purpose of harnessing the soldier's sexual desires, which have grown out of control. The absurd nature of the assignment becomes even more incongruous, not to mention funny, as the reader watches Captain Pantaleón Pantoja try to make the sex trade a legitimate and institutional activity of the army. A parallel story develops around the growing spiritual conversion of hundreds of people to Brother Francisco's kinky fanatical religious cult, the "Brotherhood of the Ark." The irony that emanates from the organization of the text quickly transforms the humor of its language and the comic nature of the narrative situations into not only an amusing tale of woe but also another commentary on fanaticism, a standard theme of Vargas Llosa, which brings into opposition the rational and irrational nature of human behavior.

Most readers and literary critics were surprised at Vargas Llosa's sudden turnabout in narrative perspective after his earlier works, which in no way include humor. Six years before this novel was published, Luis Harss and Barbara Dohmann (1967) declared that "anything approaching humor in any way is taboo for Vargas Llosa." Vargas Llosa had told them in conversation, "I've always been completely immune to humor in literature," thus underscoring his belief that "in general humor is unreal. Reality contradicts humor" (363). But in an interview with José Miguel Oviedo, following the publication of *Captain Pantoja and the Special Service,* Vargas Llosa explains that his ideas about the use of humor in literature have changed radically. Now he believes that humor is an important aspect of human experience, which provides a different means for exploring human nature and for representing it in a literary sense. In addition, humor is for fiction writing a "formidable source of technical resources" (Oviedo 1974b, 67).

Vargas Llosa feels that humor may be too bluntly or directly incorporated into *Captain Pantoja and the Special Service.* Although humor helps to mitigate or to soften certain situations, the reader could easily reject it entirely because of the truculent nature of certain scenes that are generally typical of his novels and the seemingly exaggerated albeit highly probable tale that is told in this novel. He adds that in his future novels the humor will be rendered much more subtly in order to create believable characters and to provide a sense of tragedy to accompany the reader's laughter. Nevertheless, many readers of *Captain Pantoja and the Special Service* find that the absurd scheme of the plot, the irony produced from the humorous situations, and the grotesque character of certain events also capture the author's continuing and unswerving concern for and critical stance toward certain aspects of human nature in general, and the realities of his native Peru in particular.

The basic conflict that sets the novel's action into motion is the inimitable problem that the Peruvian army faces in the sparsely populated Amazon jungle: sex-starved soldiers assigned to lonely, isolated military garrisons throughout the region have resorted to raping women in nearby villages, causing the local inhabitants to protest the soldiers' illicit behavior. The alarming news reaches across the Andes to Lima, Peru's capital, where the army's high command decides to devise a way to pacify the soldiers' sexual appetites. Hence, the decision is made to send someone to the jungle region to hire secretly a group of prostitutes and to transport them into the backwater outposts where the problem of satisfying the soldiers' sexual drives will be alleviated if not eliminated.

The responsibility for organizing such an unlikely operation falls on the shoulders of Captain Pantoja (also known as Panta to some and as Pantita to others). The unassuming officer—who has just been promoted to the rank of captain and is already recognized in the Quartermaster Corps for his amazing organizational capabilities—is transferred to the Peruvian jungle city of Iquitos. Here, in clandestine fashion, he conceives, expertly brings to maturity, and unwittingly precipitates the destruction of the armed forces' most efficient branch: the Special Service for Garrisons, Frontier, and Related Installations. From the outset, the army's clergyman foresees the apocalyptic end of the seemingly innocuous operation: " 'I wanted to cure a disease, not cause one,' Commander Beltrán reads and rereads General Scavino's flushed face. 'I never imagined the medicine would be worse than the sickness, General. Unthinkable, terrible. Are you going to permit this atrocity?' " (10).

Pantoja's wife, Pochita, and his mother, Leonor, accompany him to Iquitos, but they know nothing about his confidential activities—for the officer must wear civilian clothes and avoid making direct contact with the army—until the operation finally becomes a public scandal and it can no longer be kept secret. By the end of the novel a series of events has undone the burgeoning three-year-old traveling prostitution ring as quickly as it had been initiated. While the operation grows, however, Pantoja dedicates himself to the job with such vehemence—utilizing precise mathematical calculations and marketing strategies in order to make the commerce between the prostitutes and the soldiers as efficient as possible—that the results far exceed the expectations of his superiors. At one point in the novel, Pantoja even scrutinizes and runs calculations on his own lovemaking with his wife in an effort to acquire certain information that will help him achieve the utmost efficiency for the Special Service.

Once the clandestine operation has been discovered and publicly denounced, an army general laments the situation to a local bishop (who visits him in protest): "At least he could have organized the thing in a mediocre, defective way. But that idiot has converted the Special Service into the most efficient unit of the armed forces" (174). As Marvin Lewis (1977) states, "Pantaleón, another in a long line of Vargas Llosa's anti-heroes, finds himself in one absurd situation after another. As he seeks, unsuccessfully, to justify his existence, his state of affairs becomes somewhat tragic" (78). It is at this point that the novel's epigraph—a quotation from Flaubert's *Sentimental Education*—becomes significant: "There are some men who serve as intermediaries among others; they are treated like bridges and they advance further along." Although Pantaleón's story is finally a parody of military organization, Vargas Llosa himself views the novel as a "parable about the bureaucratic spirit itself" (Schwartz 1980, 57). He is a pawn in a ludicrous situation.

As one might expect, Pantaleón's organizational zeal and his dedication to serving his country through compliance with the suspect military orders are not enough to prevent his emotions from influencing his actions. Without realizing it at first, he becomes personally involved with one of the girls of his entourage, Olga Arellano Rosaura, alias the Brazilian. The relationship nearly destroys Pantoja's married life (and at one point in the novel Pochita and Leonor do leave Iquitos, embarrassed because everyone in the jungle but them knows what Pantoja does for the army), and it certainly brings the Special Service to an abrupt end.

In particular, an incident that brings the action in the novel to culmination occurs one day when the Special Service's boat returns from one of its garrison visits: a group of drunken civilians, outraged by the military command's denial of their request for similar privileges with the prostitutes, attacks the boat, and in an exchange of gunfire the Brazilian is mortally wounded. Since the assailants fear reprisals from the military, they make the incident appear to be the work of the fanatical religious sect that has grown in popularity throughout the region: they crucify the dead body of the Brazilian by nailing it to a tree. Pantoja, feeling remorse and pain (although "it was a decision made calmly and rationally," he says), subverts everything that he has worked for when he dons his military uniform, orders a military escort, and reads a formal eulogy at his lover's funeral. The question of Pantoja's rational or irrational behavior is a source of debate.

After the funeral, in a confrontation with General Scavino, Pantoja tries to justify his actions to his superior by explaining that the Special Service had been no secret to anyone.

"So appearing dressed as an Army officer, in a cortege of prostitutes and pimps, is an unimportant incident," General Scavino becomes theatrical, understanding, benevolent, even pleasant. "So paying tribute to a streetwalker as if it were a matter—." "Of a soldier fallen in action." Captain

Pantoja raises his voice, gestures, steps forward, "I'm sorry, but that is, neither more nor less, the status of specialist Olga Arellano Rosaura." (224)

During the same conversation, General Scavino discovers Pantoja's motives: "Are you trying to insinuate that whores in the Special Service are in the same position as doctors assigned to the Army? . . . . Pantoja, Pantoja, come down to earth." Pantoja retorts: "The specialists render the armed forces a service no less important than the assigned doctors, lawyers or priests" (225).

The high command suggests that the erring captain request a discharge from the army for his imprudent act, but Pantoja insists that he cannot because "the Army is the most important thing in my life" (228). After dismantling the base of operations, packing up at home, and getting ready to leave Iquitos for a new assignment, the chastised captain (who at the end of the novel finds himself in charge of the mess hall at a lonely outpost high in the Andes mountains) "spends his last night in Iquitos wandering the deserted streets of Iquitos by himself and with his head down. 'After all, it's three years of my life. They gave me a very difficult assignment and I executed it. Despite the difficulties, the lack of understanding, I did good work. I built something that had life, that was growing, that was useful. Now they destroy it with one blow and don't even thank me' " (235).

Similar in its plot construction to other novels by Vargas Llosa, *Captain Pantoja and the Special Service* includes the development of a parallel story to Pantoja's Special Service, involving the gruesome activities of a religious sect led by Brother Francisco that mixes Christian ideals and pagan rituals. Just as the Special Service story provides a humorous look at Pantoja's fanaticism toward organization that satirizes in turn the concept of military organizational hierarchy, the tale of Brother Francisco's sect—whose trademark is the crucifixion first of harmless insects, then of animals, and later of human infants and even the visionary mystic himself—exposes another dangerous human trait, religious fanaticism.

The two stories become interrelated only superficially at the beginning of the novel, while later they envelop each other finally to merge in the scene in which the Brazilian is killed. In the first scene of the novel, as Captain Pantoja gets dressed to go receive his new assignment, Pochita comments on a newspaper article about a man in the Amazon jungle who "crucified himself to announce the end of the world. They put him in a nuthouse but people took him out by force because they think he's a saint" (1). Not only does the Brazilian attain a certain aura of sainthood after the funeral because of her symbolic crucifixion; but the same symbolic act marks the lives of Captain Pantoja, who is also sacrificed to the system, and of Brother Francisco, who is crucified outright by his followers after they have helped him escape from the army (which has decided to hunt him down and put him in jail for the sect's homicidal acts).

The parallel symbolism between the two men is based on a common trait: the fanatic nature of their endeavors. They become equally famous at the same time in the Peruvian jungle; and while Captain Pantoja's activities are definitely physical in nature (because he deals in sex), those of Brother Francisco are purely spiritual (because he saves souls). But the irony in the relationship between the two men is revealed in Pantoja's view of his part in the operation of the Special Service as a spiritual role—as an idealist dedicated to his country—and in Brother Francisco's embodiment of his ideals in physical activities through his crucifixion of living things.

The two men's activities are equally outrageous, and although they produce consternation among the local inhabitants they somehow become a part of the ambience until, suddenly, a curious turn of events occurs, which is usually precipitated by an individual's desire to take advantage of the situation. For example, the hypocritical radio announcer Sinchi exposes the "Pantiland" operation on his daily talk show, after he has unsuccessfully attempted to blackmail Captain Pantoja (who was to pay him for remaining silent about the Special Service). In another instance, one of the seven "pirates"—while trying to escape from a military patrol after attacking the Special Service's boat and raping the girls—unexpectedly suggests that instead of an animal they should nail the body of the dead Brazilian to a nearby tree. These seemingly insignificant kinks in the chain of events alter the course of action and establish the destinies of many characters in the novel. Pantoja reacts to his lover's death in such a way that destroys his future. He becomes a Christ figure who symbolically dies on the cross, sacrificing his life for others by resigning himself to an inglorious future with an institution—the army—which he fervently admires while it ruthlessly condemns him to ignominy.

Remaining above it all, however, is the captain's sense of dedication and his refusal to capitulate in the face of heavy odds. Through it, all that remains his single virtue. At the end of the novel, when Pantoja is reunited with his wife, the final lines provide an almost exact replica of the opening lines, in which Pochita attempts to wake her husband; and in this way a circular effect is created in the structure of the work, indicating that Pantoja's semitarnished ideals have remained intact. This circularity, in fact, does suggest to the reader the thematic seriousness of this humorous, even fantastic story.

While it is true that in the end Pantoja returns to his manic drive for organization by continuing his blind dedication to an ideal, he has nevertheless changed. Pantoja, the novel's protagonist, is viewed at one point in his life as a victim of his own fanatic nature, moving forward in life without any definite moral criteria that would permit him to react not only for the benefit of himself but for others as well. By the end of the novel, however, a significant change has taken place in Pantaleón Pantoja. George McMurray (1978) states that "Pantaleón's refusal to leave the military service and his banishment to the *puna* illuminate facets of his character that lend philosophical significance and esthetic enrichment to the novel." With this rebellious act, "Pantaleón ceases to be a victim of irony and begins to emerge as an absurd hero" (52). By the end of the novel, he has become more than a comic dupe and is finally revealed as a character whose human frailties and admirable courage set him in a more believable light. As a matter of fact, McMurray states that his

role as an absurd hero acquires even greater relief by the juxtaposition of his fate with that of Brother Francisco. While one dialogue [in the last chapter] relates the religious fanatic's capture, liberation and crucifixion, an adjacent dialogue communicates Pantaleón's determination to remain in the Army and suffer the consequences of his action. In a sense, then, both Brother Francisco and Pantaleón emerge as martyrs, but from the existentialist point of view their fates are antithetical. Brother Francisco's death epitomizes the Camusian 'leap of faith' of philosophical suicide, i.e., an escape from the absurd by surrendering one's freedom to God. Pantaleón, on the other hand, faces the absurd squarely and never ceases to struggle against the overwhelming odds. (52)

According to Bobs Tusa (1977), the change that Pantaleón Pantoja undergoes in the novel suggests that he has acquired a new perspective on life, created from "the idea of a religion of mankind, based not on the Christian concept of sinful humanity's love of God but rather on the oriental idea of the love of humanity freed from the concept of sin" (27). In fact, Tusa adds, "the Oriental education of the compassionate Wise Man is the theme of *Pantaleón y las visitadoras,* as the protagonist's name suggests. 'Pantaleón' (from the Greek *pantaleemon,* 'all-compassionate') is, according to hagiographic tradition, the new name given by god to Saint Pantoleón in recognition of his compassion toward those who were torturing him to death" (29). William Siemens (1977) sees the change that Pantoja undergoes in the novel as a metamorphosis from the model of the Greek god Apollo, who represents the preservation of order in the universe, to Dionysus, who portrays chaos (489–90). As provocative and possible as these interpretations may be, it is certainly true that at bottom Vargas Llosa still relies on his personal experiences and obsessions to provide another perspective on a recurring theme that appears in most of his narrative works; according to José Miguel Oviedo (1974a), it is a problem of "imposition," that is, the infringement or invasion by authority (for example) of one person over another, one idea over another, sin over love, hate over compassion, order over chaos (5).

## Humor and Irony through Structure and Language

Without a doubt, the organization of the narrative material in *Captain Pantoja and the Special Service* is primarily responsible for the creation of the novel's humor and irony. But the narrative material itself and the re-creation of conventional linguistic behavioral patterns go far toward creating an amusing and frankly laughable context. The novel is composed of ten chapters. Chapters 1, 5, 8, and 10 are organized around sets of interpolated dialogues among different characters in different places and during moments that are temporally connected to the present action. The other chapters contain radically different narrative materials, such as official military communiqués, personal letters, dispatches, newspaper articles, radio broadcasts, and dreams.

The juxtaposed nature of the diverse dialogues in the four chapters mentioned above is similar to the treatment of the narrative material in Vargas Llosa's earlier novels—for example, in Fushía's story in *The Green House* or in the political rally scene in *Conversation in The Cathedral*. Luis Díez (1978a) maintains that in *Captain Pantoja and the Special Service* Vargas Llosa has established once again a "pattern of gliding dialogues that include a whole gamut of people and places in Peru" (56). The abrupt changes that take place between the different scenes—disrupting for the reader the logical expectancy of what is to follow and creating a sense of incongruity—are primarily responsible for the humor and consequent irony in these chapters.

Within the first few pages several scenes are interpolated to show the reader different perspectives of the situation that already exists when the novel begins. For example, the first scene presents typical early-morning dialogue among the members of the Pantoja household: Pantaleón Pantoja's wife wakes him up (just as she is trying to do in the final lines of the novel, except that at the end it is five rather than eight o'clock in the morning); he gets dressed and eats the breakfast that his mother has prepared for him before going to headquarters to receive his new military assignment. Pochita's curiosity, upon reading the newspaper account of a wild man in the jungle who crucifies himself, has, as we have seen, significant ironic implications later on in the novel and even hints at one of its thematic concerns: Pantoja's crucifixion by the system to ensure its continuity. This scene ends as Pantoja's wife and mother send him on his way, with the latter saying, "Get going, boy. Good luck. You have my blessing" (2). A radically different scene follows immediately: " 'In the name of the Father and the Holy Ghost and the Son WHO DIED ON THE CROSS," Brother Francisco raises his eyes to the night, lowers his eyes to the torches. "My hands are tied, the wood is an offering, make the sign of the cross for me' " (2). Vargas Llosa's narrative strategy produces an interpolated relationship between the blessing given by Pantoja's mother (in Lima) and Brother Francisco's prayer (in the jungle); the result is ironic and while the reader smiles both the blessing and the prayer acquire new significance.

The next scene places Pantoja at military headquarters, where he meets with the officers of the high command, who heap praise on him for his excellent service record: "Born organizer, mathematical sense of order, executive capacity" (3). This narrative scene expands into other scenes in which the problem that the army faces in the jungle, examples of this problem, and the remedy that has been devised are presented through separate sequences of dialogue. Luis Díez (1978a) states that

the narrative telescopes in several directions so that the nature of the mission is not directly briefed to Pantoja but conveyed to us through its escalating background. Like ripples on a tranquil pond, we follow the popular indignation from village mayors to junior officers and on to enraged patriotic chaplains, Iquitos commanders and Lima generals. We see a frightened girl trying to identify her two violators as a whole army company is paraded in front of her eyes; we listen to the irate voice of Sinchi, the most popular and feared of the Iquitos newscasters; we hear testimonies from angry relatives of the ravished women and we even learn of a failed attempt to quell the troop's sexual aggressiveness by employing the services of a world-famous Swiss dietitian, whose "Operation Swiss Ration" almost succeeds in curing the plague by killing the patients with hunger and consumption. (57)

It is worth noting once again that a major part of the novel's humor and irony occurs as the structural ironies of the plot become apparent. For example, early on in the novel, when Pantoja informs his wife and mother of his new assignment in Iquitos, his mother responds to Pochita's disdain of the jungle city: "Don't make such a face. Wouldn't the mountains be worse?" (7). As it turns out, in the closing pages of the novel Pantaleón is banished to the most remote military outpost in the Andes. In another scene the hot jungle environment and the type of work that Pantaleón is involved in arouse his hidden sexual passion, and he tells his wife, "Oh, babe, I can't tell who I am" (10). The succeeding lines of the text present a dialogue between Pantaleón and an army general in Iquitos who is hostile to the idea of the Special Service: " 'I know very well who you are and why you've come to Iquitos," mutters General Roger Scavino. "And straight off I'll tell you that your presence in this city doesn't please me one bit' " (10). These interpolated relationships of unrelated dialogues are based on special techniques, states Ronald Christ (1978), that make *Captain Pantoja and the Special Service* a "cinematographic novel" (39). A montage effect is created, and "we see that Vargas Llosa is linking one episode to another by means of an image that not only connects but actually reinforces, extends and even creates a significance where none existed in the discrete, sequential fragments themselves" (Christ 1978, 41).

While it is true that the procedure of abruptly meshing different spatial and temporal levels of narration is already well known in his novels, Vargas Llosa adds a new dimension to this narrative strategy by condensing the description of the action, and references to space and time that accompany the speaker's words, into an abridged version of part of the character's life. The sudden jumps in action, space, and time are distilled into a list of words that suggest rapid movement similar to the effects produced in cinematographic montage. The growing intensity of the concern for the problems that the Special Service is creating for the army, and in parallel fashion, the need to increase military patrols to search for the Brothers of the Ark, is captured through this cinematographic technique that Vargas Llosa has adapted to his narratives:

"Don't forget, it'll be necessary to divert people and money for the pursuit and repression of the crazy people from the Ark," Coloniel López López takes planes, jeeps and launches, travels through the Amazon region, returns to Lima, makes the officers in Accounting and Finance work overtime, edits a report, appears at Tiger Collazos' office. (186)

George McMurray (1978) claims that this procedure not only maximizes economy, but "it can also serve to reinforce the theme of the absurd by substituting frenetic movement for temporal progression, often reversing the normal sequence of cause and effect and thus underscoring the impression of chaos" (49). This narrative technique is also employed to communicate information that ordinarily would be presented in a more traditional way and consequently would more easily identify the presence of an omniscient narrator. In the following example the thoughts and feelings of the character who speaks are included in the accompanying description:

". . . but I warn that your son will never be forgiven for this last dirty trick, Mother Leonor," Pochita hears radios, reads magazines, listens to gossip, feels they are pointing at her on the street, thinks she is the talk of Chiclayo. (234)

This narrative compactness culminates in a scene in which fragments suggesting a type of interior monologue are compressed into the descriptions that accompany the dialogue; for example, when marital differences between Pantoja and his wife are settled and he talks to her on the phone, the reader senses the melodramatic nature of the scene in a few well-chosen, short, and simple phrases:

"Pocha, how are you, honey?" Panta feels his heart beating, thinks I love her, she's my wife, we'll never be separated. "A kiss for the baby and another big one for you. I'm dying to see you. I couldn't make it to the airport; forgive me." (238)

Chapters 2, 4, and 6 are made up mainly of military reports, communiqués, and official messages. Here the humor is based on the exact reproduction of the style and tone of a typical military document that explains the statistical organization of the Special Service. Luis Díez (1978a) invites the reader to consider the result: "Just try to imagine deadpan officialese applied to statistical-logistic considerations such as the optimum conditions for precoital readiness of the average enlisted man, or whether twelve minutes constitutes a more desirable time than twenty for satisfying the individual soldier's libido. . . . The task of rendering this rich variety of officialese and convoluted syntax without losing its humorous substance is one of the many credits the translators of *Pantaleón* justly deserve" (59).

Chapters 3, 7, and 9 contain a personal letter from Pochita to her sister, radio broadcasts, and newspaper articles, respectively. These documents, among others, create shifting points of view with regard to the development of the situation in Iquitos. For example, in that jungle city Pantoja becomes sexually aggressive (because of his job, one supposes), and in the letter to her sister, Pochita states the problem in her typically euphemistic fashion:

Do you remember how he's always been so formal ever since we got married so you always joked a lot and told me I'm sure with Panta you must be doing without, Pocha? Well, you can't laugh at your brother-in-law anymore in that respect, you badmouth, because since he stepped foot in Iquitos he's become a savage. Something terrible, Chichi, at times I get scared and wonder if it isn't an illness, because imagine that before, I've told you, I only got him to tend to his business once every ten or fifteen days (how embarrassing to talk to you about this, Chichi) and now the little bandit's excited every two, three days and I have to put the brakes on his passion, because it isn't right, no, really, with this heat and sticky humidity. . . . I have to tell you it makes me laugh seeing your little brother-in-law so horny. Sometimes he's itching to do a little business during the daytime, right after lunch, with the siesta as an excuse, but of course I don't let him, and sometimes he wakes me at dawn with that craziness. Picture this, the other night I caught him with a stopwatch timing how long our business took. I asked him about it and he got very confused. Later he confessed to me he had to know how long a little business like that took for a normal couple. Do you think he's turning into a pervert? (50)

By altering the verbal medium through the distortion of linguistic, orthographic, and grammatical elements, the humor of the novel makes it even more ludicrous and unreal. Moreover, the grammatical formality of the military documents that Pantaleón writes; the personalized, colloquial, and oral qualities that make Pocha's letter so entertaining, and the phonetic mispronunciation by certain jungle inhabitants of the *ch* in words by using the *sh* sound, evoke a humor created by the mimetic exactness of certain natural and typical verbal cultural markers that are transferred to a purely fictive environment.

Simultaneously, the thematic foci of the work become more apparent. In each case, the characters are defined by certain sociolinguistic codes. Reduced in many cases to clichés, proverbial sayings, and current euphemisms, the characters' speech patterns in the letters, radio broadcasts, and newspaper articles indicate, according to Sara Castro-Klarén (1978), the existence of a rigid social class structure and "explain to the reader, but not to themselves, their false consciousness [because they are] unable to escape the stiff mental structure which the language imposes on them" (74). George McMurray (1978) points out that, in chapter 7, "Sinchi's demagogic radio broadcasts and the newspaper reports of la Brasileña's death parody sensational journalism, the ossified, cliché-ridden language often conveying gossip rather than factual news" (48).

In addition to the materials already mentioned, chapters 2, 3, and 7 also contain three separate dream or nightmare episodes that Pantaleón Pantoja experiences during his Iquitos assignment. These episodes are signficant in revealing another level of fictional reality: whereas the interpolated dialogues suggest an objective presentation of reality, Pantoja's dreams correspond directly to the subjective level of reality that is equally important to Vargas Llosa's desire to create a "total" reality (Díez 1978b, 59). According to George McMurray (1978)

organizing his fictional material in this manner has enabled the author to vary the point of view, all the while maintaining the narrative distance typical of the detached ironic observer. The shifting perspective also lays the groundwork for a wide variety of styles, which not only provide verbal irony but also create striking ironic contrasts. Thus the pompous technical jargon used by military personnel in official reports differs radically from the vulgar slang of their dialogues. The coarse vernacular employed by the *visitadoras* [a euphemism for prostitutes] and the confidential, witty tone of Pocha's letter to her sister are antitheses of the conventional middle-class idiom that serves as a means of communication among Pantaleón, his wife and his mother. (48)

And the exactness with which the author recreates these verbal phenomena of real life in fiction is best seen in the Spanish version of the novel, where the right-hand margins of the text are purposely unjustified so as to give the appearance of a handwritten letter, in Pocha's case, or of a typewritten document in the case of Pantaleón's military reports.

The narrative and thematic significance that Mario Vargas Llosa gives to characters' names is as important in *Captain Pantoja and the Special Service* as the constant reference to animals representing the savage world of the cadets is in *The Time of the Hero*, or as the name changes representing different stages in the characters' lives are in *The Green House*. In a revealing study of nomenclature in this novel, Sara Castro-Klarén (1978) states that "to a great extent, the satirical content rests, and even depends upon, the repertory of names and nicknames of the characters" (65). The play on words in naming characters not only serves to delineate their personalities humorously but also reveals other more serious aspects about contemporary life. Castro-Klarén carefully analyzes each name and shows that

in a class-conscious society such as Peru, almost anything can be interpreted as a symbol of one's place in the social hierarchy. For example, General Scavino would avoid identification with a symbol like Peter Casahuanqui, fearing the ridicule this name implies within the social logic of the classes in Peru. It is not unusual for a president to be named Guillermo Billing-hurst, or for an intellectual to be named Doris Gibson, or for the archbishop to be named Juan Ricketts. The combination of Spanish names and Nordic surnames seems logical, and without doubt, it is prestigious. But the combination of Peter Casahuanqui is considered ridiculous, or even "corny" *(huachafa)* in that it signifies a desire for imitation, an aspiration for equality through purely linguistic analogy, and above all a misunderstanding of the class system. To accept the name Peter Casahuanqui would be to deny history and the place that Indians, that is the lower classes, have occupied within the power structure in Peru. To call oneself Peter Casahuanqui is evidence of a naive faith in the power of the word. An Indian (Casahuanqui) is ridiculously misleading himself if he believes that by adopting an Anglo-Saxon name he will be able to better his position and improve his chances of mobility into the dominant class. The Peter Casahuanquis do not understand that to abandon Casahuanqui is more important than to adopt Peter. The Peter Casahuanquis are also laughable because they do not seem to realize that upward mobility, if at all possible, depends on a good deal more than mere onomastic analogies. Their insufficient understanding of reality as much as their skill for "formal" imitation makes them fall into ridicule and pushes them into the endless lines of comic *huachafos,* hoping and waiting to be admitted into the house of their oppressors. (Castro-Klarén 1978, 66)

Equally significant is Castro-Klarén's phonetic and semantic analysis of the protagonist's name. She points out, for example, that the phonetic similarity between Panta*león* and Napo*león* leads to "a perception of ridicule" when the reader discovers that "with his role of procurer for the national armed forces, Pantaleón's thoughtless minutious planning negates and inverts the courage and strategic genius of the French model." His first name can be divided into *Panta* and *león,* with one suggesting a reference to "pants" and the other evoking the "lion," the king of beasts. Called "Panta" by his wife and mother, the protagonist is viewed as a lion without pants; and when they call him "Pantita" (the diminutive of Panta), he is cast in the image of a little boy dressed in short pants (Castro-Klarén 1978, 67). Along with other interpretive examples, Castro-Klarén's study shows how the references to masculine codes in the protagonist's name are subverted, revealing a latent presence of the female component of the self.

For many readers, then, the three-year series of episodes in the protagonist's life reveals a struggle to find harmony between the male and the female components of the self, with the male characterized as determinate and transitory and the female as ambiguous and eternal (Tusa 1977, 28–29). Despite the farcical nature of this novel, the interior conflict that almost destroys Pantoja, the clash between "the masculine and domineering nature of the military rank in society and the feminine social structure of the character" (Castro-Klarén 1978, 70), leads to strong social commentary and a continual indictment of the imposition of destructive social values and harmful cultural traits on the human being. In a society that determines itself through extreme acts of irrational behavior—that is, through fanaticism—the role of Pantaleón Pantoja in this novel may be viewed as one in which the fusion of opposing sex codes, which stereotype men and women in society, leads to the creation of an androgynous personality that is better equipped for survival. Finally, the seriousness of this possible thematic concern does not detract from the fact that, as George McMurray (1978) says, "Pantaleón has to be the funniest absurd hero in Latin American literature. His hilarious attempts to impose meaning on existence and his unique demonstration that man's struggle constitutes his only definition" (53), combined with the verbal and situational humor and the resulting irony of his mission in Iquitos, provide the special ingredients that make *Captain Pantoja and the Special Service* one of Vargas Llosa's most widely read novels.

## Chapter Eight
# *Aunt Julia and the Scriptwriter:* Fiction as Artifact

With the publication of *La tía Julia y el escribidor (Aunt Julia and the Scriptwriter)* in 1977, Mario Vargas Llosa added completely new dimensions to his thematic concerns and narrative style. His first novels reflect a cohesive period covering the 1960s, in which the neorealist presentation of Peru's sociopolitical problems, increasingly complex with each successive novel, culminated in *Conversation in The Cathedral.* Although *Captain Pantoja and the Special Service,* published in 1973, provided another in-depth look at Peruvian society from a critical perspective, its humor and parody were new to Vargas Llosa's novelistic opus, forshadowing *Aunt Julia and the Scriptwriter.* Until that point in his literary career, Vargas Llosa believed that humor detracted from the creation of an objective reality in literature. *Captain Pantoja and the Special Service* revealed his change in attitude, and the humor in *Aunt Julia and the Scriptwriter* is so well wrought that no reader can resist breaking into laughter as the "real'" world of autobiography and the "imaginary" world of radio soap opera envelop each other to produce parody that is an important statement about the nature of the creative act and of literature.

## Plot: Autobiography and Soap Operas

*Aunt Julia and the Scriptwriter* is a humorous inside look at a short but crucial period in everyone's life, the passage from adolescence to adulthood. The novel is based on Vargas Llosa's experiences during the mid-1950s, when he made two significant decisions that greatly affected his life: to marry at the tender age of eighteen and to become a writer. Hence the title of the novel refers to the two people most directly related to those decisions: Vargas Llosa's Aunt Julia, whom he married in an act of defiance against his family's wishes; and Raúl Salmón (the fictional scriptwriter, Pedro Camacho, in the novel), an eccentric Bolivian author of soap operas whom

130

Vargas Llosa met while working at a Lima radio station in 1954 and began to admire for his feverish capacity to write round the clock.

The duality suggested in the title extends to the novel's structure as well. The novel's symmetrical precision and its structural dualities were by then standard parts of Vargas Llosa's narrative repertoire. In this novel two alternating poles of narrative are established from the beginning. Of the twenty chapters that make up the novel, the ten odd-numbered chapters and the last chapter, which functions as an epilogue, present the biographical events of a short period during Vargas Llosa's life, a kind of bildungsroman. The nine even-numbered chapters narrate isolated episodes of truculent soap-opera intrigues (rebellion, violence, melodrama, and sex) written by Pedro Camacho. As a result, the chapters alternate between two apparently unrelated modes of writing: autobiography and fiction. Whereas the former works with representational materials, the latter is seemingly antirepresentational. In Camacho's world, Vargas Llosa would say, "reality is *only* melodramatic, there is only bad taste in life: its exclusivity makes it unreal" (*La orgía perpétua,* 28).

At first sight, the two worlds could not seem farther apart, yet the juxtaposition of the two modes of writing causes one world to intrude upon the other, so that by the end of the novel the relationship between reality and fiction is deeply in question and has become the essence of the novel's major theme. José Miguel Oviedo (1978b) has correctly stated that

these intense contrasts, fusions, and parallels among the subliterature of Camacho, the work of the young writer, and the lives of both make it clear that the dominant novelistic technique of the book is that of *vasos comunicantes,* the narrative art of emptying one level of the story into another, while conjugating and contrasting them constantly in a humorous way. Even if unreal and unlikely, Camacho's world comes in contact with the private world of the narrator and his love affair with tía Julia, and there is a mutual effect: in both, reality generates the artificial and exaggerated mood of melodrama; in both, the humorous perspective redeems (almost always) the grossness of the subject matter. (179)

The novel's epigraph indicates its thematic concern. Vargas Llosa quotes from a novel by Salvador Elizondo, in which the narrator says, "I write. I write that I write. Mentally I see myself writing and I can also see myself watching me write. I remember myself writing and also watching me write. . . ." Thus *Aunt Julia and the Scriptwriter* is seen as an artifact through which the process of writing, the role of the novelist, and the relationship between the writer and the reader are examined. Vargas Llosa states that the novel's significance goes deeper than soap operas and melodrama: "On a deeper level, it deals with something that has always fascinated me, something to which I devote most of my life but which I have never understood: Why do I write and what does writing mean?" ("A Passion for Peru," 108). These concerns place the novel squarely in the middle of a contemporary trend called metaart, which, according to Inger Christensen (1981), is art that "turns its attention upon the work of art itself" ( . . . 9–10).

When asked by José Miguel Oviedo how the story of *Aunt Julia and the Scriptwriter* came about, Vargas Llosa replied that

it took shape, like almost everything else I've written, from my old memories. In this case, memories of the year that I worked for Radio Panamericana in Lima, that is 1955 or 54. I've always remembered this period as linked to a man [Raúl Salmón] who used to work, not for Radio Panamericana where I was in charge of the news bulletins, but for a neighboring radio station, Radio Central. . . . He was in charge of all the soap operas of that radio station, not only writing the scripts but also directing and acting the male leads. He was truly a picturesque character who worked like the devil, who had an extraordinary sense of professional responsibility, and who was very absorbed by his role as writer and performer. But at the same time, judging him from a literary perspective, let's say, he was sort of a parody or caricature, a pedestrian version, twisted and somewhat pathetic, of a "writer." Still the man was quite popular. I understand that his soap operas were a real success on Radio Central. He greatly amused me, even fascinated me, because it was precisely at this time that I was feeling a stronger and stronger urge to become a writer myself; I was thinking that what I wanted most in my life was to be a writer. And I think that the only writer I knew at that time—who could really be called a "writer" because of the amount of time dedicated to writing, and because of the public which followed and appreciated his work—was this literary caricature, the writer of the Bolivian soap operas, Raúl Salmón. (Oviedo 1978a, 155)

Vargas Llosa goes on to explain that the obsessive nature of Salmón's dedication to his work drove Ramón literally crazy. Since he was writing day in and day out the episodes for different scripts, Salmón began to get them mixed up. Vargas Llosa recalls that things became so absurd that one day listeners called the radio station to complain that the soap operas had become distorted and illogical. These real events from Salmón's life become, in parallel fashion, part of Pedro Camacho's life in the novel.

Each of the even-numbered chapters narrates a different episode from a soap opera created by Camacho. Together, they make up the whole gamut of fictionalized fantasies of which soap operas are composed. They are described as a "torrent of adulteries, suicides, passionate love affairs, unexpected encounters, inheritances, devotions, coincidences, and crimes" (6). The first soap-opera episode (chapter 2) narrates the jolt that an upper-class, middle-aged gynecologist suffers when he discovers, after attending his niece's wedding reception, that the niece is already very pregnant—not because of any premarital relations with her fiancé but as the result of an incestuous relationship between the bride and her brother. The second soap-opera episode (chapter 4) puts a Civil Guard sergeant's courage, honor, and sense of morality to the test: one evening, as he patrols on foot the docks of Lima's port Callao, he discovers a naked, scarred, and terrified black man hiding in an abandoned building. Unable to communicate with anyone, the foreigner becomes a problem for the authorities, and the sergeant is ordered to kill him and dispose of the body. First the sergeant tries to justify his orders. Then a conversation ensues between the sergeant and his assistant, as they begin to carry out the execution. Opposing points of view become manifest in the conflict between the morality of "thou shalt not kill" and the police order to expedite the problem by simply eliminating the unidentifiable person. This episode, like others, ends in typical soap-opera fashion, just at the moment of maximum tension, with a burning question unresolved: whether the sergeant will or will not shoot the man. The third episode takes place in a courtroom at the Palace of Justice in Lima. A magistrate hears his first case of the day, in which a preacher of the Jehovah's Witnesses sect is accused of raping a minor. What begins as the presentation and deliberation of a criminal case ends as the victim's pornographic re-creation of the incident: she lies on the floor, pulls up her dress, and repeats the lurid things the accused had said to her. The judge begins to think she is a Lolita type and probably had lured the accused into the sexual act. The accused declares his innocence and avoids the facts by suffusing the hearing in religious symbolism. He reaches a state of mental frenzy, takes the judge's letter opener, and threatens to sever his penis to prove his innocence. The language used in these episodes makes them humorous.

The fourth episode is the story of one man's insanity, caused by a phobia of mice and rats, that eventually consumes his life. His complete devotion to the extermination of rodents, combined with certain repugnant childhood events, distorts his sense of reality. He becomes obsessed with his daughters' moral laxity and punishes them severely. In the end, his family turns on him, beats him, and runs away.

Tying these dissimilar stories together is the fact that they are all creations of Pedro Camacho's obsessive and distorted mind. By this time, the reader begins to see through the darker side of Camacho's nature, laughing at it all. His concern for his age, for example, becomes evident as the protagonists in every soap-opera plot are described in the same humorous telltale way: "He was in the prime of his life, his fifties, and [he had] distinguishing traits— a broad forehead, an aquiline nose, a penetrating gaze, the very soul of rectitude and goodness" (137). Other such cases are dredged up from Camacho's pathological mind. In the fifth soap-opera plot the focus is a psychodrama involving the insane treatment of a man who suffers from "infantophobia" and "herodism" (child abuse).

The sixth soap-opera plot presents the degeneration of an old aristocratic family, whose colonial mansion in the center of Lima has been converted into a boardinghouse where insidious crimes of sex and violence take place. From this point forward in Camacho's stories, he begins to confuse the characters' names and identities and to insert them indiscriminately into other plots. The absurdity of these soap operas begins to reach a climax in the radio program in which a priest transforms slum-area residents into small entrepreneurs who openly perpetuate crime. The priest converts the slum into a commune, practicing "archaic Christian living" (258), which fails miserably. The names of characters from the four previous soap operas are introduced at this point, indicating the growing frenzy and confusion in Camacho's mind.

The last two soap-opera plots present two different stories: a wealthy young man turned alcoholic becomes a famous soccer referee; and a downtown Lima street urchin becomes a popular singer while trying to maintain a spiritual relationship with a nun. The absurd nature of these episodes is curiously based more on reality than imagination; in the soccer referee segment, for example, the spectators become frenzied over an arbitrary ruling in a game and stampede the stadium's exits. In the melee hundreds of people are trampled to death. It almost seems unreal but the gory scene is based on historical fact. In the latter story, an earthquake occurs when all of the characters from the previous eight plots are being confused, switched, and altered in the final moments of total destruction. Earth tremors, of course, are a real part of daily life in Peru.

The conventional use of the open ending at the conclusion of the last plot not only establishes Camacho's crazed state but also indicates the use of narrative strategies that absorb the reader. Here, the narrator asks: "Had this story of blood, song, mysticism, and fire ended, or would it have an extra-terrestrial sequel?" (334). Vargas Llosa delineates these elements of narrative in his study of Gustave Flaubert's fiction: "seductive novels are produced by a skillful combination of rebellion, violence, melodrama, and sex. For me, a novel gives satisfaction when in the course of reading it, it provokes my admiration for something anomalous, strange, out of the ordinary, my rage at stupidity and injustice, my fascination for those situations of distorted dramatism, excessive emotionalism that romanticism seemed to have invented because it used and abused these elements; but they have always existed in literature and, without a doubt, they have always existed in reality, and in my desire" (*La orgía perpétua*, 20).

José Miguel Oviedo (1978b) provides a rationale for the use of this material by indicating that the reader is confronted with a "catalogue of horrors, not syrupy or romantic versions of everyday life. The subliterature of the 'scribbler' consists of a series of perverse variations of his own life, itself very limited and mediocre. What happens to him happens only in the realm of his own imagination, and that allows us to know him better than through his appearances in the autobiographical tales of Vargas Llosa and tía Julia: Camacho's biography literally is in his 'scripts,' that is, he lives at a completely imaginary level" (174). Oviedo adds that "the free flow of Camacho's fantasies . . . is in reality a coded record of his perturbed mind. Camacho believes that he is imagining, that he is working with unreal and absurd material, that he is inventing and dreaming, but what he is actually doing, obliquely, is revealing himself . . ." (175).

Turning now to the autobiographical part of *Aunt Julia and the Scriptwriter,* the author states that it "serves as a kind of counterpoint, that anchors in the tangible, verifiable world of the imaginary, purely fantastic, mad world of the protagonist and his soap operas" (Oviedo 1978a, 157). Vargas Llosa seeks to uncover or to discover the hidden relationships that exist between the real world of lived experience and the purely fictional worlds of fantasy and imagination. So, he asks himself:

Why couldn't the story of Raúl Salmón be intermingled with personal experience? The Raúl Salmón story happened during a very important time in my life because, in the first place, it was at that time after feeling the urge for years, my vocation was decided, although until then I had not dared to pursue it totally. Secondly, it was then that I got married for the first time, and that marriage was in certain ways a very daring act, because I was only 18, and also because it caused me many practical problems and even family problems. Then it occurred to me that the delirious stories of the protagonist who writes the melodramas and who has a disturbed imagination could perhaps be inter-twined with a story which was precisely the opposite, something absolutely objective and absolutely true. (Oviedo 1978, 157)

Seemingly, the novel is built upon two conflicting levels of reality, one based on actual lived experience and the other comprised of imagination and fiction. As the two levels interpenetrate and become less identifiable, problems of interpretation quickly emerge for the reader. Thus the story accurately reflects a basic aesthetic concern of Vargas Llosa in his literary and critical works, that is, how to deal with the contagion of these at once divergent and yet paradoxically similar levels of reality.

The autobiographical part of the novel begins with chapter 1, as an adult narrator recounts his past: "In those long-ago days, I was very young and lived with my grandparents in a villa with white walls in the Calle Ocharán, in Miraflores. I was studying at the University of San Marcos, law, as I remember, resigned to earning myself a living later on by practicing a liberal profession, although deep down what I really wanted was to become a writer someday. I had a job with a pompous-sounding title, a modest salary, duties as a plagiarist, and flexible working hours: News director of Radio Panamericana" (3). In these initial lines of *Aunt Julia and the Scriptwriter*, Oviedo has identified three aspects about the narrator that are essential for the making of the biographical document: the all-encompassing familiar world to which tía Julia herself belongs ('La tía Julia' is the way she is identified before and after the marriage with the narrator, Vargas Llosa); the grim world of the radio station (which connects the narrator with the character Pedro Camacho, on the other level of the book); and the fascinating world of literature, which will, in turn, obscurely connect with the first two. Of those three versions—the family member, the newscaster, and the writer—which Vargas Llosa gives of himself, the one which seems to dominate from the start is the first one, and doubtless the reader will prefer it with eagerness and curiosity: its central episode is the marriage adventure of the author and tía Julia. (Oviedo 1978b, 174)

Although the desire to get married is treated explicitly in the novel, the main concern of the narrator—to enter the world of literature and to become a writer—is treated implicitly. To become a part of the intriguing world of literature is the ultimate concern of the writer; it is, in effect, a framing device for the rest of the novel's content. Beginning with the initial lines of the novel— "although deep down what I really wanted was to become a writer someday"— and ending with the epilogue, when the narrator says twelve years later that "for better or for worse I had become a writer and published several books" (358), the narrator's desire forms the narrative and thematic backbone of the novel. Overall, however, the worlds of family, newcasting, and writing interpenetrate each other, providing the narrator with a sense of purpose in life and clearly highlighting Vargas Llosa's theory about the writer's vocation.

Early in the novel the links among Aunt Julia, Pedro Camacho, and the narrator are complete. Unable to obtain soap-opera scripts with any regularity, the owners of the radio station hire Camacho from Bolivia to write the scripts himself. Looking back, the narrator says: "I remember very well the day he [the station owner] spoke to me of this genius of the airwaves, because that very day, at lunchtime, I saw Aunt Julia for the first time. She was my Uncle Lucho's sister-in-law and had arrived from Bolivia the night before" (7). From here on, the events in the novel's autobiographical chapters alternate between sections of text narrating his growing love relationship with Aunt Julia and others that present his professional relationship with and admiration for the scriptwriter. Both influence him enormously.

The reader begins to make the association between the first-person adult narrator and the author Mario Vargas Llosa, who says, in the present tense, "I remember very well." First, however, the reader is given an early clue about the identity of the narrator as a young man when Aunt Julia calls him "Marito" (the diminutive of Mario, or "Varguitas" because his surname is Vargas). The author's mature voice as the first-person narrator quickly gives way to Marito's first-person narration in the preterit tense, and it is Marito who experiences the major part of the novel's action. In this way, the young Vargas Llosa, who relives his becoming a successful writer, fuses with the mature Vargas Llosa, who narrates it. In the last chapter the narrators Marito and Mario coalesce into one mature, successful, and proud narrator. In the last line of the novel the mature narrator returns to the present tense, mentioning that his second wife, Patricia, "is a girl with spirit" (374), which in effect provides a link back to the present moment of the narration in the novel's initial pages.

In the succeeding autobiographical chapters the reader learns how Marito and Aunt Julia become romantically involved. All along he is working at the radio station and struggling to write some meaningful short stories that he shares with Aunt Julia and his friend Javier. Despite a romantic and almost hopeless love affair—after all, he is eighteen years old and Aunt Julia is a thirty-two-year-old divorcée from out of town—they do marry and remain together for a total of eight years. That period proves crucial in making a writer out of Marito. Although the marriage adventure is presented in a straightforward, unemotional, and matter-of-fact way, it is rendered in a nostalgic tone and experienced as a sentimental love story.

In fact, the whole affair possesses all the ingredients of a melodramatic soap opera; for one thing, there is the conventional theme of prohibited love: a boy falls for his older aunt and she for him (although she is not a blood relative). Their romantic adventure is the subject of parody from its beginning. On their first outing together, for example, Marito and Aunt Julia coincidentally see a sentimental Mexican melodrama called *Mother and Mistress*.

The difference between reality (or autobiography) and fantasy (or soap operas) begins to blur when the reader is almost forced to make connections, due to the juxtaposition of the chapters, between the autobiographical love affair (between nephew and aunt) and the soap-opera episodes, such as the first one in which an incestuous love affair (between brother and sister) is presented. When the brother states to his uncle that he wants to kill himself (chapter 2) the reader may smirk, seeing Marito's moment of internal crisis parodied, when he lists the options before him: to marry Aunt Julia, to leave the country with her, or to kill himself (chapter 15).

The "insurmountable obstacles" imposed on the characters of this universal soap opera enhance the story. Marito and Aunt Julia's struggles to get married are narrated in great detail and with mounting intrigue. Since Marito is a minor and, of course, lacks his parents' consent, they travel to small towns outside Lima, hoping to bribe some local mayor to conduct a civil ceremony and to provide a marriage license. When they begin to realize the possibility of failure, their search for a mayor takes on highly melodramatic qualities. Moreover, because this story is interrupted by the chapters narrating Camacho's soap-opera episodes, the reader's curiosity to learn how the marriage adventure turns out is heightened by obstacles throughout the novel. On one level, this narrative procedure parodies the episodic presentation of daily soap operas on radio or television, segmenting the story and thereby holding back information from the reader; on another level, this device makes a trite, clichéd, and pathetic story come alive and take on special meaning for the reader.

The narrative simplicity of Marito's style, however, makes the situation humorous to the point of farce:

We talked with three or four mayors of districts and as many deputy mayors of hamlets that at times consisted of no more than twenty shacks. They were simple rural types whom we had to hunt up at their little farms where they were at work in the fields, or in their little village shops where they were selling cooking oil and cigarettes to their constituents; we found one of them, the mayor of Sunampe, lying in a ditch sleeping off a hangover and had to shake him awake. Once we'd located the municipal authority in question, I would get out of the taxi, accompanied sometimes by Pascual, sometimes by the driver, sometimes by Javier—we eventually learned by experience that the more of us there were, the more intimidated the mayor tended to be—to explain the situation. No matter what arguments I put forward, I would invariably see a look of mistrust come over the face, a gleam of alarm appear in the eye of the farmer, fisherman, or shopkeeper (the mayor of Chincha Baja introduced himself as a "healer"). Only two of them turned us down flat: The mayor of Alto Larán, an old man who went on loading his pack mules with bales of alfalfa as I talked to him, and informed us that he never married anyone who wasn't from the village; and the mayor of San Juan de Yanac, a mestizo farmer who was terrified when he saw us, thinking that we were the police coming to question him about some misdeed. When he found out what we wanted, he was furious. "No, not a chance, there's something fishy going on if a white couple come to get married in this godforsaken village." The others all gave us more or less the same excuses. The most common: The civil register had been lost or was filled up, and until they sent a new one from Chincha there was no way of registering deaths or births or marrying anybody at the town hall. It was the mayor of Chavín who came up with the most imaginative reply: he couldn't marry us because he was too pressed for time; he had to go out right then and shoot a fox that had been killing two or three hens a night in the district. (311–12)

Such scenes build up to the scandalous situation that develops among the members of the newlyweds' family in Lima. The final autobiographical chapter brings the reader to the melodramatic confrontation between the couple and Marito's father and family. It begins when Javier, who had helped the pair elope, returns to Lima after the marriage ceremony, which had finally taken place, several hours of travel by car away, in an out-of-the-way hamlet south of Lima. Back at his boardinghouse, Javier finds Marito's father waiting for him: "Livid with rage, he had approached Javier, brandishing a revolver and threatening to shoot him if he didn't reveal instantly where Aunt Julia and I were. Utterly panic-stricken ('Till that moment, the only time I'd ever seen revolvers was in the movies, old pal'), Javier swears to him, in taking as his witnesses his mother and all the saints, that he had no idea, that he hadn't seen me for a week" (335). Upon Aunt Julia and Marito's return to Lima, his uncle admonishes Marito for causing a scandal and ruining his future. Marito assures his uncle that he is cognizant of his actions. Other scenes with different family members are replicas of typical soap-opera episodes. His mother, who has not seen Marito for some time, says: "My baby, my little darling, my treasure, what have they done to you, what has that woman done to you?" (339). Amid the emotional outbursts, however, Marito seems continually to view the whole affair as a learning experience: "Everytime the name of her [Marito's mother] brand-new daughter-in-law came up in the conversation, she burst into tears all over again; she fell into fits of rage in which she referred to Julia as 'that old lady,' 'that brazen hussy,' 'that divorcée.' All at once, in the middle of this scene, I realized something that had never crossed my mind before: it wasn't so much what people would say but religion that was making her feel so heartbroken. She was a fervent Catholic and it wasn't the

fact that Aunt Julia was older than I was that was upsetting her so
much as the fact that she was divorced—in other words, forbidden
to remarry within the Church" (339–40).

Marito's primary concern, however, revolves around his father,
who is on the rampage. He sends a message that is replete with
farcical elements: "I'm giving that woman forty-eight hours to leave
the country. If she does not do so, I shall use my influence and
personally see to it that she pays dearly for her effrontery. As for
you, I should like to inform you that I am armed and will not allow
you to make a fool of me. If you do not obey to the letter and this
woman does not leave the country within the time limit I have
indicated above, I shall put five bullets through you and kill you
like a dog, right in the middle of the street" (345). Precisely as
Marito's problems culminate in a travesty, Pedro Camacho goes
insane. The proximity of these two particular moments in the novel
(chapter 19) marks the total fusion of reality (or autobiography) and
fiction (or soap opera). Marito's father tries to have the marriage
annulled, and pulls some political strings that force Aunt Julia to
leave the country. She ends up in Chile, and during her month-
long absence, Marito acquires several part-time jobs, confronts his
father, and eventually demonstrates to everyone that he is not throwing his life away. In a tension-riddled scene, father and son confront
each other, and in the course of a lengthy conversation most of the
problems are solved. Of concern to his father all along has been
Marito's attitude: "My rebellion and my defiance would be the ruin
of me" (355–56). Finally, Marito's father gives Aunt Julia permission to return to Peru.

In the last chapter and the epilogue, the narrator recounts briefly
the years that he and Aunt Julia had lived together in Europe, where
Marito/Mario wrote his first novels. Soon after they are divorced,
Vargas Llosa marries his cousin Patricia in an official church wedding. He discusses his periodic and brief visits to Peru and his self-
exiled status in Europe: he needs time to write, and in Peru he is
not able to find time; yet

Everything I wrote had to do with life in Peru. As time and distance
began to blur my perspective, I felt more and more insecure about my
writing (at the time I was obsessed with the idea that fiction should be
'realistic'). But I found the very thought of living in Lima inconceivable.
When I remembered the seven simultaneous jobs I'd held there, which

together had earned me barely enough to feed us, left me scarcely any time to read, and given me no opportunity to write except on the sly in the few slack moments during my work day or at night when I was already dead tired, my hair stood on end and I vowed to myself I'd never live that way again, even if it meant dying of starvation. Moreover, Peru had always seemed to me a country of sad people. (359)

In this final chapter the reader may detect a transition from the melodramatic elements of the marriage adventure to a serious commentary by a mature writer on the results of that period of youthful rebellion and search for the writer's vocation. Nevertheless, the author remains faithful to his literary mission, and until the end of the novel, he has the reader walk a narrow line between autobiography and fantasy, reality and fiction. This tightrope act is accomplished in the novel's last major scene, in which the narrator presents one of those chance encounters, during a brief visit to Peru, with his former colleagues from the earlier radio station years; their lives, in contrast to the author's, have been all but destroyed in the interim. Pablo has been demoted from radio announcer to doorman; Pascual has descended to the job of copy editor of a weekly scandal sheet; and Pedro Camacho is now an errand boy. Having been cured in a mental institution of his insanity—attributed to the pressures of producing so many soap-opera scripts, but in reality produced by his personal obsessions—Camacho has been rendered a mental vegetable, "a caricature of the caricature he had been twelve years ago" (369).

In this scene everyone except Camacho, whose wife is expecting him, agrees to go out and relive old times with Marito/Mario over lunch. Upon the departure of Camacho, the director of the weekly, Dr. Rebagliati, Pablo, and Pascual immediately break into laughter: "He's not as dumb as he pretends to be, he comes on as the devoted spouse to hide the fact that his wife makes him wear horns,' Doctor Rebagliati crowed" (371). One source of Camacho's psychological problems—one that had determined his odd behavior and had found its way into his soap-opera scripts—is revealed here when Pascual says that Camacho's wife, who had left him years earlier and then suddenly returned when Camacho went insane, is "an Argentine years past middle age, fat as a sow, with bleached hair and makeup an inch thick. She sings tangos half-naked, at the Mezzanine, that nightclub for penniless wretches on the skids" (371). This explains why Camacho, from the beginning, has always displayed an aversion toward Argentines: "His hatred of Argentines in general, and of Argentine actors and actresses in particular, appeared to be entirely disinterested" (48). This obsession goes unexplained throughout the novel and conforms to the narrative strategy that Vargas Llosa calls the *dato escondido,* which keeps the reader anchored not only in the world of creation and fantasy—because of its structural function— but also in the realm of reality—because no character, and surely not the narrator, is ever privy to such information about Camacho's obsessions. As it turns out, this ironic scene forms yet another link between the relatively objective world of autobiography and the crazy, disturbed world of Camacho's soap operas. The *dato escondido* encloses the autobiographical narration within a world of literary creation and fiction in the same way that Vargas Llosa's more important narrative strategy of *vasos comunicantes* works to imbue each of the contrasting worlds of autobiography and imagination with the characteristics of the other.

On another level, Vargas Llosa has made a profound statement about his own youthful rebellion, his early vocation, and his final success—he goes to Europe, writes successful novels, and returns to Peru the true writer he has always wanted to become. In the final scene, his situation is compared to that of his earlier colleagues who have been destroyed by the sociopolitical situation of Peru in the 1950s, when the Manuel Odría dictatorship maintained power through corruption and vice (in this case, by manipulating journalists and their publications). The autobiographical elements of Vargas Llosa's life—his periodic visits to Peru during that period— are enriched and embellished via the fictionalized scene of his chance meeting with old friends, and the noticeable contrast between his success and their failure is strikingly apparent.

Furthermore, when Vargas Llosa's ideas about the writer's vocation are taken into consideration, additional interpretive significance can be seen emanating from the final scene and, by extension, from the whole novel. Briefly, he has stated that novels are two things: "a reconstruction of reality and a testimony of the writer's disagreement with the world. Indivisibly united, two ingredients appear in the novel, one objective and the other subjective, that is, reality with which the writer finds himself at odds and that which the writer wants to eliminate, add, or change in life. A novel is a coded testimony: it constitutes a representation of the real world in addition to which something more has been *added:* the writer's resentment, nostalgia, criticism. This *added element* is what makes a novel a work of art and not just information; it's what we justly call the originality of the novelist" (*Historia de un deicidio,* 86). The structural organization and content of the last scene, like others in the novel, not to mention the overall parallel construct of autobiographical and imaginary chapters in the beginning of the novel, become significant in light of Vargas Llosa's theoretical comments, for the final scene represents a combination of the writer's subjective and objective worlds and highlights the author's narrative strategies.

The relationship between the writer's vocation and the text he produces, which is revealed in the culmination of *Aunt Julia and the Scriptwriter,* can be further understood by considering additional comments that Vargas Llosa has made about writing. He states that although it is not easy to detect the origin of a writer's vocation, the only way to discover it is by pitting life against work: "this is revealed at the point in which the two become confused. Why a novelist writes is viscerally connected to *what* he writes: The obsessions of his life are the themes of his work. His obsessions: facts, persons, dreams, myths, whose presence or absence, whose life or death make him an enemy of reality" (*Historia de un deicidio,* 86–87). Vargas Llosa concludes that "the process of narrative creation is the transformation of obsessions into themes, a process by which subjective content is converted, thanks to language, into objective content, the transition from individual experience to universal experience" (87).

By examining the unique relationship between the primary narrative focus (the autobiography) and the secondary narrative focus (the soap operas), which parallel each other in the novel, the reader may be led to make two observations: first, a person's obsessions (for example, Camacho's fantasies and fears) are an integral part of the process of revealing one's own "biography"; and, second, the autobiographical re-creation of a past period in one's life (in Mario Vargas Llosa's, specifically) is subject to strong doses of fictionalization, as memory gives way to imagination and desire. The novel is rife with humorous and ironic crossovers between the "real" world of autobiography and the "creative" world of melodrama. In essence, Vargas Llosa has worked out an ingenious narrative scheme in which subjective and objective levels of reality are played off against each other, paradoxically canceling and sustaining each other in a kaleidoscope of reflecting mirrors that create new, changing, and theretofore unused perspectives on a total reality.

## Metafiction: The Novel as a Process of Its Own Making

The reference to the act of writing in the novel's epigraph alerts the reader to a central thematic concern: the preoccupation with fiction making itself. This theme locates the novel within a contemporary phenomenon in art known as "metafiction." Inger Christensen (1981) states that metafiction is not defined just as the "exploration of the theory of fiction through fiction itself," but more as a theory of fiction "whose primary concern is to express the novelist's vision of experience by exploring the process of its own making. This definition indicates that only those works are considered metafiction where the novelist has a message to convey and is not merely displaying technical brilliance" (10–11).

The narrative world of *Aunt Julia and the Scriptwriter* is, without doubt, a literary one. The novel even has a fairy-tale beginning. Constant references to literature throughout the work accent the fictitiousness of its content. Christensen states that the most modern metafictionists share a "deep concern for verbal creation and communication". The possibilities of communication and the creation of fiction, however, differ for each writer, and "their different conceptions are revealed in their attitudes to the narrator, narrative, and narratee [reader] in their works" (Christensen 1981, 151). In *Aunt Julia and the Scriptwriter,* Vargas Llosa demonstrates the possibility of creating an "ideal" narrator who, in reality, is a composite of several different narrators in the novel, all of whom have special relationships with each other.

The relationships among four different narrators in *Aunt Julia and the Scriptwriter,* all of whom share the common bond of being writers, have been lucidly discussed and analyzed by Raymond L. Williams in his study *"La tía Julia y el escribidor:* escritores y lectores," which reveals the true significance of Vargas Llosa's novel. Williams presents a visual diagram of the relationships in the following way:

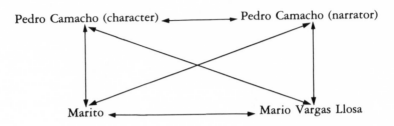

The first narrator/writer is Pedro Camacho, a character described by
Marito in the autobiographical chapters; the second writer is Marito,
who narrates those chapters, presenting his love affair with Aunt
Julia and his desire to become a writer; the third writer is the Pedro
Camacho who creates nine soap-opera episodes in the even-numbered
chapters of the novel (Williams makes an important distinction
between Camacho the author—that is, the character described by
Marito—and Camacho the soap-opera narrator); and the fourth writer
is the author Mario Vargas Llosa, whose name appears on the cover
of the novel.

Williams analyzes each of the six possible relationships indicated
by the arrows in the diagram. The first relationship is the one
between Marito and Pedro Camacho the character. It underlines the
whole problem of writing; for Marito, who is about to embark on
a literary career, seeks to find a model of discipline and profession-
alism in the figure of a real writer. Ironically, he finds his model
in Camacho, who is described throughout the novel as anything but
real: "A most unusual silhouette appeared in the doorway of the
[radio] shack: a minuscule figure, on the very borderline between
a man extremely short in stature and a dwarf, with a huge nose and
unusually bright eyes with a disturbing, downright abnormal gleam
in them" (14). Although he is viewed by Marito as odd—a puppet,
an elf, and a madman—his seriousness and lack of humor provoke
Marito's curiosity: "His every word was uttered with extraordinary
solemnity, all of which—along with his perfect diction, his dwarf-
like stature, his bizarre attire, and his theatrical gestures—made
him appear to be an odd sort indeed. It was obvious that he took
everything he said to be the gospel truth, and he thus gave the
impression of being at once the most affected and the most sincere
man in the world" (42). At another point in the novel, Marito states

that "the scriptwriter was a man of unshakable convictions. I had come to feel genuine friendship for him; above and beyond the entomological curiosity he aroused in me, I truly respected him" (127). Finally, Marito provides a list of Camacho's characteristics that he admires: "three things about Pedro Camacho fascinated me: what he said; the austerity of his life, entirely devoted to an obsession; and his capacity for work. This latter especially" (127). For Marito, Camacho is a living model of the professional writer, just what he himself wants to be; what is true for Camacho is true for Marito: "For him to live was to write" (130). At another point in the novel, Marito finally puts the Camacho literary phenomenon into perspective:

How could he be, at one and the same time, a parody of the writer and the only person in Peru who, by virtue of the time he devoted to his craft and the works he produced, was worthy of that name? Were all those politicians, attorneys, professors who went by the name of poets, novelists, dramatists really *writers,* simply because, during brief parentheses in lives in which four fifths of their time was spent at activities having nothing to do with literature, they had produced one slim volume of verses or one niggardly collection of stories? Why should those persons who used literature as an ornament or a pretext have any more right to be considered real writers than Pedro Camacho, who lived *only* to write? Because they had read (or at least knew that they should have read) Proust, Faulkner, Joyce, while Pedro Camacho was very nearly illiterate? When I thought about such things, I felt sad and upset. It was becoming clearer and clearer to me each day that the only thing I wanted to be in life was a writer, and I was also becoming more and more convinced each day that the only way to be one was to devote oneself heart and soul to literature. (195)

The second relationship involves Marito and Mario Vargas Llosa. Marito is the young first-person narrator who experiences the action, while Mario Vargas Llosa is the mature adult narrator who presents the story. Differences between them exist, although the two narrators merge at moments several years after the narrated events (the epilogue); that is, at those points at the beginning and the end of novel when the narrator employs the present tense. The principal common bond between the two narrators is their concept of the writer in society, which Marito becomes aware of during the course of events in the novel and which Mario Vargas Llosa discusses in his theoretical essays. Basically the writer is perceived as an outsider and a rebel who cannot conform to the norms of society. For example, after an outing with his neighborhood friends, Marito discovers that he thinks differently than they do; he doesn't belong because he is a writer:

> My pals were still the same as ever, cracking the same jokes, talking of the same girls, but I couldn't share with them the things that mattered most to me: literature and Aunt Julia. If I'd told them that I was writing stories and dreamed of being a writer, they would doubtless have thought, just as my cousin Nancy did, that I had a screw loose. And if I'd told them about my romance—as they told me about their conquests—with a divorcée, who was not my mistress but my sweetheart, my *enamorada* (in the most Miraflorine sense of that word), they would have taken me for (as a poetic, esoteric, very popular expression of those days went) a *cojudo a la vela*—an ass under full sail. I didn't feel the slightest scorn for them for not reading literature, nor did I consider myself superior because I was having a romance with a real, grownup woman who'd had lots of experience, but the truth of the matter was that on those nights, as we poked around graves under the eucalyptus and pepper trees of Surco, or splashed about beneath the stars of Santa Rosa, or drank beer and haggled over prices with the whores at Nanette's, I was bored, and found my thoughts dwelling more on my "Dangerous Games" (which had not appeared in *El Comercio* this week either) and on Aunt Julia than on what they were saying. (205)

At another point in the novel, Marito experiences jealousy when Aunt Julia steps out on him; so he consults with the scriptwriter, revealing the importance of art to life that Vargas Llosa has discussed in several literary essays: " 'I've got love troubles, my friend Camacho,' I said to him straight out, surprised at hearing myself use a soap opera cliché; but it seemed to me that by speaking in this way I distanced myself from my own story and at the same time managed to vent my feelings" (157). In his study of *Madame Bovary*, Vargas Llosa alludes to the redeeming qualities of literature by stating that at one point in his life he became so dejected that he contemplated suicide. At about the same time in his life, Vargas Llosa remembers reading the passage about Emma Bovary's suicide in Flaubert's novel; the scene proved to be therapeutic for him because Vargas Llosa absorbed from those frightening pages the feelings of consolation and balance, a repugnance for chaos, a pleasure for life; accordingly, he states, "the fictitious suffering neutralized my real suffering" (25).

The third relationship, between Mario Vargas Llosa and the character Pedro Camacho, reveals another aspect—parody—that, according to Christensen (1981), plays a major role in metafiction (154–55). Vargas Llosa discovers in Camacho's attitudes toward writing a distorted mirror, a caricaturized version of his own literary obsessions. The relationship reveals a self-parody of the serious writer. Whereas Marito admires Camacho, Vargas Llosa turns him into a caricature, thereby deflating some of his own literary attitudes by representing them, through Camacho, in a distorted fashion. In the same chapter, while Marito discovers why he admires Camacho so much, the latter begins to lose control of his soap-opera creations. One day, the radio-station owner complains that Camacho has taken "to pulling people's legs, shifting characters from one serial to an entirely different one or changing their names all of a sudden so as to get our listeners all confused" (200). Vargas Llosa's penchant for changing characters' names in many of his own novels is parodied here, and the irony deepens when Marito innocently responds by saying that "perhaps these interchangeable characters and mixed-up plots were Pedro Camacho's highly original way of telling a story" (201). In not understanding the aesthetic possibilities for such narrative strategies, the radio-station owner—who is not looking for originality but pure entertainment—orders Marito to tell Camacho "to cut out these modernist gimmicks, or else he's liable to end up without a job" (201).

A fourth relationship is established between the character Camacho and the narrator Camacho. An apparent dichotomy arises between the person as author (the character whom Marito admires) and the same person as narrator (the originator of the soap-opera scripts). The first Camacho is a "full-time writer, obsessed and impassioned by his vocation" (195), while the second Camacho is a fanatic "scribbler" who lays bare the perverse nature of his own life. In fact, José Miguel Oviedo (1978b) points out that

it is not only his stories that show us that the internal world of Camacho is an inferno of psychopathic obsessions looking for a way to express themselves (anal fixation and incestuous, masturbatory, sadistic, pornographic, destructive compulsions are always part of them) but, also, his own relationship with his own created characters is morbid and neurotic. On the one hand, his characters depend upon him like slaves depend upon their master; they are disjointed, deformed marionettes whom he subjects to the worst abuse, with a ruthlessness reminiscent of the inexorable discipline of military hierarchies; each and every one zealously performs his duty in the name of unassailable principles. On the other hand, the characters engage in compulsive activities and fanatical endeavors which are part of a fixed pattern—someone discovers a truth or a myth, a religion or a hobby, and gives himself over to it completely—which is adhered to despite the obvious thematic or geographical differences of the plots. They are heroically given over to their vocation, to the point of insanity and death. They identify with their vocation to the point of being crushed and destroyed by it. Most of them are dogmatic militants: the crusader of the antirodent campaign, the unorthodox preacher from Mendocita, the uncompromising soccer referee, etc., are alike because, with the fixed stare of the possessed or the mystic, they all search for one objective, and they fail in their endeavor. (174–75)

In the relationship between the narrator Camacho and the author Vargas Llosa, the differences between the narrative styles of each writer become clear. On the one hand, Camacho's writing is romantically inspired, quite simple, and totally without any purpose other than the creation of pleasure; "hence, when writing stories, it was important that contrast, not continuity, be the ruling principle of composition: the complete change of place, milieu, mood, subject, and characters reinforced the exhilarating sensation that one was starting afresh. Moreover, cups of mint-and-verbena tea were helpful" (133). On the other hand, Vargas Llosa has written extensively about his theories of writing, with many of them appearing in his studies of Gabriel García Márquez and Gustave Flaubert. He declares that the best novels are those constructed with a rigorous symmetrical order (*La orgía perpétua*, 18). In the construction of his fictitious worlds, he places a large burden on the concept of binary opposites (170). These ideas emphasize the need for a precise structural organization of the narrative material, the organization of time, the gauging of desire effects, and the concealment or exposure of certain narrative facts (95). He goes on to state that a sign of bad writing is the excessive use of repetition, incorrect grammar, and cacophony. Camacho, of course, falls into this category when he repeatedly describes his characters as fifty years of age and in the prime of their lives. The repeated clichés make his narratives thoroughly subjective, revealing them as the reverse side of Vargas Llosa's personal goal of creating objectivity in his own prose works. Vargas Llosa learned from Flaubert that the novelist must inform himself completely about his subject by traveling, reading voraciously, interviewing, and studying before he can begin to write adequately about it. In other words, one must consciously plunder reality in order to be able to construct a convincing fictitious reality (88). Camacho works differently; he has a suitcase stuffed with props and disguises that he wears in order to play out the roles of his soap-opera characters as he writes the scripts. He asks: "What is realism, ladies and gentlemen—that famous realism we hear so much about? What better way is there of creating realistic art than by materially identifying oneself with reality? And doesn't the day's work thereby become more tolerable, more pleasant, more varied, more dynamic?" (*Aunt Julia*, 135–36). Vargas Llosa's rigorous control over the narrative material by working from organizational concepts of a rational nature is the opposite of Camacho's ideas of completely and utterly immersing oneself, even to the point of dressing the part, in the subjective world of his characters. Camacho makes it impossible for his "literature" to provide anything more than cheap pleasure and an endless repetition of the feeling of always starting over again.

The last possible relationship between writers—the one between Marito and the narrator Camacho—offers further implications with regard to the metafictional theme in *Aunt Julia and the Scriptwriter*. Williams points out that this relationship is less significant than the others because Marito, who never listens to the soap operas when they are presented on the radio, cannot gain access to the fictional narratives except through the power that they wield over the listening audience. What happens, in fact, is that Marito learns almost all there is to know about them through the commentaries about them, for the soap operas are a constant topic of discussion among the members of his family and his coworkers at the radio station. As Camacho loses control of his mind and begins to confuse the scripts, greater commentary and more revealing information about them filter into the autobiographical chapters of the novel. By receiving information about Camacho's "other" world in an indirect or secondhand way, Marito is learning, in practical fashion, about the ambiguous nature of reality, just as the characters (and readers) in most of Vargas Llosa's novels learn about and accept reality in oblique or roundabout ways.

The significance of the relationship between the two men is necessary for an understanding of Vargas Llosa's theory of narrative. One principal idea in this theory holds that between man and his grasp of reality stands a wall of differing perspectives that, when expressed in words, will taint one's understanding of that reality. Ironically Camacho, while discussing how he creates characters by wearing different disguises, exclaims to Marito, "Don't you know that in the beginning is the Word—always?" (135). The relationship must also be viewed in light of the fact that while Camacho is writing his scripts Marito is also struggling to write short stories. Throughout the autobiographical parts of the novel, Marito discusses with Aunt Julia his own creative attempts, and to his friend Javier he describes his narrative problems. One story, ironically entitled "The Qualitative Leap" (the term for an important narrative strategy that Vargas Llosa uses), contains an entire set of linguistic influences and perspectives. For one thing, it has all the ingredients of a soap opera: devils, magic, murder, and intrigue; in addition, it contains the perspective of a Jorge Luis Borges story that he wants to imitate: "I wanted it to be as coldly objective, intellectual, terse, and ironic as one of Borges's—an author whom I had just discovered at that time" (44). In contrast to Camacho's loosely defined creative method, Marito's narrative attempts begin to reflect influences of the great masters and not simply the reference guide, *Ten Thousand Literary Quotations Drawn from the Hundred Best Writers in the World,* that Camacho consults. In another story Marito tries to write about a Spanish actor who, while performing the Passion Play, falls to the stage floor and, tied to a wooden cross, screams obscene remarks. This time Marito wants to create humor: "It was, above all, this very last scene that I wanted to re-create; my story, too, would end up with a bang, with Jesus cursing like a trooper. I wanted it to be a funny story, and to learn the techniques of writing humor, I read—on jitneys, express buses, and in bed before falling asleep— all the witty authors I could get my hands on, from Mark Twain and Bernard Shaw to Jardiel Poncela and Flórez" (96). While discussing the story with Aunt Julia, he defends a narrative procedure that Vargas Llosa has written about extensively, the *elemento añadido.* When she tells Marito that he has gotten the story all wrong, he becomes upset and informs her "that what she was listening to was not a faithful, word-for-word recounting of the incident she'd told me about, but *a story, a story,* and that all the things that I'd either added or left out were ways of achieving certain effects: 'Comic effects,' I emphasized, hoping she'd see what I was getting at" (123). Later, he tries to write a completely realistic story after he has been influenced by that technique in a Buñuel film and by Hemingway's writing style. Other attempts are described, and in general Marito reveals in a metafictional way how the crucial relationship between the artist's intense experience of reality and his obligation to render it through a literary form creates certain desired effects. Doubtlessly, Marito/Vargas Llosa could not agree more with Camacho when he says that "I work from life; my writings are firmly rooted in reality, as the grapevine is rooted in the vinestock" (48). But the relationship between Marito and the narrator Camacho exposes a grave difference between them: Marito struggles to objectify his narrative material through the use of certain narrative strategies, whereas Camacho remains trapped in a subliterary world of distortion, cliché, repetition, and cacophony.

In conclusion, *Aunt Julia and the Scriptwriter* is a fine example of contemporary metafiction. The novel highlights several aspects about literature that writers must confront constantly. For one thing, it is impossible for art to become a true copy of reality; literature does not hide the disparity between them but exposes it. Irony, parody, and humor—which form an integral part of metafictive novels— provide a spoof on literary practices that strive in vain to create the appearance of reality. Equally important is the attention that Vargas Llosa's novel gives to certain fundamentals of fiction writing itself. An important difference is established, for example, between the concept of "author" and that of "narrator." In addition, certain problems involving the reader come to the forefront in metafiction. The significance of the multiple relationships among the four narrators in Vargas Llosa's novel depends on the reader's involvement and interpretation. Different levels of reading attention are required, producing varied reactions and interpretations. Whereas curiosity attracts some readers to the novel, the richly autobiographical portions and the humor in the soap opera narratives of *Aunt Julia and the Scriptwriter* provide the major attractions for other readers; and yet another type of reader responds to the ambiguous relationship between the two types of narration—autobiography and soap operas—that ultimately creates the quintessence of narrative art in general.

## Chapter Nine

# La señorita de Tacna and Kathie y el hipopótamo: Storytelling as Dramatized Art

In the early 1980s Mario Vargas Llosa added a new dimension to his literary career: he wrote and published two plays, *La señorita de Tacna* (The señorita from Tacna) (1981) and *Kathie y el hipopótamo* (Katy and the hippopotamus) (1983). Both are two-act plays—the former an intense work that probes the nature of the creative act, also a significant theme in *Aunt Julia and the Scriptwriter;* and the latter a glib comic farce about people who deceive themselves while living part of their lives in make-believe worlds created through stories in order to escape their own suffocating mediocrity and insignificance. *La señorita de Tacna* premiered in Buenos Aires in May 1981, and *Kathie y el hipopótamo* opened in Caracas in 1983 at the VI International Theatre Festival. *La señorita de Tacna* was presented in English in New York City by the INTAR Hispanic American Theatre Company in 1983. Both plays hve been successfully produced in several major world capitals, bearing witness to their success as engaging art forms.

Vargas Llosa's biographers indicate that the Peruvian's first incursion into literature came through the production of a play, entitled *La huída del Inca* (The escape of the Inca), which he wrote as a teenager in Piura in the early 1950s. Practically nothing is known about the play's literary merits. Yet the fact that Vargas Llosa made an attempt to write drama at the beginning of his career is at least a good indication of his long-standing interest in the theater as a viable literary genre and in its literary importance within the performing arts.

In fact, some of Vargas Llosa's theoretical notions about the writing process and certain techniques that he employs in his novels, and now in these plays, suggest that he recognizes a strong kinship between the two literary genres. The curious mixture of narrative and dramatic elements in the two texts makes the experience of reading them as important as viewing the stage production of the plays. This should not come as a surprise to his readers, for all of Vargas Llosa's novels are heavily laden with dialogue and its variants, all of which create in prose fiction an intense dramatic quality about them. However, it is possible to consider these plays as discussions in dialogue form of abstract questions rather than as dramas of concrete action. In essence, Vargas Llosa has merged concepts of "literature" and "drama" in these works.

The two plays challenge their audiences with regard to the nature of how and why human beings tell stories, a major theme in both plays. As in his narrative fiction, Vargas Llosa has pushed the dramatic art form toward new limits through incorporating diverse techniques as he searches to find answers to such universal questions as the need for art, its purpose in life, and the process involved in creating fiction. As a fiction writer, playwright, film producer, and intellectual, Vargas Llosa seeks to show his readers and audiences ways in which art contributes to the quality of one's life and to a better understanding of oneself. In his works, the fictional realities encompass the spectator, and in the fascinating encounter between fantasy and reality one is brought face to face with some of the human race's deepest concerns: the enigmatic relationship between past and present, memory and oblivion, truth and deception, adolescence and maturity, love and hate, jealousy and vengeance, and morality and immorality.

The task of fully comprehending the process of creating fiction is a primary concern for Mario Vargas Llosa at this stage of his career, and it is the prevailing theme of *La señorita de Tacna* and *Kathie y el hipopótamo*. In the 1983 *New York Times Magazine* article "A Passion for Peru," he poses serious questions to himself with regard to fiction writing and what it means:

Why do I write and what does writing mean? Ever since I was a boy, I have been pursued by the temptation to fictionalize everything that happens to me. I sometimes have the impression that what I do, what is done to me—my whole life—is only a pretext for inventing stories. What lies behind this incessant transmutation of reality into fiction? Is it an effort to save what I have loved from ravenous time, or the desire to exorcize painful and terrible events by transfiguring them? Or is it simply a game, a drunken orgy of words and fantasies? The longer I write, the more difficult it becomes to find the answer. (108)

It is possible to view both plays as attempts in explaining his desire to transfigure reality, however perplexing it may be to find satisfactory answers to those burning questions. *La señorita de Tacna* is an admirable effort on Vargas Llosa's part to recapture and save from oblivion cherished moments of the past, while *Kathie y el hipopótamo* approaches the creative act almost as a game, that seemingly farcical yet almost primitive and deathlike "drunken orgy of words and fantasies" that human beings so desperately need in order to give structure to life's overriding sense of chaos.

*La señorita de Tacna* is a two-act play about the past and present lives of several members of one family spanning three generations. Although the title of the play alludes to one of its female characters, the true protagonist is Belisario, a seasoned writer in his forties. The year is 1980. In his study, he grapples with the problem of how to write a love story by using, on the one hand, strong doses of personal experience and, on the other, the power of imagination as a narrative catalyst. Once again, Vargas Llosa relies on a fortuitous mixture of melodrama, violence, sex, and rebellion to produce a distorted but convincing mirror of reality reflecting the world beyond the stage and bringing into focus the spectator's world. As in the novel *Aunt Julia and the Scriptwriter*, in which the life of the character Marito Vargas is tied closely to the author's life, here the reader-spectator is tempted to link the character Belisario with the author Mario Vargas Llosa. The title of the play refers to the story that Belisario struggles to write, which is based on his memories of his now dead great aunt, who told him stories as a child in the 1940s. While he labors to make her come alive in his memory, Belisario attempts to write a romantic love story about her, while commenting throughout on the problematic nature of the creative act.

The stage is divided into two parts; in addition to Belisario's study, we see the interior of a modest household of the 1950s in Lima. Here, scenes re-create the period when the señorita from Tacna, now old and decrepit, dies. Through other scenes that re-create the señorita's youth, the spectator learns that she was born sometime after 1850 and mysteriously adopted by the family around whom the play revolves. She grows up with Belisario's grandmother, Carmen, who marries Pedro and has three children, Agustín, César, and Amelia, Belisario's mother. Belisario's father is noticeably absent. At the courting age, the señorita become engaged to a Chilean army officer, Joaquín. Historically, Peru had lost the War of the Pacific (1879–83) to Chile, and the province and city of Tacna, situated on the border, was occupied by Chile for over a decade (Peruvian sovereignty was not reestablished until much later). Just days before the marriage is to take place, she learns directly from Joaquín's lover, Carlota, that she will have to share Joaquín's love after she marries him. Overtaken by rage, she burns her new wedding dress and calls off the marriage. Immediately, the señorita begins to play the role of a pious spinster, which will last for the rest of her life. Deep inside, however, her yearning to be loved torments her. She becomes a permanent member of the Carmen-Pedro household, helping to raise the three children.

Although the passionate romance between Elvira and Joaquín has all the ingredients of a sentimental love story, which leaves Elvira's desires to be fed long afterwards by the smoldering remnants of her memory, Belisario finally begins to sense that the real love story involves the señorita and someone else. As in his novels, Vargas Llosa hides enough necessary information in order to inhibit the reader or spectator from fully knowing the truth. But one clue, which suggests the possibility that such a secret relationship, if not consummated, is nonetheless desired, but never directly revealed in the play, is found in the repeated use of two seemingly simple yet interrelated words: *señorita* (or young lady) and *caballero* (or gentleman), with the former referring to Elvira and the latter to Carmen's husband, Pedro.

Structurally, the two acts of the play are composed of temporally and spatially diverse scenes, which capture in montage fashion different moments in the lives of Elvira and others. Similar to the characters in Vargas Llosa's novels who possess different names at different moments in their lives—for example, Bonifacia–La Selvática in *The Green House,* Cuéllar-P.P. in *The Cubs,* Santiago-Zavalita-Skinny-Superbrain in *Conversation in The Cathedral,* or Pantoja-Panta-Pantita in *Captain Pantoja and the Special Service*—Belisario's aunt has different names that correspond to different stages in her life and in her relationship with others. As a young woman growing up with Carmen and Pedro, she is Elvira; as a middle-aged woman helping to raise their children, she is known as Mamaé (a word coined by one of the three children, which is a combination of Mama and Elvira); and, finally, when she tells stories (about herself) to young Belisario, she refers to herself as the señorita from Tacna.

The temporally diverse scenes of the play—for example, a secret midnight meeting at the open barred window between Joaquín and Elvira prior to the wedding in the 1880s; Mamaé telling stories about the young lady from Tacna to young Belisario in the 1940s; the grownup children arguing about how to continue caring for their aging parents and Mamaé in the 1950s; and Belisario arguing with himself about what constitutes a romantic love story in the 1980s—are organized to allow the spectator to view the action as a process of Belisario remembering, having heard or actually experienced those moments and gaining from them the imagination he needs to fill the lacunae left by the past's unremembered or, more likely, misunderstood events. The fragmented temporal sequencing destroys any sense of chronology of the events, while providing structural independence and relevance to each scene. By placing the scenes on equal par with each other, the dramatist provides an important clue to the interpretation of the work. In effect, the scenes jump back and forth in time, flowing in and around each other in much the same way that Belisario experiences them in his mind, regardless of whether they are real or imagined. The scenes function for him as atemporal, living realities, and he searches intensely yet randomly to find connections, relationships, answers, and meanings for his own life, about which the spectator knows practically nothing.

At one crucial point, however, he does mention his present status. He remembers the period in his childhood when he got the chicken pox. Mamaé would apply some ointment to the sores and pull his hands away from his face so that he would not scratch the skin eruptions and leave permanent scars on his face. Moreover, this was the time when she first began to tell him stories in order to distract him from scratching himself. As if the romantic concept of destiny plays a role in determining his future (and now present moment in life), Belisario cries out, "Despite all she did, I'm still ugly" (67). As a result, the kaleidoscopic patterns of interwoven time planes, which provide the play's organization, reduce or mask the present moment and make it seem unimportant among the confluence of the other moments in the past. Taken together, however, these moments determine Belisario's position in life. Although he seems unable to confront the present and therefore turns to the past, he discovers that by focusing his imagination upon forgotten or misunderstood past realities he can rescue something intimately important in his life: his apprenticeship with Mamaé in the art of storytelling. Therefore, he reasons, the need to tell her story (now that he is a professional writer) is based on his desire to clear a longstanding debt to her.

The theoretical implications of the play are indeed intriguing, for Vargas Llosa has fused literary devices that, on the one hand, belong to the early epic theatre mode and, on the other, point to the concept of dramatized self-referentiality and metafiction. Of primary importance for the epic mode is the basic situation of telling a story. The technique of narrative art involves three ingredients: a narrated incident, an audience, and a narrator. In this sense, Belisario is the narrator of the young lady's story; but as a character in a fictitious setting, he presents facts and events of the past not as they probably or could have happened but more "as if" they had happened, thereby creating the feeling of the historical present in the play.

Within this context the epic narrator assumes a position of serene reflection, judging the play with regard to his relationship to the content of the narrative. His epic monologues, which are interspersed throughout the other scenes of the play, work not only to communicate to the audience past events in a meaningful present context but also to comment on the process of writing stories. At the same time, Belisario's monologues question the nature of imaginary past events as if they had actually occurred; and they also separate the narrator from the action, permitting the audience greater accessibility to the events that are viewed within the play as fictitious. As a result, the audience's sense of anticipation is stimulated, which, in turn, tends to confirm and give a heightened sense of reality to the scenes that occur in the play. Although the epic mode tends to treat events as past action, while the overall effect of drama is to re-create a sense of the present moment of action, the combination of these two aspects in *La señorita de Tacna* allows the narrator to recall his personal experiences as past events and to judge them in order to reach moral conclusions about them; at the same time, he presents them dramatically as part of a historical present, creating different and even conflicting points of view. The first point of view to emerge in the play is important for setting the tone of the play. Here Mamaé babbles to herself in lyrical, even symbolic, imagery suggestive of dream or fantasy worlds. The scene, when viewed in relation to the last one (of the play), in which Belisario contemplates the meaning of narratives, provides a framing device for the creation of a totally "poetic" world in the play, pointing to the universal theme of life as a dream. In addition, the poetic flow of highly suggestive imagery at the beginning, which is substantiated by Belisario at the end, reflects the idea that time not only obstructs a clear understanding of reality, but also obliterates memory. For a creative writer, then, the nature of writing is complex: as memory is lost with the passage of time, fantasy intensifies its intrusion into the writer's reality.

Belisario's role as the epic narrator of a love story grows as he takes on other roles in the play. He is the protagonist of the play, and he assumes momentarily the role of other characters, such as the secret dancing partner at a masquerade ball to whom Elvira feels sexually attracted until she learns of his black identity, or the priest confessor to whom she reveals remorse for the sin of thinking evil and libidinous thoughts. In this way, Belisario becomes a character of his own fiction, and consequently, his text becomes a justification of Mamaé's attempt to justify the stories that she told him as a child.

The second important theoretical consideration contained in the play is its totally self-conscious nature that demonstrates an awareness of its own existence, actions, and purpose. But Belisario's intrusions into the action as narrator do not destroy the audience's sensitivity toward the dramatic nature of the work because he plays an important part in the development of the action. Nevertheless, the play fits perfectly into the realm of metafiction, of works that comment on the fiction-making process itself in order to provide some proof that art has a purpose. Inger Christensen's explanation of the nature of metafiction as it applies to novelists is equally important for Vargas Llosa as a playwright: "metafiction deals with questions essential to any novelist: the narrator's conception of his own role and art, and of the reader. Writers are . . . conscious of these relations, but the metafictionist differs by making these questions the subject of his work. Thus metafiction sheds light on

fundamental issues in connection with fictional creation in general"
(Christensen 1981, 13).

In *La señorita de Tacna* diverse narrators—principally Mamaé,
Belisario, and the implied author—re-create parts of their own pasts,
set into motion the conflict between memory and desire, and, collectively, suggest certain truths about the nature of fiction writing.
Vargas Llosa employs two literary strategies—the "added element"
and the "hidden fact," as well as the concept of duality—to organize
the play's fictional material in such a way that the characters' pasts,
memories, desires, and certain basic truths about writing ultimately
envelop each other, therefore not only highlighting themes dealing
with old age, family relationships, morality, and individual destiny,
but also seeking answers as to why and how stories originate. The
intertextual relationship between this play and Vargas Llosa's previous works, for example, goes far toward understanding the complexities involved in writing fiction. The narrative world of the play
is virtually built on the fictitious realities of Vargas Llosa's previous
novels. For example, in one scene that occurs in the 1950s, the
aging couple and Mamaé listen to a radio soap opera by Pedro
Camacho, a central character in *Aunt Julia and the Scriptwriter* who
was also a creator of real and fictitious realities. The relationship
established here becomes complex, but basically members of the
audience who know the novel will be able to appreciate the commentary about the characters from the soap operas, who, in turn,
provide a counterpoint to the characters in the play. In another
scene, in which Carlota visits Elvira and tells her about Joaquín's
love for Carlota—knowing that this will cause the little worm to
begin to gnaw away at Elvira's heart—one is reminded of Santiago
in *Conversation in The Cathedral,* whose conscience forces him to cling
desperately to destructive values. In both cases, their lives are ruined
by a false sense of pride. Not only is there a sense of self-referentiality
within the play, but an intertextual relationship with other works
highlights the play's fictional basis, which has the curious influence
of making Vargas Llosa's previous novels seem historically true. In
the process, Vargas Llosa has revealed to himself the true nature of
art; Gustave Flaubert, a writer he fervently admires, describes it
this way: "The day before yesterday, in the woods of Touques, in
a charming spot beside a spring, I found old cigar butts and scraps
of pate. People had been picnicking. I described such a scene in
*Novembre,* eleven years ago; it was entirely imagined, and the other

day it came true. Everything one invents is true, you may be sure. Poetry is as precise as geometry. Induction is as accurate as deduction; and besides, after reaching a certain point one no longer makes any mistake about the things of the soul. My poor Bovary, without a doubt, is suffering and weeping at this very instant in twenty villages of France" (letter to Louise Colet, 1853).

In an introduction to the play, "Las mentiras verdaderas" (Authentic lies), Vargas Llosa discusses this complex process, which is based less on the logic of reason than on obscure irrational impulses. A person's experiences in life include, says Vargas Llosa, frustrated desires, broken dreams, happiness, and rage. It was Henry James who said that aspiring writers should write from experience and experience only. Storytelling, then, is for Vargas Llosa the art of using experience to create pious frauds about oneself and about life; in the process of creation, however, deeply cherished truths about individuals, in particular, and about human beings, in general, are surprisingly revealed.

In addition to the fact that both *La señorita de Tacna* and *Kathie y el hipopótamo* are plays, the two works possess structural and thematic similiarities. In fact, the reader senses that the search deepens in the second play for answers to the questions about fiction writing that Vargas Llosa poses in the earlier play and in *Aunt Julia and the Scriptwriter*. The author's preface to *Kathie y el hipopótamo* immediately alerts the reader to the basic conflicts and the major themes of the play. Entitled "El teatro como ficción" (Theater as fiction), Vargas Llosa's preface informs the reader that one's dull, mediocre, and at times stultified life is enriched, first, by digging through memories, exposing desires, giving free reign to impulses, and listening to one's emotional palpitations, and second, by imagining and creating worlds that go beyond the frontiers of known reality. As a result, fictions are created that hardly reflect real life but create the life that never was, the life that everyone always wanted but never had, or the life that would make a person do anything in order not to have it. Another point that Vargas Llosa makes in the essay is concerned with the nature of theater. Even though a dramatic production might seem real enough, it has the same mission as all other fiction, "to contrive illusions, to deceive" (11). Fiction does not reproduce life but contradicts it; like a photographic negative, Vargas Llosa declares, a work of fiction systematically rectifies life and documents human history. Finally, Vargas Llosa repeats here that "to dream, to write fiction (similar to reading, seeing or believing it) is an oblique protest against the mediocrity of our lives and a transitory but effective way to ridicule it" (12).

With this in mind, it should come as no surprise that *Kathie y el hipopótamo* fits perfectly within the scope of the theater of the absurd (which originated in France in the 1950s and included such playwrights as Samuel Beckett, Eugene Ionesco, and Fernando Arrabal). Here the concept of absurd theater is not meant to be defined in a narrow sense; for what seems to be simply absurd to a French bourgeois audience is, in the context of Latin America, an oppressive sociocultural reality. Nevertheless, the basic ingredient of this dramatic mode (and Vargas Llosa's play) is the idea that everything is a game. In absurd theater, fundamentally, two persons enter into a tacit agreement to play out a monodrama based on mental games. This play, set in the 1960s, is organized around two people—Kathie Kennety and Santiago Zavala—who meet secretly everyday for two hours at her clandestine apartment in Lima (decorated like a Paris bohemian loft) in order to fantasize about their lives, indulging in a game that reveals the basic mechanisms of deception to which the human mind is subjected when one invents, pretends, or feigns situations. In this play, the author adds another component: the atmosphere of the soap opera conflict. Kathie, the wife of a rich Peruvian playboy and mother of two children, hires Santiago to embellish—rewrite—her travel memoirs about an exotic trip to Africa that never took place. Kathie is personally frustrated and sexually estranged because of her husband's infantile dedication to surfing, partying, and his young female admirers. In short, her life mirrors a typical Pedro Camacho soap opera episode in *Aunt Julia and the Scriptwriter.* Kathie fantasizes about a boyhood sweetheart whom she turned down for the man she married, a rich and debonair man of her own social class.

Santiago, whose name immediately suggests an intertextual relationship with the primary character in *Conversation in The Cathedral* (whose name is also Santiago Zavala) is a poorly paid, insignificant newspaper journalist. In addition, he plays out the role of a liberal university literature professor. But just as Kathie's exotic trip is probably more desire than reality, it is suggested that Santiago never was a real professor. His life has been consumed with rebellion against crass bourgeois mentalities and attitudes, and in his fantasies he has been obsessed by his supposed sexual prowess with young and liberated college coeds.

Similar problems arise in the case of Kathie and Santiago. The themes of jealousy, envy, contempt, and hatred, among others, surface as the basic conflict—the commonplace love triangle—creating a sense of plot in the play; normally, this theme is the basis for the development of a sentimental romantic plot. Here, in fact, the love triangle functions as a structural device for the play. Vargas Llosa takes this hackneyed, banal, yet destructive relationship, which is the source of those themes, and reduces it to its most base, instinctual, and animalistic level by euphemistically associating it with the grotesque grunting sex act between two slovenly hippopotamuses after one male has defeated another in order to take his prize. Kathie mentions these animals while describing her imaginary trip to Africa; Santiago enriches the scene by making lurid associations to the same conflict among human beings. As a matter of fact, the whole play is built upon the special use of euphemistic language that deflects and disguises the true nature of the characters' problems.

Historically the theater of the absurd represents the period of bourgeois crisis in Western societies. Faced with the complete lack of communication among human beings, individuals seek ways to pass the time, which leads to their invention of games. Masked taboo language creates humor, irony, and tension. Just as the numerous euphemisms magically transform the meaning of language in the play, the characters experience transformations as well. In addition to the two principal characters, two others—Juan, Kathie's husband, and Ana, Santiago's wife (also a character in *Conversation in The Cathedral*)—appear on stage; however, they are not meant to function as flesh-and-blood characters who participate in the daily encounters between Kathie and Santiago; rather, they are mental creations with whom Kathie and Santiago enter into conversations, playing out their secret desires. Kathie envisions a way out of her sordid situation by leading her husband to discover her love affairs with several men and to threaten to commit suicide because his machismo has been impugned. In a highly emotional scene, he gets drunk, pulls a gun, threatens first to kill Kathie, and when he cannot do it, puts the gun to his head. Kathie helps him pull the trigger. Santiago imagines a new life after leaving his wife and their two small daughters. In the discussions that ensue with Ana, after he has tried to adapt to a new life-style of free love and independence, he uses hypocrisy and the double standard toward her and his political convictions in declaring that he is not to blame for the fact that men are sexually aroused by bourgeois frivolity. He states that moral and political convictions have no power over man's instinct. Ana reminds him that he had told her that human nature is nonexistent. He responds by declaring that it does not exist but that it is exploitatively convenient for the bourgeois to say that it does. She calls him a deceiver and a liar. He lectures her about man's malleable nature, saying that man is what he chooses to be. He advises her to read Jean-Paul Sartre. Even though he might sound sincere, everything he says is made false when he begins to view reality in terms of "human nature"; apparently, he is not able to maintain his abnormal sexual potency for long, and the liberated coeds become bored with him. Hence, he falls back on his antibourgeois rhetoric about fighting sex appeal—the same diatribe he had thrust on Ana, which eventually made her less desirable to Santiago—and tries to convince himself of the need for love through solidarity rather than sex. At bottom, finally, the problem is not the lack of communication between two real characters who face each other in order to play out a game, but rather the inability of Santiago to communicate with himself and his own fantasies.

A key to understanding the absurdist theater is the different roles that the basic characters undertake in the play. Several transformations occur among the four characters. These actions take on a ritual quality and indicate the degree of alienation that the characters feel toward others and toward themselves. The transformations not only show a rejection of reality but an intense search for identity, which is never forthcoming. At different moments in the creation of Kathie's hackneyed adolescent romance, Santiago becomes Víctor, the outsider of the love triangle. In the same way, Kathie plays the role of Adéle, one of Santiago's liberated students. In another scene, Kathie imagines the moment when she is persuaded by her older children to take the African tour to get away from the mediocrity of Lima's upper crust. Here, Ana and Juan play the children's parts.

Another type of transformation that occurs in the play is the designation of certain characters with different names—a technique long used by Vargas Llosa—which, in this case, indicate more than social relationships among characters; rather, they function to designate the characters' private worlds of desire, imagination, and fantasy. Kathie Kennety is a fictitious name that she invents in order to play out the role of the author of her travel memoirs (her real name is never revealed). Santiago's name, already the name of a character in another Vargas Llosa novel, is transformed at certain points into other names that represent the character's desire to be something more than he is. This relatively insignificant technique points toward the overall thematic significance of the work: the awesome power of language to transform reality to match one's desires or vice versa. Kathie tells Santiago that she chose the name because if she uses her real name no one will take her book seriously. Peruvian names, she says, do not sound like writers' names; Kathie Kennety sounds foreign, musical, and cosmopolitan (the social implications of nomenclature is discussed by Sara Castro-Klarén and mentioned in chapter 7 of this book).

Other transformations take place throughout the play, which immediately point toward the thematic importance of the impossible nature of adequately distinguishing between fantasy and reality. The opening scene sets the conflict in motion and creates, as in the first scene in *La señorita de Tacna,* a lyrical and symbolic world of dream and fantasy: first, when the music heard in the background changes from a French melody (in the Parisian writer's loft) to Arabian music (during the trip to Africa); second, when the audience realizes that Santiago is reinterpreting—transforming—her narrative about her experiences; and third, when it is noted that the scene described—in which a woman (Kathie, in her imagination) contemplates a majestic sphinx in Egypt—immediately creates a mysterious situation and symbolic nuances. At one point near the end of the first act, the different levels of desire and imagination of the two characters begin to envelop each other. One character comments on the other's fantasies. Since they are actually playing out their fantasies on stage, it is important to realize that the play itself can only represent one more level of unreality. By the end of the play, numerous transformations have taken place, and the audience cannot distinguish between fantasy and reality. The distinction between truth and lie has been erased, and the destructive truths are exchanged for pious lies so that some of the characters may continue to live. Kathie and Santiago pretend to recognize each other's problems, and their game seems to take on therapeutic implications. While they do recognize the banality of their game, Santiago justifies the purpose of their sport: "at least, we haven't lost our imagination, our desires. We shouldn't let them take this little game away from us because we don't have any other" (143). Kathie agrees and declares that they understand each other well and that they are good friends now. Santiago replies, "Friends and accomplices" (143). Because the audience is an integral part of a play's performance, they too are accomplices to the characters' need to give life to their desires through dreams and fantasies. Characters and members of the audience become one in the final scene in which Santiago once again begins to embellish Kathie's adventure with lyrical imagery and symbolic overtones, and everyone becomes trapped in a prison house of language, slaves to the enchanting mystery of words. Ironically, Vargas Llosa has effectively communicated this theme on a real-life level, which brings the make-believe world of Kathie's secret bohemian loft back to the world of serious social comment. In effect, the constant use of the purposely funny yet crass and infantile middle-class Peruvian euphemisms and melodramatic responses referring to sex in society provides the perfect example of people who are slaves to a language that distorts meaning and, in this case, prevents a clear understanding of social realities among men and women. The enigma that lies behind all this is the possibility that for Vargas Llosa this is the only game that gives recourse to imagination and the displacement of desire.

In conclusion, *La señorita de Tacna* and *Kathie y el hipopótamo* are strikingly similar in some respects, but they differ radically in terms of the theatrical mode employed in each play. The first play is an earnest attempt to provide an important commentary on life that depends on an epic component to question the relationship of reality and fantasy. The second play is based on humor that stems from the absurdist mode of ineffectual language—euphemisms—which is totally ridiculous and sadly pathetic. Despite the different approaches, both plays communicate the same idea: there is no reality other than the one created by fiction.

## Chapter Ten

# The War of the End of the World: A Modern Romance

By the time Mario Vargas Llosa's sixth novel *La guerra del fin del mundo* (*The War of the End of the World*) was published in 1981, his popularity had grown immensely. Readers of previous novels who had been captivated by his sheer mastery in rendering contemporary themes with innovative narrative techniques would once again discover an awesome story of epic proportions. This novel deals with events that occurred in Brazil at the turn of the century. The inhospitable and impoverished backlands of northeastern Brazil become the setting for a ghastly massacre of thousands of religious fanatics by the Brazilian army.

Beginning in October 1896 and lasting for a year, the recently formed republican government of Brazil (where a monarchy had existed from Independence until 1889) sends four military expeditions to the Canudos region in northwest Bahía to suppress a "promonarchist" rebellion of *jagunços*—reformed bandits, assassins, outcasts, and downtrodden backlanders. The Canudos rebellion is inspired by the spiritual fanaticism of the nineteenth century's last apocalyptic visionary, António Conselheiro (Anthony, the Counselor, or *Consejero* in Spanish). He miraculously transforms the backlanders into a tightly structured, paramilitary, ultra-Catholic religious cult that valiantly resists, in guerrilla fashion, the advances of the Brazilian army until it is finally decimated, leaving few survivors. The intensity of the novel's action and the symbolic progression toward apocalypse grow as the first small military expedition is repelled, replacements are added, and the military operations grow in size, only to be driven off again. Now a crusade, a third attempt led by Colonel Moreira César, a national military hero, is repulsed as well. Finally, several army divisions and modern armaments are mobilized from around the country to rout the rebels, leaving in their wake nothing but stories, legends, and myths about the war.

Artistically, the formation of the cult and the resistance it meets are the primary narrative generators for the many stories that make up the plot of the novel. Aesthetically, the reader experiences the novel's conflict through multiple viewpoints, many of which are based on known historical figures, ranging from army generals to common foot soldiers, from hardened criminals turned saints to visionary political anarchists; from journalists to aristocratic land-owners; from gypsy circus misfits like the Bearded Lady, the Midget, and Spider Man to rebellious Catholic priests who assist Antonio; and from rustic backland guides and common rural folk to cagey and sly city politicians. Just as *Conversation in The Cathedral* presents the whole social milieu of contemporary urban life in Peru, a complete social spectrum of nineteenth-century Brazil appears in *The War of the End of the World.*

## The Historical Setting

The historicity of Vargas Llosa's novel is based in part on Euclides da Cunha's classic work *Os sertões (Rebellion in the Backlands)* (1902). During the late 1970s, Vargas Llosa traveled to Brazil to conduct further research on the topic. His findings were astonishing.

Early on, the Canudos rebellion had acquired political overtones, and its spiritual leader was labeled a monarchist. Political factions began to distort the significance of the incident and to portray it as a danger to the nation. They claimed that the cult was an attempt to thwart republicanism, to restore the abolished monarchy of Don Pedro II, and to return to the primitive religion called Sebastianism. The situation had become exaggerated well beyond reality. The problem began to weigh heavily on the national conscience. But, as far as the rebellion was concerned, a visionary mystic had simply gone about gathering up the region's poor people for several years, and finally he had established a community that was going to form the last bastion of zealous Christian ideals. It was a nineteenth-century version of the New Jerusalem that religious anarchists had hoped would bring prosperity and justice to the world. But the new edicts of the republican government caused alarm, and António preached that the devil was roaming the earth, seeking to destroy everything and precipitating an apocalypse.

Brazilians had learned that Canudos was based on a primitive form of socialism; its inhabitants practiced free love yet fervently believed in God. Apparently, the cult would not recognize the new constitution, participate in a national census, adopt the concept of divorce, use the metric system, or accept money as a unit of exchange. Even the Conselheiro's promise to provide the basic necessities of life and to establish communal happiness for the impoverished backlanders began to worry the rich landowners of the region as their lands were seized and their goods plundered. The source from which Brazilians became aware generally—if only partially—of the aims of the Canudos enclave was mainly through the leading newspapers that were controlled by the country's political party interests. The politicians were determined to show how the cult was a political force that endangered the new republican movement.

The Canudos cult became a scapegoat for underhanded political machinations by the Bahían Progressive Republican party, which wanted to undermine the local conservatives who controlled state government. The liberals connived to show that the old-guard conservatives had purposely sought the aid of the English Crown in order to promote the rebellion and in that way to weaken the federal republican cause. Supposedly the rebels, like the local conservatives, were promonarchist.

Political machination and intrigue eventually led to genocide in Canudos. By early October 1897, the devastation, extreme hardships, and consequent demoralization of the army, on the one hand, and the total annihilation of the renegade spiritual cult, on the other, were complete.

## Plot and Structure

The novel begins with a legendary vision of Antonio, the future cult leader. Although he is seen only indirectly, he creates a biblical atmosphere of mystery, magic, and miracle. In this way, the tenor of the novel is set in the first few pages. The reader is told that this man, whom no one knew, possessed certain magnetic qualities that made people gravitate toward him. When he first appears, he is alone, a single silhouette covered with dust and walking the back roads of Brazil's northeastern desert. He does not remain alone for long, however, because by the time the army begins its fourth and final assault on Canudos thousands of people have congregated around Antonio. The pulsating movement of the novel flows outward from

Antonio's unseen but strongly felt presence, reaching a high pitch of emotional intensity as the stories of several characters' immediate and remote pasts become entwined with and engulfed by the armed hostilities.

In fact, the first few pages not only set the general tone of the novel, but also create the cumulative process of action becoming events, events becoming stories, stories turning into legends, and legends contributing to the creation of a mythology or a sense of cultural history. A mystic, Antonio composes his own prayers, and the backlanders memorize them. Wherever Antonio travels, the local inhabitants gather around and listen to him as he predicts the future. He seems to employ a strange and magical metaphoric language— in 1900 the lights will go out and it will rain stars—that leaves his listeners spellbound. The enigmatic use of religious and cultural archetypes, for example, requires Antonio's listeners "to animate their collective memory in order to remember the future." The transformation from act to cultural myth is complete by the end of the novel's first short segment: The skinny, purple-robed specter whose worldly name was Antonio Vicente Mendes Maciel becomes known as the *Consejero,* that is, the advisor, counselor, minister.

The narrative substance of the novel is distributed into four basic parts. Part 1 contains seven chapters, and each is divided into four segments. A pattern of interrelated episodes appears throughout most of the chapters and individual chapter segments. Apparent from the beginning is a measure of congruity and order in the segments of the chapters. The first and third segments of the chapters in the first part narrate similar material. These segments refer to Antonio Consejero, the historical period in question, and the first encounter between the rebels and the army. In addition, half of these segments present the past lives of the principal characters who gravitate toward Antonio's utopian community in Canudos. The stories of seven characters (one from each chapter)—some of whom are historical figures and all of whom provide the key to the organization and administration of the Canudos enclave in the novel— are narrated and told as flashbacks, relative to the novelistic present, in the other parallel segments. The stories center on the miraculous conversion to religious piety that each character undergoes.

Just as Antonio becomes the Consejero, the seven characters who turn out to be his closest followers and advisers also undergo name and role changes in Canudos. The spiritual young orphan Antônio

(not the Consejero) is denied the right to join the priesthood; instead
he becomes known as the Devout One and takes on administrative
duties at the growing Canudos complex. João Grande is a pampered
black slave who turns on his owner and butchers her; he joins the
Consejero's band, and later becomes Captain of the Catholic Guard
for the Consejero. María Quadrado becomes the Mother of Men,
but her sensational past is not revealed until much later in the novel.
João, the Devil, who has previously raped, plundered, and murdered
while roaming the backlands as a bandit becomes João Abade (the
Abbot) and forms part of the Canudos government structure. The
entrepreneur Antonio Vilanova has failed three times to become
successful in his business dealings; he interprets this as a sign from
God and joins the Consejero to become his logistical aide. Felicio,
later known as León de Natuba, is transformed from an unsightly
creature who walks on all fours into a person who miraculously
learns to read and write; he joins the growing entourage and becomes
the Consejero's scribe. Finally, Father Joaquim, once a corrupt Catholic priest, senses spiritual rebellion in his heart and serves as a
contact with the outside world for the Canudos group, bringing in
supplies, weapons, and news.

In contrast, the second and fourth segments of the seven chapters
of part 1 all converge upon the past and present life of one character:
Galileo Gall. Equally as mysterious and utopian-minded as the
Consejero, Gall is a composite figure created from mostly fictional
material. The only relationship Gall bears to reality is his last name,
but the narrator says even that is not his real name. Franz Joseph
Gall (1758–1828), however, was an actual person. He developed
the science of phrenology, which undertook to show how a person's
character and intelligence could be analyzed by studying the shape
and protuberances of the human skull. In the novel, the scientist
is a teacher of Galileo Gall's father. Galileo learns from an early age
that revolution will free society from its calamities and science will
free the individual from his or her problems. He dedicates his life
to the pursuit of these ends.

Galileo Gall is a man driven by ideas—a freedom fighter, anarchist, and phrenologist. His past is told as a succession of escapes
from different jails for allegedly setting fire to a church in France,
for participating in the 1871 French revolution, and for attacking
an army post in Spain. After adopting the name Galileo Gall he
writes political articles for a French journal; he describes his adven-

tures in Brazil, where he fled after being wounded in Spain. In Bahia (Brazil) he preaches that all human virtues are compatible if one makes reason, not faith, the nucleus of his or her life; Satan, not God, is the true rebel, the real prince of freedom. Yet his presence in the novel is not incongruous with its story. Obsessed by what he has read about Canudos, he sets out for the community. In part 3 he innocently gets caught up in political intrigue during his journey and dies needlessly in a fight with the revenge-seeking Rufino, a backlander trail guide whose wife had been raped earlier by Gall.

Structurally, part 1 is extremely important for the development of the underlying themes of the novel. The first and third segments (the religious world of Canudos, the evangelical nature of sinners turned saints) in each chapter are intercalated with the second and fourth segments (the wild scientific and political ideas of Gall) to create a strong reaction in the reader. The two ideological stances are juxtaposed in such a way that each is altered, enlarged, and corrupted through its structural meshing with a religious stance, as the reader switches back and forth between segments. The religious segments are presented in the past tense, and the political-scientific segments in the present. Gall's story in the present actualizes the past events surrounding the religious nature of the Canudos group. The use of structural parallels is a narrative strategy that Vargas Llosa relies on heavily in the novel. In this way, divergent points of view are contrasted, highlighted, or destroyed so that, by the end of the novel, several principal characters will have embodied a different form of what Vargas Llosa considers a basic frailty of man: the ignorant surrender to dogma (Vargas Llosa speaks of Camus's "horror of dogma"). Vargas Llosa condemns humanity for delivering itself over to flagrant fanaticism—be it religious, political, or cultural—which suffocates the moderating voice of tolerance and prudence.

The structure of part 2 is unlike the others. Its three short unsegmented chapters are, however, significant for the development of the plot. First, the reader is given a closer look at another character who appears only briefly in the segments dealing with Galileo Gall in the first part: the young, anonymous, scarecrow-like newspaper journalist who wears thick glasses and always sneezes. He is an amusing yet pitiful human figure who accompanies the army to Canudos, writing articles about the campaign along the way. Second, the political situation of the period in question is outlined in this part. In all three chapters, the journalist is seen writing, reading, and, commenting on an article for the republican newspaper, an article in which the Liberals accuse the Conservatives of conspiring with the English to arm Canudos in order to restore the old monarchy. At the time that the myopic journalist writes this article, two expeditions have already been turned back by the Canudos enclave. The chronicle explains that the Bahian population, fearing a threat to peace in the region, has requested the assistance of Brazil's greatest military hero, Colonel Moreira César, to lead the national army into battle against Canudos. Proof of the alliance between the promonarchists and the English lies in the alleged discovery of Gall's body. Gall had been duped into taking a shipment of arms to Canudos, but for the liberals, who were really arming Canudos. A corpse is produced, but only a few locks of Gall's red hair are exhibited as actual evidence of his participation in the gunrunning scheme. Actually, he does not die until later and of another cause. The political duplicity involved in all this makes itself apparent as the novel progresses, leaving little sympathy for the political process of the times.

Humor and irony provide Vargas Llosa with a critical stance vis à vis the hypocritical nature of politics. The last chapter of part 2 presents a dialogue between the myopic journalist and Epaminondas Gonçalves, the newspaper's director and head of the Liberal party. As in *Captain Pantoja and the Special Service,* Vargas Llosa has transcribed mimetically the vocabulary, the phraseology, and the tone of a typical political newspaper article. By means of the mimetical exactness of the piece, the chapter satirizes the politics of yellow journalism and condemns its corruption.

A third aspect of part 2 provides the infrastructure for the presence of the myopic journalist from that point forward in the novel. He represents a fictional parallel to the historical biography of Euclides da Cunha, the intellectual who wrote about the Canudos incident in *Rebellion in the Backlands.* This book, composed of both rigorous eyewitness documentation and a visionary regional nostalgia, has been lauded for its rich description of the backlands and for the author's attempt, as a journalist, to present what he experienced, and, as an intellectual, to analyze what he felt had caused the gruesome incident.

In the novel the unassuming journalist is a fictional creation whose presence serves to highlight not the historical person but the situation da Cunha faced as an intellectual and as a writer in the midst of political turmoil and human chaos. Vargas Llosa is fascinated by the process in which an intellectual's convictions or ideological perspective on reality can be suddenly altered or even destroyed by the volatile nature of the situation, which, in turn, requires him or her to assume a previously untenable position. To that point in the novel the journalist's indirect involvement in the whole affair has piqued his curiosity, and he requests permission to travel with the military hero to Canudos. The myopic journalist possesses a secret desire to discover what it is that makes a hero—a myth, actually— of an individual. He says he does not really admire the army colonel, but he is curious about something: "To see a hero in the flesh, to be close to someone so famous is very tempting. It's like seeing or touching a character in a novel" (140). The myopic journalist establishes himself from the beginning as an indirect voice for the author's views on the relationship between appearance and reality. Vargas Llosa has always maintained the belief that art and life are indistinguishable. By the end of the campaign, the journalist's ideas about life have changed drastically. After the war ends, the journalist declares that the incident changed his ideas about history, about Brazil, about mankind, and above all about himself.

Each of the seven chapters of part 3 contains five segments. New plot lines are added. Basically the first segment of each chapter describes the advances of Moreira César's army on Canudos. From the beginning the colonel is depicted as a mythical figure, despite his small, frail stature. The second segment develops around another group of characters: the members of a traveling circus, including the Midget, the Idiot, the Frog Eater, and others. Meanwhile Gall, who has barely escaped with his life after an ambush by bandits looking for the arms he was supposed to deliver to Canudos, rapes his guide's wife, Jurema, in a scene of violence and lust. Then Gall decides to continue his journey toward Canudos alone. Jurema follows him, knowing that her husband, Rufino, will hunt them down like animals to avenge his loss of honor. On the way, Gall and Jurema join the circus group. She reveals her past, announcing that she had been a maid for the wife of the Barón de Cañabrava before she married Rufino. The Barón's point of view is developed throughout the fifth or last narrative segment of each chapter. As in Vargas

176 MARIO VARGAS LLOSA

Llosa's other novels, the intricate relationships between dozens of characters create a complex mosaic of intrigue and suspense.

The Midget is the one circus character who becomes important for the development of the rest of the novel. The other circus freaks simply drop out of sight. The Midget turns out to be an archetypal miniature bard or storyteller. The magical nature of his art and the spells cast over his listeners by his stories of legendary figures eventually save him and others from death.

The third segment of each chapter develops further the stories and activities of the people in Canudos. The fourth segment presents Rufino's point of view as he sets out to seek revenge for his loss of honor. The marriage vows that Rufino and Jurema made to the Virgin and to the Barón, who gave them permission to marry, have been broken. In order to avenge his honor, the backlander's code of ethics requires that the avenger place his hand over or slap the culprit's face; in the case of his wife, he could kill her. The problem of seeking revenge in compliance with a simple code of honor becomes ironically insignificant on a personal level as Rufino's story develops in the midst of an explosive tragedy. Nevertheless, a sense of anticipation builds as the reader wonders if Rufino will catch up with Gall and Jurema before they reach Canudos.

In the fifth and final segment of each chapter of the third part the rich landowner and conservative politician from Bahia, Barón de Cañabrava, returns from his travels abroad to learn of the accusations of conspiracy against his political party. The Barón's concern for his personal losses (the religious sect occupies a large portion of his landholdings and demands supplies from him), the dogmatic nature of the liberals, and the destructive nature of the war are clarified, in part 4, via a long conversation with the myopic journalist after the war. By this point in the novel, however, the chaotic nature of the events and the structural intricacies of the plot symbolize the distortion of reality: unclear motives, personal misconceptions, and imposing dogmatic positions.

The clash of differing points of view about the nature of the truth of the events in Canudos only leads to greater chaos. A conservative party member tells the Barón that "there are no facts, only incredible fantasies and intrigue" (164). The religious fanatics in Canudos, for example, see the new republican government as the devil; likewise, the republican army sees Canudos as the work of Satan. As it turns out, misconceptions about the ideas of the new republican govern-

ment cause the cult members to rebel, while the army fights simply
to avenge the earlier deaths of fellow soldiers. The Barón is viewed
as a courteous, level-headed, calm, and intelligent person; and, at
several points in the novel, he emits judgments that seem to parallel
Vargas Llosa's own viewpoints on reality. The Barón sums up a
general feeling when he says that "the times are confusing" (185).
From all this misunderstanding and confusion emanating from the
arbitrary nature of each individual's value system, the reader garners
a sense of the hatred and contempt that some characters have for
others. When some innocent civilians are ruthlessly executed by the
army, the journalist asks himself if their actions do not mirror the
same violence that the backland bandits have inflicted on innocent
bystanders. The journalist begins to doubt what he has seen and
heard. He cannot be sure of anything, and the truth becomes impossible to discover. The personal parameters of each character's
viewpoint invariably lead to an exclusive point of view, in opposition
to other points of view, but no one character—neither the Consejero,
Colonel Moreira César, Galileo Gall, Rufino, the Barón, nor the
journalist—is presented in completely negative or positive terms;
they are not seen as defending any one utterly bad or completely
worthwhile position.

By the end of part 3 the action, like the numerous characters'
lives, has reached different levels of involvement and conflict. Some
relationships end, characters even disappear, and new relationships
are created. Rufino finally catches up with Gall, and they kill each
other like mad dogs. The legendary hero Moreira César dies in a
heroic battle charge, but the third attempt to wipe out Canudos
fails. At center stage by this time is the curious alliance of three
characters who finally scurry away to survive, Jurema, the Midget,
and the myopic journalist. Each one finds security in the other two.
Jurema is alone now without a husband to protect her; the Midget
has lost his circus friends along the way; and shortly before they all
meet the journalist is rendered blind and helpless when he sneezes
and his glasses fall and shatter. The last thing he sees is the severed
head of Moreira César, who dies when the Canudos guerrillas overrun
the army positions.

Beyond the fascinating complexity of the action, achieved with
less structural rigor than *Conversation in The Cathedral* but still difficult to summarize, the multilayered significance of the author's
views regarding Canudos and its implications for any era become

increasingly apparent. The problem of verifying the truth about what happens, let alone why it happens, occupies the observations and thoughts of several characters. As the novel moves into part 4, however, it becomes evident that the myopic journalist and the Barón—rather than protagonists like Gall, Moreira César, and the Consejero, all of whom die in the novel—present coinciding views that the reader will associate with the overall philosophical position or ideological stance that Mario Vargas Llosa has clarified for himself since reaching a new level of maturity in the early 1970s.

Part 4 is composed of six chapters, each containing four separate narrative segments. The first segment of each chapter presents a long conversation betweeen the myopic journalist and the Barón in Salvador, after the war has finally ended. The journalist, Jurema (who lives with him), and the Midget escaped from Canudos shortly before it was overrun by military forces and burned to the ground. Back on the coast, the journalist goes to seek employment with the Barón's conservative newspaper so that he can pay for the treatment of the Midget's tuberculosis. The journalist owes his life to the Midget, who was able to tell stories in Canudos and thereby keep the desperate, potentially violent men like João Abade at bay. The conversation between the two men takes on decidedly philosophical implications with respect to the significance of Canudos. Both begin to see Canudos more as a history of misunderstandings than as a history of lunacy. The journalist has decided not to let the incident that occurred in Canudos be forgotten, thus creating possible future misunderstandings about its significance. When the Baron asks him how he will achieve this, the journalist responds that the only way to conserve things is to write about them. Ironically, the journalist had broken his glasses before entering Canudos and never witnessed the bellicose events; therefore, his future book will necessarily be a mixture of appearance and reality, of fact and fiction. The irony becomes even stronger when one realizes that Vargas Llosa's position as a writer about the Canudos incident is exactly the same as the myopic journalist. It is important to realize, however, that Vargas Llosa is completely aware of his tenuous situation as a writer, which indicates to the reader that the mixture of fantasy and reality is not an end in itself but merely a means for communicating an idea or profound belief about the nature of the historical incident.

The conversation becomes even more philosophically complex as the two men discuss life, fate, good and evil, fanaticism, the value of history, and the importance of love and understanding as an antidote to humanity's problems. After the journalist leaves, the Barón contemplates his present situation: he thinks about his wife, who has lost her mind because of the losses they have suffered; and he decides to break a long period of sexual abstinence caused by his wife's sickness and to make love to her servant while his wife looks on. This scene is juxtaposed with a gory battle scene of violence during the fourth assault on Canudos (in another segment), just as Gall's sexual abstinence is broken with Jurema immediately after they have been violently attacked by thieves looking for arms.

Segments two, three, and four are concerned with the last assault on Canudos by the army. Each segment deals with a different character, but the focus remains the same. The longest battle scenes of the novel appear in the second chapter of this part. They are re-created with a strong penchant for detail, and yet they are presented from a comprehensive perspective that involves the movement of hundreds of soldiers and the hidden presence of the innumerable guerrilla forces from Canudos. The individual stories relate the events and the thoughts of different characters. The power of love and understanding becomes the central concern of the new relationship between João Abade and his companion, Catarina. João Grande contemplates the Consejero's philosophy as the group makes last-minute preparations for the final battle. Antônio Vilanova considers the fate of Canudos, finding consolation in his people, who always manage to reach beyond the limits of reality to find either a miracle or death. He is called to the Consejero's deathbed and is appointed the leader's successor. In another segment the scribe León de Natuba pronounces the death of the Consejero. Near the end, the Midget's storytelling charm is conveyed. João Abade, however, demands that the Midget explain the moral significance of the French legend about Robert the Devil, who was converted to a saint—a legend that parallels his life. The Midget explains that it is his job only to tell the story, and not to ascribe to it moral interpretation. Basically, the third segment narrates the efforts of the threesome to escape from Canudos. The Midget, Jurema, and the journalist protect each other; and their mutual understanding reaches a profound level of intimacy as the girl and the journalist make love in Canudos while the Midget looks on.

The fourth series of segments captures the battle from the point of view of the armed forces. A lieutenant who led the first expedition against Canudos (depicted in the first part of the novel) is now wounded grotesquely and pleads for someone to put an end to his misery; in another scene, an army sergeant asks himself why he is fighting, only to meet his death in ironic fashion when another soldier seeks revenge upon the sergeant who had been sexually abusing his wife back home; and in still another scene, an army medical student documents the human destruction and the severe nature of the casualties. Upon entering Canudos an army general asks himself what the whole affair really means; a foot soldier accidentally captures one of the Consejero's converted bandits, Pajeu, who dies laughing at an army colonel, after which the cadaver is morbidly destroyed.

The last scene, and final segment of the novel, focuses on the confrontation between the southern and northern regional armies of Brazil that overrun Canudos. In the final scene the reader comes face to face with the differences and the hatred that run deep among the regional forces. The local Bahian volunteer police force (from the north) is led by a bounty hunter who is mentioned throughout the novel, rising from lieutenant in the opening pages, then to captain, and finally to colonel. The southern forces are portrayed not as true soldiers of a disciplined army but rather as a group of violent gaucho bandits who are known for their habit of slitting their captives' throats. The colonel slaps the face of an officer of the southern forces and then urinates on him for having ridiculed his men. The rivalry between them makes a profound statement about the future of Brazil after the 1897 Canudos war. The significance of this scene is important for an interpretation of Vargas Llosa's views on history. He seems to be saying that twentieth-century Brazilian history has been determined by the destructive effects of false regional pride and regional honor, which have mitigated against the creation of cohesive human values and the cultivation of solidarity among all men and women—be they regional Brazilians, national Brazilians, or going beyond their national confines, Latin Americans.

The novel ends, finally, when an old woman explains to the bounty-hunter colonel, who has roamed far and wide over many years in search of João "Satan"/Abade, that she saw some archangels take him to heaven. Her statement, which closes the novel, opens the door to the miracles, legends, and cultural myths that will provide the most significant type of historical interpretation of events for future generations. Again, Vargas Llosa seems to be saying that most of what is known about what actually happened in Canudos and why it occurred is based not on factual data and scientific research but on an interpretation of reality that falls into the realm of fantasy. Factual history is reduced to a schematic and predictive realm of knowledge; beyond this, the reader of *The War of the End of the World* is presented with other equally significant determinants such as stories and legends, not to mention the press, which, for Vargas Llosa, are ambiguous but far more influential than factual documentation in the making of history.

## Form and Meaning

*The War of the End of the World* is an aesthetically diverse novel. First, it is a modern epic. Second, it is a monumental work of art that re-creates the inner mechanisms of the way history is made, communicated, and understood. The story is told from intriguing perspectives, creating a special view of reality. At first glance the novel appears to be little more than a reworking of the da Cunha text; furthermore, its narrative mode is much more conventional than that of previous works. Yet the third-person omniscient point of view, which provides a special backdrop to the multiple character perspectives, and the seemingly transparent narrative style attest once again to Vargas Llosa's struggle to find a functional narrative format that gives significance to the novel's content. Finally, *The War of the End of the World* makes a profound statement with regard to Mario Vargas Llosa's now mature personal outlook on life.

All these aspects converge in the novel as it brings into question the nature of the artist's ability and indeed his obligation to invent stories or to remake both lived and imagined experiences in order to create an ambiguous yet seemingly true human experience. The problem of writing fiction about historical events is complex. It is important to note that the historical elements in this novel, when compared to its fictional content, do not assume the major role they take in the traditional historical novel. The fictional re-creation of characters about whom little is actually known, on the one hand, and the overriding significance that Vargas Llosa gives to the structure of the novel, on the other, plays a far greater role than do the historical events included in the novel.

The Consejero's rapid transformation into a person with the stature and power of Jesus Christ is complete by the end of the novel.

Vargas Llosa indicates this metamorphosis in subtle ways; for example, in the first part of the novel the Consejero's followers, upon hearing one of his sermons, cross themselves and say, "Alabado sea Nuestro Señor Jesucristo" (Jesus Christ be praised). By the end of the novel his followers are saying, "Alabado sea el Buen Jesus Consejero" (Jesus Christ the minister be praised). The fusion of Antonio the mortal and the mysterious presence of the son of God has taken place through the power and substitution of words. Actually, it is important to point out here that words take on magical qualities. They become highly "poetic" and are understood as particular kinds of signs. Since words express a common power or energy, verbal expression casts spells over the people. Powerful words control the way human beings think and they become the very focus of mental activity.

An oral teacher, Antonio uses electrifying prose that is accepted and pondered by his followers. His aphorisms are cosmologically oriented, and yet they remain very physical in nature. Concepts of soul, time, courage, and emotion are imbued with emotionally charged physical imagery. The relationship between man and nature becomes highly metaphoric. But this process is not presented directly through what the Consejero says in the text (except in isolated instances) but is communicated implicitly through Vargas Llosa's prose style. The Consejero's presence comes alive through Vargas Llosa's creation of the magical quality and dynamic forces of verbal elements. Vargas Llosa creates this effect in the first few pages of the novel; his use of the imperfect past tense in Spanish places the reader in a trance; and he sprinkles exotic-sounding, yet actual Brazilian Portuguese words throughout the Spanish text. The words sound mysterious and connote magical qualities. The words seem to expand in time, giving the language a millennial status and mythic power. In addition, the process of simply naming things, places, and people takes on a special significance. The names of the places that the Consejero visits throughout his travels—Toucano, Soure, Amparo, Cumbe, Natuba, Mocambo—are cited, and the strange nature of the words themselves communicates a kind of enchantment that metaphorically envelops the story, transcending its regional nature and suggesting a completely religious, miraculous, and Holy Land ambience. In fact, the prose style generally has a notable tendency toward the process of naming things by the repeated use of parts of speech in series of three or four elements.

As such, the prose seems more complete, harmonious, unified, and indivisible: it is simple and transparent; it does not call attention to itself, but reaches out to the world beyond language. Vargas Llosa's style captures the multiplicity of experience, and distance is controlled without losing contact with the world that the novel's language describes. As a result, Vargas Llosa's prose clearly communicates a feeling of strength and assurance, all of which endows the omniscient narrator with a kind of wisdom and an oracular vision. For these reasons, Vargas Llosa's prose calls to mind a sense of moral goodness. It represents a kind of literary morality, and in this way its form closely follows its function in the novel.

In fact, the relationship between *The War of the End of the World* and da Cunha's book, which is itself a curious mixture of fact and interpretation, makes possible a greater transformation from history to fiction. The relationship between the two texts, however, is best understood in terms of their place within the cultural and intellectual history of Latin America. Uruguayan critic Angel Rama (1982) sees strong philosophical ties among Domingo F. Sarmiento's *Facundo* (1845), da Cunha's *Rebellion in the Backlands* (1902), and Vargas Llosa's novel (625–26). Just as the latter is a recent reworking of certain historical and philosophical elements of da Cunha's book, written eighty years earlier, da Cunha's book is an interpretation of a historical event based on an intricate intertextual relationship with the Sarmiento text. Sarmiento, da Cunha, and Vargas Llosa are captivated by the enigmatic nature of the human being caught historically between the opposing forces of change and permanence. Sarmiento discovered a contradictory irrational behavior among the gauchos and caudillos (regional political bosses) in Argentina after Independence (once the conflicting emancipatory forces of the revolutionary colonists and the reactionary colonizers had been destroyed). Rama states that da Cunha also discovered this new heterogeneous force of popular dissidence in society once the modernizing and positivistic republicans had replaced the monarchists in Brazil. Finally, Vargas Llosa modernizes this theme by making the Canudos incident a paradigm of the long succession of revolutionary and counterrevolutionary movements that have characterized twentieth-century Latin America. Therefore, Vargas Llosa's novel might be interpreted as pointing to the continual failure of popular movements to provoke social changes. Yet the deep significance of *The War of the End of the World* brings the reader face to face with the baser struggles of men and women that take place not in society but in the more private human arenas.

Externally, the novel is organized around the basic historical conflict between the spiritual converts at Canudos and the modern republican army of Brazil. As a spin-off, this opposition immediately throws light on the differences that exist between the northern region of the country (poor, backward, rural, and superstitious) and the southern parts of Brazil (modern, urban, liberal, and progressive). This basic conflict is reduced in scope and at the same time intensified by focusing on the regional confrontation between local pro-monarchist conservatives and the Liberal Progressive party. In Vargas Llosa's novel, both ideologies converge in the defense of the same regional economic interests, indicating their mutual defense of the status quo. Different ideological stances are played off against one another through the different characters. The different perspectives include Gall's anarchism and pseudoscientific beliefs; Moreira César's military utopianism; the republican party's progressive positivism; the myopic journalist's free-thinking intellectualism; Rufino's rural, folk traditions of ironclad honor codes; the Barón's mediating, gentlemanly pragmatism; and, of course, the Consejero's evangelical prophecies. The structural fragmentation of the episodes pits the differing perspectives against each other, and the effect neutralizes some, destroys others, and strengthens still others. The fanatical position held by the legendary colonel is symbolically destroyed when he dies in the novel; in his place, the bounty-hunter leader of the Bahia volunteer police force rises to the rank of colonel. The significance of the roles that the two colonels play in the novel is interpreted in historical terms. Vargas Llosa probably feels that there is little possibility that in the future the countries of Latin America will move toward any global concept of nationalism, and beyond nationalism to some form of hemispheric unity, but only regress into a splintered society composed of stifling regional differences, hatred, and degeneration.

In similar fashion, Gall's dedication to social change through anarchism and pseudoscientific beliefs is thwarted by his death at the hands of another fanatically driven man, Rufino, who in turn must conform to the rural backlander's honor code. In other words, ideas that are alien to the reality of the situation will not survive. Although the Consejero dies near the end of the novel, the evangelical process of miraculous metamorphosis of his people from sinners to saints will live on, as the old woman says in the novel's last line that she has seen João Abade go to heaven. The reader is left with the thoughts and ideas of two of the principal characters who do survive the historical moment: the journalist and the Barón. Their points of view strengthen each other and go beyond the immediate circumstances to find new meaning for their own lives and, by extension, for all mankind.

This interpretive dimension of *The War of the End of the World* becomes especially clear once certain distinctions are made between the concepts of the medieval romance and the modern realistic novel. Whereas the latter focuses on the representational qualities of reality, the former is concerned with the fabular or antirepresentational nature of reality. Robert Scholes (1979) claims that the fabular approach allows the creative writer to move "from the base of specific events toward some satisfying artistic shape and some universal aspect of the human situation. He seeks to make a myth" (201). The fabular aspect of early romance narrative, as well as its referential tie to actual history, provide ample room for the interpolation of fact and fantasy. Vargas Llosa has not necessarily distorted history nor eliminated its meaning; rather, he has retrieved a part of the process that gives shape not only to historical events but, more importantly, to culture. Although it may seem as though Vargas Llosa has achieved a harmonious balance between empirical and fictional writing, he situates the novel within the realm of romance and even allegory. For one thing, medieval romances employ multiple narrators, dislocations of time, and tales within tales. Early in his writing career, Vargas Llosa relied heavily on these narrative elements. The critic Frank Dauster deals with the relationship between these earlier works and the romance of chivalry in which multiple levels of reality create the "total" novel. Beyond this, Vargas Llosa's latest novel even contains all the spectacular elements found in the romances, such as battles, rituals, magic, and celebrations. Of greater significance is the fact that although *The War of the End of the World* utilizes several narrative techniques that Vargas Llosa had perfected as far back as *The Green House,* this historical novel does communicate a much greater sense of purpose in its use of a fabular approach to writing.

By linking Vargas Llosa's novel to certain narrative strategies of the romance, the reader gains a perspective vastly different from that of the modern novel: the panoramic perspective of reality for the romancer dominates the modern novel's use of minute detail; action dominates character development; causality of events and a sense of coherence are lacking; the plot is composed of astonishing events that possess symbolic undertones, making myth and allegory more important; the presence of an omniscient narrator who creates a background of mystery and wonder dominates the characters' diverse points of view; experience for the romancer can never be directly known or fully understood; and life fluctuates among extremes or opposites. Beyond these visions of reality, modes of characterization, points of view, and setting, lies the central concern of the early and now modern-day romancers: the role of the artist as discoverer of truth. The truth of the romancer is not derived from the purely intellectual realm of scientifically observable and verifiable human experience but from its totally opposite realm, that is, the world of inspiration and even mystical and visionary experience. Like the romancer, Vargas Llosa seeks to behold something inherent or innate in humanity that is never exteriorized in reality. He seeks to communicate a profound truth that will possess moral significance for the novel's readers. Long ago, Vargas Llosa discovered that the romancer does not shun reality or truth by incorporating into his work unusual circumstances, eccentric points of view, or fantastic landscapes; rather, he creates a fictional reality in which individual peculiarities and a fascination with the sensational and even bizarre acts in life play an equally important role. Northrop Frye (1976) views the romance as purely sensational violent stimuli, at the heart of which is the love story. In addition, the numerous and exciting adventures that are narrated throughout the work prepare the reader for some type of sexual union. Moreover, Frye adds, the romance even seems bent on encouraging irregular or excessive sexual behavior (152). In similar fashion, Vargas Llosa's novel culminates on a symbolic level that brings love and adventure dangerously close to pornography and bloodlust. The interpolation of segments dealing with love, on the one hand, and the fury of the war, on the other, bring sexuality and violence together. The symbolic import of two parallel scenes, groups of characters, and actions brings the thematic significance of Vargas Llosa's novel into focus. At one point in *The War of the End of the World* the three pitiful characters Jurema, the Midget, and the journalist huddle together, wondering if they will leave Canudos alive; Jurema and the journalist make love while the Midget looks on. The other scene involves the Barón, who makes love to his wife's servant while she consentingly observes the sexual act. Like the romancer, Vargas Llosa is reaching into the farthest depths of human nature to tap the unconscious and to bring to the surface certain dark yet vital impulses that represent uncontrollable human forces. Although these drives may be seen as a part of humanity's evil side, they are intimately connected to the hidden workings of such basic impulses as love and hate. These love relationships serve to provide new perspectives on life for the journalist and the Barón. According to Frye, the romance involves the reader in the Eros theme, whereby the lover is driven by his or her love to ascend to a higher world, to self-recognition (152). The Barón, for example, wakes up the next day to birdsong and the hushed murmur of the sea nearby. From a window overlooking the city of Salvador, the Barón feels sensations of tenderness, melancholy, and gratitude as he contemplates the "majestic spectacle" of color, beauty, harmony, and understanding. Peace, it seems, has returned.

Following the romance tradition, Vargas Llosa's novel creates a struggle between rationalism and irrationalism, with the latter gaining the upper hand as a response to man's problems. The stance taken in the novel forms the basis not only for Vargas Llosa's interpretation of the historical moment but also for his views on reality, the problems humanity faces today, and the possible solutions. One might ask if Vargas Llosa is signaling the need for the triumph of irrationalism over rationalism, in which a profound comprehension of love and its mediating powers counters the destructiveness to which apparently rational but overtly fanatic ideologies seem to lead man. The irrational impulses of the body are deemed good, while forms of rational thought that lead to ideological fanaticism are considered evil.

Although this interpretation may seem plausible enough, a touch of irony is added to the scene in which the Barón finds himself at peace with the world. Suddenly, he becomes uneasy when he sees through binoculars a group of fishing boats in the distance, from which people are dropping wreaths and flowers into the bay while they cross themselves and—he imagines—sing. The fact is that the people in the boats are performing a funeral rite. After the Consejero's body has been exhumed and decapitated, his head is sent to the coast where scientists attempt to determine the constitution of its evil; it is then dumped into a sack and tossed into the ocean. The Consejero thus becomes an important cultural myth, a symbol of rebellion for the masses. At another point in the novel, when Canudos is being destroyed, Antônio Vilanova ponders the hopes and dreams of the downtrodden who "come to mind in moments like these, when a limit or an extreme beyond which only miracles or death is possible" (443). The novel seems to tell the reader that certain religious phenomena might be more important than historical influences in determining human conduct. The truth of Canudos is found less in its historical documentation than in the myths, speculation, and superstitions that still live today.

The historicity of the Canudos war not only sums up the visible presence of diverse types of thinking in the world at the turn of the century, stretching from the progress of civilization to utopian primitivism, but also a period of crisis for the Peruvian novelist. He tells Ana María Moix that "I discovered the history of Canudos about the time of the Padilla case, which represented for me a period of political and ideological crisis, and many beliefs I had crumbled and I began to doubt many things that I had firmly believed. To discover in that moment an historical event of these characteristics which flagrantly showed the degree to which everything becomes deformed when one submits life to an ideological vision was very illuminating and decisive, and it imposed itself on me as a theme to write about" (Moix 1981, 12).

At bottom, Vargas Llosa's perspective on contemporary man parallels the romancer's sense of the profound and unfathomable discrepancy between appearance and reality. Mario Vargas Llosa has given a romantic vision to *The War of the End of the World,* stating an overpowering truth that he feels must be told within the romance tradition. On the one hand, Vargas Llosa continues to support Albert Camus's thesis that man's problems began when it became permissible to kill in the name of an idea, when certain abstract concepts become more important than human life; on the other hand, Vargas Llosa also maintains that man's problems are less the fault of his institutions than of himself. Vargas Llosa's earlier works seem to express the idea that some form of external revolution is necessary to combat injustice and human suffering and to eliminate or change existing social, political, and religious institutions. *The War of the End of the World* presents the view that both the origin of evil and the possibility of reform are the moral responsibility of man himself. Wars and revolution are merely outward signs of man's moral disarray and internal conflict; hence, successful political reform becomes possible only when man finds it within himself to alter the course of things, that is, by substituting love for hate. *The War of the End of the World* is not pure allegory. Yet the reader is faced with an immense and complexly organized world that seeks to communicate profound truths about the nature of man, the drive toward moral goodness, and the need to impose moderating limits on all human activity.

## Chapter Eleven
# Conclusion

After initiating his writing career at a young age in the early 1950s, Mario Vargas Llosa has become an internationally known and mature writer. His impressive literary corpus includes short stories, novels, plays, literary criticism, and journalistic work. Each endeavor represents a major undertaking for Vargas Llosa, and hardly any single literary work stands out as more important than any other. In each one, the author struggles to capture the complexity inherent in diverse personal, social, and historical worlds. To be sure, much commentary has been generated about the technical virtuosity that Vargas Llosa tenaciously displays in each work. Together, these texts share common characteristics that not only define Vargas Llosa's narrative styles, but also substantiate the fact that he has been engaged over the past thirty years in formulating a literary-philosophical credo in an effort to reach an understanding of the nature of life and, above all, of the role that art—and, specifically, literature—plays in revealing life's "hidden truths," that is, the invisible and secret motives that propel human beings through life.

The structural complexities that make his novels a challenge to read but richly reward their readers with engaging stories exemplify Vargas Llosa's view on life; for him it is violent, chaotic, complex, absurd, and undefinable. The seemingly innumerable conflicts that give rise to his convoluted plots stem from multiple colliding perspectives of several and, at times, dozens of characters who are guided by an intense set of complicated and destructive criteria, ranging from subtle to excessive behavior, from memories to dreams, and from desires to emotions and impulses. Although satisfactory answers are never forthcoming, Vargas Llosa's narratives do pose a basic question: how is life to be interpreted (by art) so that it becomes at least slightly more meaningful? Although the task may be too great for one person, Vargas Llosa's unflinching commitment to writing is, in itself, proof that reading about the complexities of life in a novel, seeing them in a play, or viewing them in a movie are valid activities like artistic creation itself, through which life's perplexing, multifaceted nature is, if not fully understood, at least seen in new perspectives. As a result, a moderating stance toward life is created that provides an alternative to the violent extremes toward which humanity is always strongly attracted.

For Vargas Llosa, the creative act involves an implicit protest of one's undesirable position in life and provides a way to ridicule it, making the less interesting parts of life more bearable. Vargas Llosa believes that art cannot be expected to provide much more, and on this point he is adamant. When literature exceeds its limits and becomes an instrument for the propagation of religious, ideological, historical, or moral truths, it creates a superficial, distorted, and untruthful view of reality. Instead, its mission is to focus on the more obscure and irrational side of man; in this way, the writer's creativeness works not to mimic life as he or she knows it but to present it as one would or would not like it to be.

In order to give focus effectively to the complex relationship between reality and fantasy and thereby lend strength to his literary-philosophical credo, Vargas Llosa has rebelled against all ideas that require literature to become something more than a means of discovering the multiplicity of conflicting perspectives that are created in all societies. One of the less obvious but decidedly profound aspects of Vargas Llosa's narrative production throughout his career—the creation of a significant statement about the nature of life and writing—points toward this continuing rebellion against the role that dogmatic concepts of institutionalized thought unjustifiably demand of literature. Most noteworthy, Vargas Llosa's works are imbued with a metaliterary quality that tends to separate literature from the realm of the real world, placing it totally within the world of imagination. This self-referential phenomenon of literature, which looks at itself in highly structured ways in Vargas Llosa's works, subverts any attempt to place fiction on an equal footing with reality; instead, when the intertextual reference of a work is literature itself, the feeling is created that "the world is a stage."

Language is a principal ingredient in the process; it is the instrument through which Vargas Llosa besieges and tests the creative act and gives language a specific purpose in each of his works. As a matter of fact, it is possible to discern a significant progression of inventive language from *The Time of the Hero* through *The War of the End of the World* that portrays and puts to the test the different ways in which language is used to achieve specific ends. In *The Time of the Hero,* Alberto, alias Poet, writes gushy love letters and pornographic stories for his classmates in return for money or small favors; although he finds the creative act a gratifying experience, it is made to seem spurious and unreal because he does not write from experience. Here, language is attractive, tantalizing, and prohibitive, but it is also unreal (nor is it explicitly presented in the text). In *Conversation in The Cathedral,* the scatological tone of the novel highlights the feeling of revenge that motivates the rebellious Santiago to write vulgar newspaper articles as he seeks to make the act of writing a way to subvert his mediocre life and to destroy it in the process.

The humorous language in *Captain Pantoja and the Special Service,* created by the protagonist who writes military documents, is a direct result of Vargas Llosa's demonstration that institutions stultify and freeze language, making it utterly absurd and robbing it of essential meaning. In *Aunt Julia and the Scriptwriter* the metaliterary theme reaches fruition. Here Vargas Llosa writes from personal experience about the period when he began to write fiction and met a soap-opera scriptwriter who went crazy. The language is humorous because, within the context of the narrative situations, it is purposely simple, tasteless, affected, and vulgar. The effect, however, is important; the comic nature of the narration immediately distances Vargas Llosa from the biographical events of the period and, while he pokes fun at himself, he is in a better position to comprehend the significance of the period in a much clearer and more objective way. In his plays, Vargas Llosa creates two more characters—Belisario in *La señorita de Tacna* and Santiago in *Kathie y el hipopótamo*—who portray his growing metaliterary concerns; here, the characters question the nature and meaning of the creative act. Styles that contrast clichéd romantic vulgarisms and deeper symbolic references in the first play serve to advance the idea that Belisario is trying to write a story based on personal experience, which, forgotten or never fully understood, leads to doubt and opens the door to fantasy. In the second play, Santiago rewrites another person's unfulfilled dreams and, in the process, distorts and exaggerates desire with fantasy. Here, language is wildly absurd, totally funny, and pathetically sad because, in part, of its almost wholly euphemistic quality.

Finally, in *The War of the End of the World,* three different positions toward language are discernible, all of which point to an equally serious side of language in the creation of reality: (1) the myopic journalist writes to discover heretofore unknown realities—be they historical, national, regional, or personal—and strives to discover the truth for moral reasons; (2) the Consejero's freak-scribe is not a discoverer but a recorder of reality, a person who documents events; and (3) the Midget uses language for a different reason: he seeks to entertain, for he is a bard—a storyteller—who is an instrument for the continuation of man's traditions, culture, beliefs, and myths. Taken together, the three characters comprise an ideal narrative stance, which is moral, objective, and entertaining. As individuals with their own points of view, each is a slave not to language necessarily but rather to his own limited perspective. But like anyone else whose life is determined by the use or misuse of language, none of them separately may ever realize the awesome power—that is, paradoxically, the inherent dangers—of language. Vargas Llosa's rebellion against convention and dogma in literature has generated a progressive continuity in his growing number of works, to creating texts that are equally balanced among the objective, entertaining, and moral perspectives. As a result, Mario Vargas Llosa's readers view humanity from several perspectives, beginning with the confining and alienating circumstances of corrupt social values such as machismo; the maladaptation to dominant values of society; violence in some works, including the view of mankind functioning within wider parameters of historical and cultural myth; and, in its extreme form in other works, deeply personal experiences and demonic obsessions.

# References

Aldrich, Earl M. 1971. "Recent Trends in the Peruvian Short Story." *Studies in Short Fiction* 7, no. 1:20–31.

Baker, Rilda L. 1978. " 'Of How to Be and What to See While You are Being': The Reader's Performance in *The Time of the Hero.*" In *Mario Vargas Llosa: A Collection of Critical Essays,* edited by Charles Rossman and Alan Warren Friedman, 3–14. Austin: University of Texas Presss.

Bevelander, Charles D. 1975. "Point of View in Mario Vargas Llosa's *Conversación en La Catedral.*" Doctoral Dissertation, University of Illinois, Urbana-Champaign.

Brushwood, John S. 1975a. *"Conversation in The Cathedral." Kansas City Star,* 2 March, 8D.

————. 1975b. *The Spanish American Novel.* Austin: University of Texas Press.

Cano Gaviria, Ricardo. 1972. *El buitre y el ave fénix: Conversaciones con Mario Vargas Llosa.* Barcelona: Editorial Anagrama, 1972.

Castro-Klarén, Sara. 1978. "Humor and Class in *Pantaleón y las visitadoras." Latin American Literary Review* 7, no. 13 (Fall-Winter) :64–79.

Charyn, Jerome. 1979. "In Vargas Llosa's Peru" [review of *The Cubs*]. *New York Times Book Review,* 23 September, 12.

Christ, Ronald. 1978. "Rhetorics of the Plot." *World Literature Today* 58, no. 1 (Winter):38–44.

Christensen, Inger. 1981. *The Meaning of Metafiction.* Oslo: Universitetsforleget.

Dauster, Frank. 1970a. "Aristotle and Vargas Llosa: Literature, History, and the Interpretation of Reality." *Hispania* 53, no. 2:273–77.

————. 1970b. "Vargas Llosa and the End of Chivalry." *Books Abroad* 44, no. 1:41–45.

Diez, Luys A. 1970. *Mario Vargas Llosa's Pursuit of the Total Novel.* Cuernavaca: Centro Intercultural de Documentacion.

————. 1978a. "Another Chapter of Peru's *Comedie Grotesque." Review* 23:54–61.

————. 1978b. "The Sources of *The Green House:* The Mythical Background of a Fabulous Novel." In Rossman and Friedman, eds., *A Collection,* 36–51.

————. 1978c. "Three Conversations and One Monologue on Human Failure." *World Literature Today* 58, no. 1 (Winter):63–67.

Donoso, José. 1977. *The Boom in Spanish American Literature.* New York: Columbia University Press.

Edwards, Jorge. 1975. "The Serpent of Remorse." *Review* 14:22–25.

Forgues, Roland. 1976. "Lectura de *Los cachorros.*" *Hispamérica* 5, no. 13:34–49.

Fowles, John. 1972. "My Recollections of Kafka." In R. G. Collins, ed. *The Novel and Its Changing Form.* Winnipeg: Manitoba University Press, 188.

Frank, Rosyln M. 1981. "El estilo de los cachorros." In José Miguel Oviedo, ed. *Mario Vargas Llosa.* Madrid: Taurus, 156–75.

Frye, Northrop. 1976. *Secular Scripture: A Study of the Structure of Romance.* Cambridge: Harvard University Press.

Hancock, Joel. 1975. "Animalization and Chiaroscuro Techniques: Descriptive Language in *La ciudad y los perros* (The City and the Dogs)." *Latin American Literary Review* 4, no. 7:37–47.

————. 1977. "Stylistic Techniques Determined by Narrative Point of View in Mario Vargas Llosa's *Los cachorros.*" *Pacific Coast Philology* 12:15–20.

Harss, Luis, and Dohmann, Barbara. 1967. "Mario Vargas Llosa, or the Revolving Door." In their *Into the Mainstream.* New York: Harper & Row, 342–76.

Hirsch, Marianne. 1981. *Beyond the Single Vision.* York, S.C.: French Literature Publications.

Johnson, Philip. 1976. "Vargas Llosa's *Conversación en la Catedral:* A Study of Frustration and Failure in Peru." *Symposium* 30, no. 3:203–12.

Lernoux, Penny. 1975. "The Latin American Disease." *Nation* 221, no. 17:522–27.

Levine, Suzanne Jill. 1975. *"Conversation in The Cathedral."* *New York Times Book Review,* 23 March, 7.

Lewis, Martin A. 1977. "Reading *Pantaleón y las visitadoras.*" *Hipanófila* 60 (May):77–81.

Lipski, John M. 1979. "Narrative Textures in *Conversation in The Cathedral.*" *Revista de Estudios Hispánicos* 13:66–79.

Luchting, Wolfgang A. 1978. "Literature as a Negative Participation in Life: Vargas Llosa's *Los cachorros/Pichula Cuéllar.*" *World Literature Today* 58, no. 1 (Winter):53–62.

————. 1968. "Recent Peruvian Fiction: Vargas Llosa, Ribeyro, and Arguedas." *Research Studies* 35:271–90.

————. 1975. "Masochism, Anyone?" *Review* 75 17:12–16.

McMurray, George R. 1971. *"Conversación en la Catedral."* *Books Abroad* 45, no. 1:83–84.

————. 1973. "Form and Content Relationships in Vargas Llosa's *La ciudad y los perros.*" *Hispania* 56, no. 3 (September):579–86.

————. 1978. "The Absurd, Irony and the Grotesque in *Pantaleón y las visitadoras.*" *World Literature Today* 58, no. 1 (Winter):44–52.

Moix, Ana María. 1981. "El arte nuevo de escribir novelas clásicas." *Quimera* 14 (December):10–13.

Moody, Michael. 1977. "Don Anselmo and the Myth of the Hero in *La casa verde.*" *International Fiction Review* 4, no. 12 (July):186–89.

O'Hara, Edgar. 1980. "Mario Vargas Llosa o el desarrollo de una involución." *Marka*, 21 febrero, 40–41; 28 febrero, 40–41.

Ortega, Julio. 1972. "Sobre *Los cachorros.*" In *Homenaje a Mario Vargas Llosa*, edited by Helmy Giacomann and José Miguel Oviedo, 265–73. New York: Las Américas.

Oviedo, Jose Miguel. 1974a. "Recurrencias y divergencias en *Pantaleón y las visitadoras.*" *Memorias del IV Congreso de la Nueva Narrativa Hispanoamericana* 1:5–8. Cali: Universidad del Valle.

————. 1974b. "Seis problemas para Mario Vargas Llosa." *Plural* 32 (May):62–67.

————. 1978a. "A Conversation with Mario Vargas Llosa about *La tía Julia y el escribidor.*" In Rossman and Friedman, eds., *A Collection*, 152–65.

————. 1978b. "*La tía Julia y el escribidor*, or the Coded Self-Portrait." In Rossman and Friedman, eds., *A Collection*, 166–81.

————. 1982. *Mario Vargas Llosa: La invención de una realidad.* Barcelona: Seix Barral.

Rama, Angel. 1982. "*La guerra del fin del mundo:* Una obra maestra del fanatismo artístico." *Eco* 15/6, no. 246 (April):600–640.

Sainz, Gustavo. 1968. "*Los cachorros* de Vargas Llosa: El más radical experimento con el lenguaje." *Siempre*, 3 April, 12.

Scholes, Robert. 1979. *Fabulation and Metafiction.* Urbana: University of Illinois Press.

Schwartz, Ronald. 1980. *Nomads, Exiles, and Emigres: The Rebirth of the Latin American Narrative, 1960–80.* Metuchen, N.J.: Scarecrow Press.

Sheppard, R. Z. 1975. "Caged Condor." *Time*, 17 February, 84.

Siemens, William L. 1977. "Apollos's Metamorphosis in *Pantaleón y las visitadoras.*" *Texas Studies in Literature and Language* 19, no. 4:481–93.

Tusa, Bobs. 1976. "Mario Vargas Llosa: The Profane Optimist." *Hispanófila* 59 (September):75–88; 60 (May 1977):59–76.

————. 1977. "An Interpretation of Mario Vargas Llosa's *Pantaleón y las visitadoras.*" *Revista de estudios hispánicos* 11:27–53.

Vargas Llosa, Mario. 1967. "¿Epopeya del sertao, Torre de Babel o manual de satanismo?" *Amaru* 2 (April–June):n.p.

————. 1969. *Antología mínima de M. Vargas Llosa.* Buenos Aires: Tiempo Contemporáneo.

————. 1977. "Letter to President Videla." *Index on Censorship* 6, no. 2 (March–April):5.

————. 1982. "El elefante y la cultura." *Vuelta* 6, no. 70 (September):13–16.

————. 1983. "A Passion for Peru." *New York Times Magazine,* 20 November, 75 and passim.

————. 1983. "Inquest in the Andes: A Latin American Writer Explores the Political Lessons of a Peruvian Massacre." *New York Times Magazine,* 31 July, 18–23.

Widmer, Kingsley. 1980. *Edges of Extremity: Some Problems of Literary Modernism.* Tulsa: University of Oklahoma Press.

Williams, Raymond L. 1981. *"La tía Julia y el escribidor:* Escritores y lectores." In José Miguel Oviedo, ed. *Mario Vargas Llosa.* Madrid: Taurus, 284–97.

# Selected Bibliography

PRIMARY SOURCES

## 1. Narrative

*Los cachorros: Pichula Cuéllar.* Barcelona: Editorial Lumen, 1967. Novella. Prologue by José Miguel Oviedo, introduction by Carlos Barral, and photographs by Xavier Miserachs. Definitive edition with prologue by author: *Los jefes. Los cachorros.* Barcelona: Seix Barral, 1980.

*La casa verde.* Barcelona: Seix Barral, 1966. Novel.

*La ciudad y los perros.* Barcelona: Seix Barral, 1963. Novel. Introduction by José María Valverde.

*Conversación en La Catedral.* Barcelona: Seix Barral, 1969. Novel.

*La guerra del fin del mundo.* Barcelona: Seix Barral, Plaza y Janés, 1981. Novel.

*Los jefes.* Barcelona: Editorial Rocas, 1959. Short stories. Prologue by Juan Planas Cerdá. Contains "Arreglo de cuentas," "Los jefes," "El abuelo," "Día domingo," and "Hermanos." Definitive edition with prologue by author: *Los jefes. Los cachorros.* Barcelona: Seix Barral, 1980. Contains "El desafío," "Los jefes," "El abuelo," "Dia domingo," "El hermano mayor," and "Un visitante."

*Obras escogidas. Novelas y cuentos.* Vol. 1. Madrid: Aguilar, 1973. Contains prologue by Alfredo Matilla Rivas, *La ciudad y los perros, La casa verde, Los cachorros,* and *Los jefes.* Vol. 2. México: Aguilar, 1979. Contains *Conversación en La Catedral, La orgía perpétua, Pantaleón y las visitadoras.*

*Pantaleón y las visitadoras.* Barcelona: Seix Barral, 1973. Novel.

*La tía Julia y el escribidor.* Barcelona: Seix Barral, 1977. Novel.


## 2. Translations (English)

*Aunt Julia and the Scriptwriter.* Translated by Helen R. Lane. New York: Farrar, Straus & Giroux, 1982.

*Captain Pantoja and the Special Service.* Translated by Ronald Christ and Gregory Kolovakos. New York: Harper & Row, 1978.

*Conversation in The Cathedral.* Translated by Gregory Rabassa. New York: Harper & Row, 1975.

*The Cubs and Other Stories.* Translated by Gregory Kolovakos and Ronald Christ. New York: Harper & Row, 1979. Includes translations of stories in *Los jefes.*

*The Green House.* Translated by Gregory Rabassa. New York: Harper & Row, 1968.

*The Time of the Hero.* Translated by Lysander Kemp. New York: Grove Press, 1966. Translation of *La ciudad y los perros.*

*The War of the End of the World.* Translated by Helen Lane. New York: Farrar, Straus & Giroux, 1984.

3. Literary Criticism and General Interest (books and journal articles)

"Carta de batalla por *Tirant lo Blanc.*" Prologue to Joanot Martorell. *Tirant lo Blanc.* Madrid: Alianza, 1969, 1:9–14.

*Contra viento y marea.* Barcelona: Seix Barral, 1983.

*Entre Sartre y Camus.* Puerto Rico: Ediciones Huracán, 1981.

*García Márquez: Historia de un deicidio.* Barcelona: Barral, 1971.

*García Márquez y la problemática de la novela.* Buenos Aires: Corregidor/Marcha, 1973.

*La historia secreta de una novela.* Barcelona: Tusquets, 1971.

*José María Arguedas, entre sapos y halcones.* Madrid: Ediciones Cultura Hispánica del Centro Iberoamericano de Cooperación, 1978.

"La literatura es fuego." Speech delivered upon receiving Rómulo Gallegos prize. *Mundo Nuevo* (Caracas) 11 (1967):93–95. Translation: "Literature Is Fire." In Hortense, Carpentier and Janet Brof, eds. *Doors and Mirrors.* New York: Grossman, 1972, 430–35.

"The Latin American Novel Today." *Books Abroad* 44, no. 1 (1970):41–45.

"Martorell y el 'elemento añadido' en *Tirant lo Blanc.*" Prologue to Martín de Riquer and Mario Vargas Llosa's *El combate imaginario: Las cartas de batalla de Joanot Martorell.* Barcelona: Barral, 1972, 9–28.

"A Media Stereotype." *Atlantic* 253, no. 2 (February 1984):20, 22, 24.

*La novela.* Buenos Aires: América Nueva, 1974.

*La novela en América Latina: diálogo.* Literary discussions with Gabriel García Márquez. Lima: Carlos Milla Batres, 1968.

*La orgía perpétua: Flaubert and 'Madame Bovary.'* Madrid: Taurus, 1975.

"Sebastián Salazar Bondy y la vocación del escritor en el Perú." Prologue to Salazar Bondy's *Obras completas.* Lima: Moncloa, 1967, 11–34.

"Social Commitment and the Latin American Writer." *World Literature Today* 52, no. 1 (Winter 1978):6–14.

"The Writer in Latin America." *Index on Censorship* 7, no. 6 (November-December 1978):34–40.

4. Drama and Films

*Kathie y el hipopótamo.* Barcelona: Seix Barral, 1983. Play.

*La señorita de Tacna.* Barcelona: Seix Barral, 1981. Play.

*Pantaleón y las visitadoras.* Film production (Dominican Republic): Paramount Pictures, 1976. Script and direction: Mario Vargas Llosa and José María Gutiérrez.

## SECONDARY SOURCES

### 1. Books

*Asedios a la realidad: Mario Vargas Llosa.* Las Palmas: Inventarios Provisionales, 1972. A series of literary essays of high quality by perceptive scholars dealing with Vargas Llosa's novels of the 1960s.

Boldori de Baldussi, Rosa. *Vargas Llosa: un narrador y sus demonios.* Buenos Aires: Fernando García Cambeiro, 1974. A general but thorough overview of the principal literary themes and techniques found in Vargas Llosa's novels.

Cano Gaviria, Ricardo. *El buitre y el ave fénix: Conversaciones con Mario Vargas Llosa.* Barcelona: Anagrama, 1972. The book is divided into two parts; the first is an extensive interview with Vargas Llosa, while the second is an analysis of certain concepts regarding real and fictional realities.

Diez, Luis A. *Mario Vargas Llosa's Pursuit of the Total Novel.* Cuernavaca: CIDOC, 1970. One of the most perceptive analyses of Vargas Llosa's works, through *Conversation in The Cathedral,* which demonstrates the relationship between technique and theme.

————, ed. *Asedios a Vargas Llosa.* Santiago de Chile: Editorial Universitaria, 1972. A series of fine studies dealing with multiple aspects of Vargas Llosa's works in the 1960s.

Fernandez, Casto M. *Aproximación formal a la novelística de Vargas Llosa.* Madrid: Editorial Nacional, 1977. Provides a convincing structuralist approach to the analysis of *Conversation in The Cathedral.*

Giacoman, Helmy F., and Oviedo, José Miguel, eds. *Homenaje a Mario Vargas Llosa.* Madrid: Las Américas, 1972. A collection of the more outstanding articles of literary analysis that have appeared earlier in other journals.

Lewis, Marvin A. *From Lima to Leticia.* Lanham: University Press of America, 1983. This revised doctoral dissertation provides valuable insights into the themes of determinism and existentialism and the social consequences of Vargas Llosa's novels, through *Aunt Julia and The Scriptwriter.*

Luchting, Wolfgang A. *Mario Vargas Llosa: Desarticulador de realidades.* Bogotá: Andes, 1978. A highly personalized version of one scholar-translator's relationship to and interpretation of the life and works of Vargas Llosa.

**Martin, José L.** *La narrative de Vargas Llosa. Acercamiento estilístico.* Madrid: Gredos, 1974. A thorough study of the major themes and techniques in Vargas Llosa's novels. Of interest is the concept of "structural realism" as it is applied to the novels.

**Oviedo, José Miguel.** *Mario Vargas Llosa: la invención de una realidad.* Barcelona: Barral Editores, 1970; Editorial Seix Barral, 1982. The most exhaustive study, to date, of Vargas Llosa and his works. The first part is an engaging inquiry into Vargas Llosa's biography; the second part discusses Vargas Llosa's literary theories, and the third part presents a chronological study of all of Vargas Llosa's fiction published through 1981. The eighty-five-page bibliography of primary and secondary works provides the principal source of bibliographical information.

————, ed. *Mario Vargas Llosa.* Madrid: Taurus, 1981. A collection of twenty-three articles by scholars and specialists who have published studies on Vargas Llosa in other journals. The first part provides a general perspective on Vargas Llosa's narrative concerns; the second part is composed of studies of individual novels; the third part includes an interview with Vargas Llosa, in which he discusses *The War of the End of the World.*

**Pereira, Armando.** *La concepción literaria de Mario Vargas Llosa.* México: Universidad Nacional Autónoma de México, 1981. An attempt to elucidate Vargas Llosa's literary concepts and to explain how certain irrational elements of the human conscience determine Vargas Llosa's interpretation of the writer's vocation.

**Rossman, Charles,** and **Friedman, Alan Warren,** eds. *Mario Vargas Llosa. A Collection of Critical Essays.* Austin: University of Texas Press, 1978. Fourteen essays present fresh ideas and contemporary interpretations of his works, providing a complementary edition to earlier collected essays.

2. Special Journal Issues

"Focus on *Conversation in The Cathedral.*" *Review* 14 (1975).

"Homenaje a Mario Vargas Llosa." *Norte* 12, nos. 5–6 (October-December 1971).

"An Issue Devoted to the Work of Mario Vargas Llosa." *Texas Studies in Literature and Language* 19, no. 4 (1977).

"Literature as Fire: The Achievement of Mario Vargas Llosa." *World Literature Today* 52, no. 1 (1978).

3. Articles

**Brown, James W.** " 'Expatriate Syndrome': Mario Vargas Llosa on Peruvian Racism." *Essays in Literature* (Western Illinois University) 3, no. 1 (1976):131–39. Analyzes the problem of racial differences in

Peru as a thematic and structural device in *The Time of the Hero, The Green House,* and *Conversation in The Cathedral.*

Coleman, Alexander. "The Transfiguration of the Chivalric Novel." *World Literature Today* 52, no. 1 (1978):24–30. An excellent article that concentrates on the relationship between Vargas Llosa as creative writer and Vargas Llosa as literary critic. Defines and links key terminology that Vargas Llosa uses to explain his attitudes toward fiction and reality: his "demons" (obsessions), dissidence, rebellion, deicide, substitution, totality (through qualitative leap and communicating vessels). Highly recommended.

Escobar, Alberto. "Impostores de sí mismos." *Revista Peruana de Cultura* 2 (1964): 119–25. One of the first critics to evaluate accurately Vargas Llosa's narrative potential. Provides a concise study of *The Time of the Hero,* showing that bipolar structures and dualities in the novel are the bases for a moral interpretation of the victimization of man by corrupt societies.

Filer, Malva E. "Vargas Llosa, the Novelist as a Critic." *Texas Studies in Language and Literature* 19, no. 4 (1977):503–13. An examination of the importance of Gustave Flaubert's literary ideas on Vargas Llosa's credo, revealing many similarities between the two writers.

Foster, David W. "Consideraciones estructurales sobre *La casa verde.*" *Norte* 12, nos. 5–6 (1971):128–36. A skillful application of Lévi-Strauss's structuralist concepts to the analysis of the creation of new myths in *The Green House.*

Fuentes, Carlos. "El afán totalizante de Vargas Llosa." In his *La nueva novela lationamericana.* México: Joaquín Mortíz, 1969, 35–48. An interesting study of the principal themes and structural elements in Vargas Llosa's earlier novels. Themes of man versus nature in *The Green House* and rites of passage in *The Time of the Hero* come alive through the use of exact language and the concept of ritual.

Gallager, David P. "Mario Vargas Llosa." In his *Modern Latin American Literature.* New York: Oxford University Press, 1973, 122–43. This perceptive examination of the novels of the 1960s attempts to unravel the complexities of the novels by analyzing narrative structure and technique. Explains how the function of parallel and shifting narrative sequences, as well as the strategical device of concealment, produces ambiguity, which results in frustration and failure.

Lafforgue, Jorge. "*La ciudad y los perros,* novela moral." In Helmy Giacoman and José Miguel Oviedo, eds. *Homenaje a Mario Vargas Llosa.* New York: Las Américas (1972):101–23. A valuable study that deciphers the novel's narrative complexities, which produce a mutilated reality in which time seems to be frozen.

**McMurray, George R.** "The Novels of Mario Vargas Llosa." *Modern Language Quarterly* 29, no. 3 (1968):329–40. A study of *The Time of the Hero* and *The Green House* for their use of symbolic elements, their reliance on the *nouveau roman* concept of time to determine characterization, and their creation of ambiguity. The article explains how two philosophies—social determinism and existentialism—are fused in the novels.

**Matillas Rivas, Alfredo.** "Sobre algunos aspectos en la obra de Mario Vargas Llosa." Prologue to Vargas Llosa's *Obras escogidas*. Madrid: Editorial Aguilar, 1973, xi–xlii. A survey of principal characteristics of Vargas Llosa's novels, such as the use of ellipses, the function of the epilogues, ways in which incidents work with each other through dialectical structures; the function of the "hidden fact"; the meaning of Vargas Llosa's personal demons, the theme of corrupted rebellion, and the overall effect of violence. States that *The Green House* is Vargas Llosa's most profound work.

**Moody, Michael.** "The Web of Defeat: A Thematic View of Characterization in Mario Vargas Llosa's *La casa verde*." *Hispania* 59, no. 1 (March 1976):11–23. Convincingly maintains that there is not a "lack" of characterization in the novel, as critics have stated, but rather an important relationship between the treatment of character and Vargas Llosa's worldview. The existential nature of the character's world reflects a sense of entrapment.

**Ortega, Julio.** "Sobre *Los cachorros.*" In Helmy Giacoman and José Miguel Oviedo, eds. *Homenaje a Mario Vargas Llosa.* New York: Las Américas, 1972, 265–73. A skillful interpretation of the novella from the point of view of its importance as a metaphor for all of Vargas Llosa's works. The theme of castration is seen more as an allegory of the "possibility" of the act happening to someone and has the effect of neutralizing the grotesque nature of reality.

**Osorio, Nelson.** "La expresión de los niveles de realidad en la narrativa de Vargas Llosa." In Helmy Giacoman and José Miguel Oviedo, eds. *Homenaje a Mario Vargas Llosa.* New York: Las Américas, 1972, 23–35. An examination of the ways in which Vargas Llosa creates a sense of multiple levels of reality in his novels. Looks at *The Time of the Hero* and *The Green House* in an attempt to show how several conflicting perspectives are created through social, linguistic, and symbolic elements. Analyzes the first paragraph of the second novel, demonstrating that dialogue works to create different spatial and temporal planes.

**Rodriguez Monegal, Emir.** "Madurez de Vargas Llosa." In Helmy Giacoman and José Miguel Oviedo, eds. *Homenaje a Mario Vargas Llosa.* New York: Las Américas, 1972, 45–67. Studies the elements of Vargas Llosa's narrative that communicate a clear and indisputable sense of commitment to reality. His success lies in the direct criticism of decadent bourgeois values and the military. Although Vargas Llosa may play with the reader by hiding certain information, the reader is captivated by being compelled to re-create an ambiguous, closed world of violence.

**Sommers, Joseph.** "Literatura e ideología: La evaluación novelística del militarismo en Vargas Llosa." *Hispamérica.* Supplement (1975):83–117. Essentially concerned with the ideological implications of Vargas Llosa's works. From *The Time of the Hero* through *Captain Pantoja and the Special Service,* the works are generally disconnected from historical reality, creating an extreme sense of individualism and obstructing the presence of a central narrative voice that might seek basic social change. Only the frailty and vulnerability of man are revealed in his novels.

# Index